COUNSELING THE TERMINALLY ILL

SERIES IN DEATH EDUCATION, AGING, AND HEALTH CARE

HANNELORE WASS, CONSULTING EDITOR

ADVISORY BOARD

Herman Feifel, Ph.D.
Jeanne Quint Benoliel, R.N., Ph.D.
Balfour Mount, M.D.

COUNSELING THE TERMINALLY ILL:
Sharing the Journey

George S. Lair
Department of Counselor Education
School of Education
Drake University
Des Moines, Iowa

Taylor & Francis
Publishers since 1798

USA	Publishing Office:	Taylor & Francis 1101 Vermont Avenue, NW, Suite 200 Washington, DC 20005-3521 Tel: (202) 289-2174 Fax: (202) 289-3665
	Distribution Center:	Taylor & Francis 1900 Frost Road, Suite 101 Bristol, PA 19007-1598 Tel: (215) 785-5800 Fax: (215) 785-5515
UK		Taylor & Francis Ltd. 1 Gunpowder Square London EC4A 3DE Tel: 0171 583 0490 Fax: 0171 583 0581

COUNSELING THE TERMINALLY ILL: Sharing the Journey

1 2 3 4 5 6 7 8 9 0   B R B R   9 8 7 6

This book was set in Times Roman by Sandra F. Watts. The editors were Christine Williams and Kathleen Sheedy. Cover design by Michelle Fleitz. Printing and binding by Braun-Brumfield, Inc.

A CIP catalog record for this book is available from the British Library.

∞ The paper in this publication meets the requirements of the ANSI Standard Z39.48-1984 (Permanence of Paper)

Library of Congress Cataloging-in-Publication Data

Lair, George S.
    Counseling the terminally ill : sharing the journey / George S. Lair.
        p.   cm. — (Series in death education, aging, and health care, ISSN 0275-3510)
    Includes bibliographical references (p.   )

    1. Death—Psychological aspects.   2. Terminally ill—Psychology.
3. Terminally ill—Counseling of.   4. Counselor and client.
I. Title.   II. Series.
    BF789.D4L34   1996
362.1'75—dc20   96-12921
                                                                                        CIP

ISBN 1-56032-516-X (case)
ISBN 1-56032-517-8 (paper)
ISSN 0275-3510

To Diane
who has taught me how to share the journey.

CONTENTS

PREFACE

Dying is an integral part of living and therefore engages the attention of all of us. For some, the attention is focused on denying the reality of death; at the other extreme, some spend their whole lives exploring its meaning. There are persons who die easily and those who struggle against the inevitable. There are those who choose to go through the final stages alone and those who seek an opportunity to share its meaning with others. As in most areas of life, the way of viewing death and the way of dying are individual matters.

This book is written for those who work in hospices and other settings that provide care for persons with terminal illness and who are concerned with the intrapsychic and spiritual needs of these persons. While social workers, psychologists, and clergy all perceive themselves to be counselors, what they perceive counseling to be is quite different from one group to another and from one individual to another. All of us who work with the terminally ill must come to our own conclusions regarding what is the appropriate way to be of help. What is presented here is a model that is based on the experience of one person, and it is offered only as a possibility for readers to measure against their own experience.

My experience in working with the terminally ill had its start in 1979 when I was invited by Dr. Fred Brunk to work as a counselor with some of his cancer patients. Almost immediately I met a young man who was dying and would likely live no more than a few months. He appeared eager to enter into counseling, yet he had no problems or concerns that he wanted to work on. I slowly became aware that what he wanted was someone to share the final stage of his journey with him. Through many hours I listened to him, trying to understand what he was experiencing and helping him become more aware of that experience. I slowly came to understand that we were working toward no solutions, no point at which we would say, "Counseling has been successful, we can now stop." Yet I also became aware that this young man was becoming less afraid of dying, and that there was a sense of joy and comfort during the final weeks of his life. At one point he stated that death was an experience that he was now looking forward to. When he died, I felt good about what we had experienced together, yet it didn't feel like what I knew counseling to be. After working as a mental health counselor for 15 years in other settings, I found this to be a different experience for me. And so began a learning process about dying, and what persons who are dying want and need.

My professional experience had been within the philosophical context of the humanistic counseling approach developed by Carl Rogers (1951, 1961). I had been attracted by his belief in people's tendency toward positive growth and his trust in individuals to direct their own lives. Yet I had seen the practice of that approach come into conflict with the needs and desires of clients I had worked with in other settings, and so while I continued to have a strong kinship with the philosophical underpinnings of the Rogerian approach, I felt, at times, uncomfortable with its method of counseling. As I began to work with persons who had a terminal illness, however, the focus of the therapeutic relationship became stronger. The idea of sharing the journey with persons who are dying and the essence of a Rogerian counseling relationship began to merge into a single concept.

Still there was more to learn. In 1982 I came across an article in the *Journal of Humanistic Psychology* that piqued my interest. It was an article by Ken Wilber, the first of his writings that I had read, and he was explaining in a very understandable way why Rogerian counseling, no matter how much I was committed to its philosophy, was not suitable for everyone (Wilber, 1982). His conceptualization of a spectrum of consciousness as the overall framework for understanding human development provided many answers for me, and along with the Rogerian conceptualization of relationship, it was to become a major component of my approach to working with terminally ill persons.

As I continued to study Wilber's theory, I came to know what it meant when one said that dying was about growing. In *The Atman Project*, he says his theme is simply that development is evolution and evolution is transcendence. The final goal of transcendence is Unity (or God) Consciousness (Wilber, 1980). The purpose for working with terminally ill persons was beginning to come into focus: to facilitate the dying person's continuing evolution through this final earthly stage.

The method was still a problem, however. I accepted the concept of the spectrum, which states that Rogerian and other humanistic approaches are appropriate only for those persons whose level of development matches the point on the spectrum at which these approaches are focused. This is generally at the high personal, or formal-reflexive level (Wilber, 1979, 1986), and many persons with a terminal illness have not reached that level of evolution. Method and relationship had to be separated. Rogers advocated that the relationship was sufficient to bring about change, and this still seemed to hold some truth. But how was I to reconcile this with the need for different approaches at different levels of the spectrum. The answer seemed to lie in the purpose; facilitation of growth during the final stage of life was different than psychotherapy as we knew it in other circumstances, where the concern might be overcoming psychoneuroses, script pathologies, or identity issues. If the purpose was facilitation, then the path was a relationship that gradually dissolved the boundaries between counselor and client, one that was characterized by empathic understanding, unconditional love, and a genuine personal honesty. The levels of the spectrum dictate different ways of communicating these conditions, but their underlying presence is a universal prerequisite for facilitation of the final stage of growth.

The theme of this book, then, is that the focus of counseling with the terminally ill should be on the psychospiritual aspects of death and dying. It is based on two assumptions: that death anxiety, not pain, is the most critical issue for the dying person, and that the time of dying is an opportunity for growth and transformation. Counseling with a terminally ill person does not call for an "expert" providing treatment or intervention for the client. It is a time in which understanding and caring are primary, where the process is one of facilitation, and where a genuine and authentic relationship is the means of accomplishing the counseling goals.

ACKNOWLEDGMENTS

In addition to the work of Carl Rogers and Ken Wilber, I owe a special gratitude to the many persons who have allowed me to share their journey and who have been my teachers. I also am indebted to Dr. S. Fred Brunk for having the vision to invite me to share in the care of some of his patients; to Dr. Mary Brunk, a colleague who shared the experience and learning with me; and to the staff of Hospice of Central Iowa who allowed me to be a member of their family.

Chapter 1

Introduction

HOLISTIC PALLIATIVE CARE

Palliative care is the process of making a person as comfortable as possible during the last stages of life, when cure is no longer possible. When deciding how to provide this type of care for patients, we must be just as concerned about their psychological and spiritual needs as we are about their medical care. It is not a question of whether we should take care of their medical needs or their social needs or whether we should take care of their psychological needs and spiritual needs. We need to be concerned about all of these. The number of persons who will die of noninfectious diseases will most likely continue to increase during the next two decades, and the need for quality palliative care will therefore also increase.

The efforts that have been made in providing palliative care for terminally ill people have been primarily in the area of medical care. With advances in drug treatment, pain control has been improved and the negative effects of other symptoms diminished. Much slower progress has been made in understanding how to help the patient from the psychological or spiritual point of view. This is not to say that no efforts in this area have been made, for there are certainly those who, in recent years, have discussed what could be described as the psycho-spiritual side of palliative care: Weisman's (1972) ideas about appropriate death,

Shneidman's (1973) conception of emotional and personal care of the patient, and D. C. Smith and Maher's (1993) concept of a healthy death are examples of this focus. Yet in spite of these efforts, articles and books on providing counseling for terminally ill persons are not numerous, nor are workshops and seminars at professional gatherings. A greater effort toward these concerns is needed if we are to provide total palliative care.

The approach described in this book is a holistic one, meaning that it is based on a belief that each person is an integrated whole. Physical, social, psychological, and spiritual concerns interact with each other and should not be seen as separate parts. Too often interdisciplinary approaches to helping involve all parts of the dying person but treat each part as a separate entity. All professionals, including nurses and medical doctors, should be concerned with and able to deal to some extent with the social, psychological, and spiritual needs of the patient as well as the medical ones.

When we work with persons who are terminally ill, our focus is on helping the person move toward a peaceful death. Socrates (Plato, 1952) offered one of the finest descriptions of dying with equanimity. He proposed that for a philosopher, meaning one who has lived thoughtfully and particularly one who has thought seriously about death, death itself cannot be frightening. When you have been preparing yourself for death all your life, you cannot be troubled when it actually comes. According to Socrates, equanimity comes not from drugs and denial but from exploring the meaning of death.

In caring for the terminally ill person, we must be just as concerned about freedom from anxiety, depression, anger, and fear as we are about freedom from pain. If preparation for dying comes through living thoughtfully, then we must focus ourselves on becoming aware of the meaning of death. The professional who has chosen to share the journey with dying persons must ask these questions: "What can I do to facilitate my patients in living thoughtfully and knowingly about death? How can I facilitate their movement toward equanimity and peaceful dying?" If we can find the answers to these questions we will become more effective in providing palliative care in our hospice programs.

There is no single meaning of death. Different people, depending on their culture, religion, and philosophical beliefs, have different ideas about what death means. Counselors must be aware of these differences when providing psychological and spiritual help to terminally ill persons. We must try to understand each person as being unique and to provide help that is appropriate to that person's way of perceiving the world, life's meaning, and the meaning of death.

Whereas medical care of the terminally ill involves diagnosis and treatment, psychospiritual care involves understanding and facilitation. Medical treatment is oriented toward care of the physical body, and psychospiritual care is focused on growth and transformation. The latter is concerned with the inner healing power of the individual, which comes through love, compassion, forgiveness, and connectedness. In a holistic approach, both medical and psychospiritual care must be involved in an integrated way.

To be healed does not mean *not* to die. The crisis that comes when a person faces death provides that person's final opportunity for healing. The healing of dying comes when a person experiences being part of a greater unity and realizes that the death of the self in this world is not the final end. This realization represents a transformation from focusing on the individual self to an experience of the interconnectedness of all people. True hospice care must facilitate the terminally ill person's journey through this period of transformation. To be healed means to have experienced the transformation.

THE PURPOSE OF HOSPICE CARE

Much of the discussion about working with the terminally ill centers around the hospice movement. This is not to deny that significant counseling and psychological and spiritual help occurs outside of hospices. Certainly, there are many counseling programs and support groups that provide help; this chapter as well as the rest of this book is intended for people who are involved in those settings as much as it is for people working in hospices. However, the hospice has become the primary institution that cares specifically for terminally ill persons, and therefore, as a matter of convenience, most references in this book are to hospices.

St. Christopher's Hospice was started in England in 1967, and since that time hospice programs have been developed all over the world as an alternative to hospital care for the terminally ill. Their purpose is (a) to provide the means for terminally ill persons who choose to do so to die at home or in a home-like setting, (b) to provide a structure designed specifically to give pain-free palliative care, and (c) to offer such care through a holistic model. The word *hospice* itself means that spiritual and emotional care of the patient are as important as is medical care (Craven & Wald, 1975).

By being able to take care of a patient in the home or a special care facility, hospice workers have certainly made the final period of a person's life more emotionally comforting and, therefore, of a higher quality. They have also provided for more cost-effective health care. Yet there are still many opportunities left to be fulfilled. Although great advances have been made in providing physical comfort to the patients, the ability to help terminally ill patients from a psychospiritual point of view remains elementary. We do not have a unified theory that brings together the dynamics of time and setting, the nature and needs of the person, and the process of helping the person to meet those needs during a period of dying.

Because hospice programs have grown so fast, practitioners have borrowed ideas and practices from other areas, adopting patterns of care that are used in other areas of the helping community. The field of thanatology has grown along with hospice care and has had to be incorporated along the way. However, we are now ready to develop ways of helping the dying person that come from an understanding of the needs of that specific person. Such efforts are being made, and the model presented in this book is one of them. It is a model specifically focused on working with terminally ill persons—one that attempts to be comprehensive and pertinent to *their* special circumstances.

The basis of this model is understanding a terminally ill person as a unique individual and as a whole person. It is an attempt to move away from making external assessments and prescribing treatment plans for the patient. It is concerned with being empathic and with creating a relationship with dying persons rather than with making decisions for them. It is based on the premise that we should work with the person as a complete human being rather than attending primarily to the physical malfunctions of the body or in any way segmenting the person into distinct physical, social, psychological, or spiritual categories. It has a greater focus on the existential and spiritual meaning that dying has for the patient and a willingness to help in the struggle to deal with this meaning.

A DIFFERENT ORIENTATION

How do you help someone who is dying? This is a question often asked of people who work in hospice programs. The answer is not found in techniques but in being aware of one's own experience of sharing the final stage of life's journey with persons who are dying. Ken Wilber wrote about his role as a support person for his wife, Treya Killam Wilber, during her battle with cancer (Wilber, 1988, 1991). He is recognized as one of the outstanding theorists in the area of transpersonal psychology, yet in these writings he doesn't simply present a theoretical or philosophical interpretation of his wife's illness and his role as a support person. Instead, he provides a very personal and existential description of who he is, who his wife is, and the relationship between them at a critical period in their lives. This is perhaps the essence of the answer to the question of how to help someone who is dying—not by following theoretical formulations and techniques, but by living with the person through the trials and joys of that period.

In the medical model of death and dying, quality care of the physical body is perceived as the essence of hospice care. Yet too often this conception does not recognize that the process of dying always involves death anxiety, which is the fear of being alienated from the source of one's being and hence of being annihilated as a separate self. If we perceive the physical to be separate from the whole person and therefore focus primarily on making the body comfortable so that we can deal with psychological and spiritual issues *if* we have the time and resources, then we may prevent the person from being able to use the crisis of dying as an opportunity for growth. From a transpersonal orientation, dying is understood to transcend the physical—the world of the body—and this provides the reason for developing approaches to helping that focus on the transformative aspect of a person's growth. These approaches enable us to provide psychospiritual care that supports dying persons as they work through the negative emotions that are a part of death anxiety.

In following a primarily medical model, hospice workers most often work with the patient from a psychosocial perspective, concerning ourselves with the interpersonal aspects associated with dying. We may want to develop goals for the patient and family, and these are likely to be goals that are most interesting to us. As professionals, we generalize about terminally ill persons, making external judgments about their reactions, feelings, and psychological processes. We then focus on controlling the process of the person's dying rather than being concerned with the far more simple but difficult process of facilitating growth during this final stage. Yet Shneidman (1973) pointed out that the interpersonal is only one part of the twofold burden facing the dying person, the other part being the intrapsychic aspects of preparing for one's own death.

A life-threatening illness may expose hidden problems and unresolved disagreements in a family. There is a tendency for counselors to want to solve these problems, but this is similar to the medical doctor's wanting to cure the terminally ill patient. A person facing death very well may not want to deal with the messy worldly problems he or she has been avoiding. Death provides the opportunity for the person to see the temporary quality of these concerns and frees psychological energy to be turned to questions of a higher order. If we focus our help only, or primarily, on these interpersonal problems, we become a party to the patient's attempt to maintain the status quo, to use the crisis of dying as a time to bargain. To do that, however, is to turn attention away from the opportunity for growth. It is very much like giving a patient drugs to stop depression instead of facilitating movement through depression so that growth can occur on the other side.

The psychospiritual help given to terminally ill persons should have only one purpose—to help the person use this final stage of life for growing. Help should be centered on the intrapsychic rather than the interpersonal aspects of the person's life and, therefore, be focused toward transcending the present level of consciousness and moving to a higher level of being. If we focus only on interpersonal concerns, we orient ourselves to the worldly self of the dying person and away from the transcendent possibilities. Yet it is necessary to understand that for the dying person, the worldly self has limited value. As counselors, we must leave our own perspective and see the future from the dying person's point of view.

Counseling with terminally ill persons is a form of death education. It should be designed to help patients increase awareness and acceptance of themselves during a time of crisis. The ultimate crisis that humans face is the one precipitated by a threat to one's very life. We have become so afraid of dying that we do not realize the potential that it holds for growth and meaning in our lives. If we can overcome the tendency to allow a life-threatening disease to overwhelm us or to ignore that it is an integral part of our lives, then we can use it as a life-promoting event. It will then contribute to our total growth, our positive movement along life's journey.

HOLISTIC COUNSELING

When we concern ourselves with providing counseling for terminally ill patients, we need an appropriate psychological model from which to work. We must begin with an understanding of our reasons for entering into a counseling relationship with someone who is dying. Grof and Halifax (1977) noted that a person working with the terminally ill does not have very much to offer in terms of a concrete positive alternative, either for the dying person or the survivors. They also noted that even the clergy find little to offer beyond words of solace and dependence on faith. Wilber (1988) talked of the helplessness that virtually everybody involved in a chronic cancer situation tends to feel. Yet a counselor's sense of helplessness comes primarily when the purpose of counseling is seen as solving a problem or correcting a situation—which, of course, may very well be beyond the counselor's power.

In the practice of caring for terminally ill persons, counselors most often use an interdisciplinary approach in which the person is seen as having emotional, social, intellectual, spiritual, and physical concerns. However, we deal with these concerns in an additive rather than an integrated way. If one has a tumor, this creates physical problems. It also may very well create emotional problems, social problems, and spiritual problems. Therefore, to be of maximum help, we must provide professionals to deal with each of these areas. But the problems, although perhaps relating to the same source, are dealt with as separate entities. A problem of interfamily communication, even though it might be precipitated by the patient's disease, is viewed as a problem in and of itself, to be dealt with by a social worker. The resolution of the problem relates primarily to the social well-being of the family and does not impinge on or alter the course of the disease.

The introduction of Medicare certification for hospices in the United States has made the struggle to provide holistic palliative care more acute. On the one side of this struggle there is a strong pull toward making hospices one more arm of the medical model of health care. Nonmedical services tend to be made ancillary to the medical care rather than an integral part of the whole. Such an orientation certainly is not holistic.

Rhymes (1990) described hospices as using an interdisciplinary approach with a basic team of nurse, physician, and social worker, as well as other professionals as needed. A physician maintains overall supervision of medical care, and the nurse is the leader of the caregiving team, often making the assessments of what the patient and family need and determining what support is required. Many services are provided by other health care professionals, and this implies an interdisciplinary focus, but it certainly is not a holistic one.

These interdisciplinary approaches are positive in the sense that they broaden the help provided to patients by involving several professionals. Yet they fall short of the integration concept that is so critical to a truly holistic approach. Simply by the personnel indicated as the primary team and the focus on the nurse as the team leader, there is an implication that hospice care is first and foremost a medical matter.

The interdisciplinary medical model and the holistic facilitative model are different orientations, and several polarities exist between them. The medical model is likely to be concerned with surface symptoms and their alleviation (e.g., anxiety and depression), whereas the facilitative model looks at the deep meanings underlying the symptoms. The former tends to deal with contents, those entities that can be labeled, rather than viewing the organism as a process. A person working with a patient from the medical perspective will make determinations as to what that person's needs are, whereas the facilitatively oriented person will work to understand the needs as perceived by the patient. Moreover, the interdisciplinary medical model operates from a role orientation, whereas the holistic facilitative model is more concerned with persons helping persons. From the latter perspective, the healing power of the individual is contained within, and the most effective growth occurs when that inner power is brought forth.

When we view the person from a holistic viewpoint, we see the concerns in one area as affecting, in a very critical way, the other parts of the person. If we treat the emotional concerns effectively, we will also be treating the physical problems. If we can facilitate patients' growth in relation to their emotional concerns, we will also facilitate physical and spiritual growth. There is now considerable evidence that consciousness is a key controlling factor in both health and disease, and, therefore, it should be possible to use the mind to bring about health. This is a major precept of holistic health care.

Psychospiritual counseling has the capacity to deal with surface structures and contents, and it also has the capacity to deal with deep structures and processes. For both clients and counselors, there is a tendency to deal with the former because this is the area we know best. However, the deep structures of separation and alienation and the process of transcending the negative effects of these deep structures begin to manifest themselves through the crisis of terminal illness. The healing that can come from such a crisis is found within the individual, and counseling can be offered in such a way as to facilitate the person in using this healing. This is counseling that is congruent with a holistic facilitative view of hospice care.

One of the best examples of this difference in viewpoint comes from recent work in hypnotherapy. Traditional development in this area in the last two decades has been in the area of behavioral psychology, where the principles of operant conditioning are applied through a trance state. Techniques have been developed for treating problems symptomatically and have found a wide range of use: eliminating undesirable behaviors, reducing general anxiety, and creating new patterns of behaving. At the same time, Milton Erickson (Erickson & Rossi, 1983) presented a different model of hypnotherapy that was focused on the inner resources of the client. Erickson termed his model *utilization* because it was designed to facilitate clients' use of their own inner powers in the process of healing. The first type of hypnotherapy is allopathic and in line with the medical model, and the second is holistic and more suited to a facilitative, psychospiritual orientation.

We must not view dying as predominantly one concern over another, whether this be medical, social, psychological, or spiritual. For the dying person, spiritual and emotional concerns are as critical to comfort as are physical concerns. Suffering is as important as is pain; anguish and despair are of as much concern as are feebleness and a lack of energy. Alienation is as critical an issue as any medical problem. Yet the suffering and anguish are dealt with only secondarily at best, and often such needs are not perceived at all, because they tend not to come to the fore when the needs of the patient are viewed from the medical paradigm. Kutscher (1980) stated that present knowledge of science and medicine, for all its benefits, has cast a shadow on medical care "for, in the quest to achieve cure, the status of giving care has been diminished" (p. xiii). As counselors, our approach is too often behavioral and reductionistic, based on an empirical perception that ignores other ways of understanding the world.

SUMMARY

We are in need of a broader perspective of palliative care for the terminally ill person. Management of pain and physical comfort are essential. For many, resolution of interpersonal concerns is necessary to their emotional comfort. Yet this is not enough. Equal to these concerns are those of the existential and spiritual realm. Cassel and Meier (1990) noted that for many people transcendent and spiritual meanings take precedence over the concerns of the dying process itself. The refusal of professionals to help patients with these concerns amounts to a narrowly focused view of the help we can offer.

Byock (1991), in discussing issues of assisting terminally ill patients in committing suicide, pointed out that there is little rationale for assuming that this should be a "physician" question. He noted that the medical profession is beset by an egocentrism in which it is presumed that anything having to do with the human body, health, or disease must be the domain of doctors and nurses. Byock suggested that in some cases, responsibility should be given over to other professionals and, I might add, even to nonprofessionals. In this light, counseling for the dying person should be viewed not as an adjunct to medical care but instead as an integral part of the assistance offered. It should be as much a part of hospice care as medical services and should not be subjected to prescription by medical personnel whose understanding of the purpose and nature of counseling is as minimal as is most counselors' knowledge of the physical care of the patient. Yet such an orientation calls for a rethinking of what counseling is, especially as it relates to the person who is dying.

As counselors (this includes mental health counselors, social work counselors, and clergy), we need to be more concerned with facilitating the person's use of the crisis of dying as an opportunity for growth and transformation.

Concerns with treatment and curing mental illnesses are inappropriate to palliative care. Our focus should be more on listening and less on problem solving, more on understanding and less on diagnosis and judging, more on empathy and less on sympathy. If palliative medical care is designed to make the patient physically comfortable at a time when cure is no longer feasible, then palliative counseling should be designed to make the person psychologically and spiritually comfortable—free of psychic pain, anxiety, and depression. We should not focus on curing psychological problems any more than we focus on curing physical disease, and in the process of helping dying persons become free of pain and anxiety, we can facilitate their use of energy for spiritual growth.

By sharing in the journey with persons who are dying, rather than trying to fix anything in them that might be broken, we are able to listen to them in a very empathic way. Being understood in this manner allows the person to know, at some level of awareness, the sense of connectedness that underlies and transcends all humanity. In this experience, feelings of alienation and aloneness may pass from the mind of the person who is dying, allowing for a quiet acceptance of the peacefulness of death.

Chapter 2

Special Concerns of the Dying Person

Counseling with persons who have a terminal illness is different in some significant ways from counseling with other clients (Shneidman, 1980). Certainly there are commonalities, but there are also special concerns that must be considered. The dying person has a different perspective, simply because dying is more imminent, or real. Everyday communication, as well as that which is specific to counseling, is different in some significant ways. And there are some psychosocial and spiritual concerns that take on a special meaning at this point in a person's life. Some of these special concerns are discussed in this chapter.

THE MEANING OF CRISIS

A psychological crisis can be defined as a situation that is perceived by an individual to be a threat to the self-concept, a threat that calls for substantial change. It is the possibility of losing the perceptions and values by which we define ourselves and therefore the meaning that life has for us. The perceived need to let go of the self of one stage and move on to the next represents a developmental crisis. It comes as a natural part of movement through life. Crises provide the impetus for moving from one major level of growth to the next. However, not every person progresses from one stage of self-growth to the next easily. If we choose not to let go of our present values or perceptions or if we choose to replace them with those that don't represent a higher self, then growth is foreclosed. We remain stuck in our current level of development.

When a natural developmental crisis occurs, the person is faced with the choice of (a) reinforcing the boundaries around the self-concept in an attempt to avoid change, (b) regressing to an earlier stage of development that is perceived as being safer, or (c) using the crisis as an impetus to move to a higher level of development. The last of these choices is the one that provides for growth and should be considered most healthy. All growth is centered around a crisis, and when a person is not experiencing a major crisis, the level of anxiety is not sufficient to cause movement toward greater wholeness.

There are crises other than those that come through the process of natural development, however—crises that are forced upon us by circumstances external to ourselves. These crises result when the values by which we define ourselves are forcibly taken away, leaving us with a temporarily incomplete self-concept. These crises also afford an opportunity to grow, but they differ in the sense that the change in self is forced by external events, and therefore we have no choice about giving up our self-concept. The choices in this case are to (a) deny that the crisis has occurred and the self-values are lost, (b) attempt to recapture the self that has been lost, or (c) use the crisis as an opportunity to grow by moving to a new level of self-development.

CRISIS FACILITATION

Many crises call for intervention on the part of human services workers, such as when a child faces the crisis of abuse or when a woman is involved in the crisis of rape. These interventions do not constitute counseling, however. Nevertheless, crisis intervention has been introduced into the field of counseling in recent years. Counselors are viewed as persons who step in when a crisis occurs and intervene to correct the situation through counseling. This implies, of course, that the individual with the crisis cannot cope with it and needs someone to intervene and take care of it. The crisis is perceived to be a difficulty that exceeds the resources and coping mechanisms of the person being helped. Such a definition, however, denies people's basic ability to live their own lives.

A counselor faces a client who threatens suicide and becomes afraid. A hospice worker sits with a patient who might die when there is no other help around and becomes overwhelmed. Crises need to be fixed, we need to heal the patient, and so we become crisis intervention workers.

A crisis hurts, there is no denying that. To have one's self, or personhood, threatened and put in danger is painful. The client wants someone to intervene and stop the pain. So the professional has a choice, just as if the client had a headache. If a headache were the problem, the counselor could intervene with aspirin, massage, or relaxation tapes and stop the pain. But if the headache is the manifestation of an unsatisfactory life, the professional helper could use the occasion of the headache to facilitate the client's understanding of the life issues that are creating the pain, and together they could explore the options that might be available for growing beyond the need to have headaches.

In the same way, a psychological crisis can be perceived as something that needs to be stopped, or it can be seen as a manifestation of an opportunity to move forward in one's life development. Seen from this latter perspective, crises provide the impetus for growth and do not necessitate intervention. Rather, they call for someone to facilitate the person's attempts to find new meaning in life within the context of the crisis and to use it in a transformative way.

The critical factor in receiving a diagnosis of terminal illness is that it constitutes a life crisis that calls for a reevaluation of values and goals. If a crisis represents a loss of the identity of one's self, then in the case of impending death it is the loss of the most basic of the values by which the person defines the self. The threat of losing one's values creates anxiety; the actual loss or the perception of loss creates depression. This is the essence of the crisis of death and dying—the threat of the loss of life values and the final acknowledgment of the reality of this loss, which creates in the person a universal pattern of anxiety and depression. The outward response will differ from person to person with respect to timing, severity, and behavioral manifestations, but the anxiety and depression will be present. This is the essence of a worldly life, the suffering of Christ, the dukkha of Buddhism, the angst of existentialism. It is not a condition to be gotten rid of but a fact of life that must be faced and transcended. It is this reality of life that should cause us to focus on the intrapsychic concerns that are associated with dying rather than only trying to alleviate medical problems.

A loss can result in retreat, in a reinforcement of the boundaries around the identity of the self at the present level of development, or in a letting go of those boundaries in an effort to move to a higher level. One patient, in describing her own battle with a life-threatening illness, said, "We've all heard stories about people who have used a confrontation with catastrophic illness to change themselves radically, to turn their lives more toward service, to learn to treat themselves and others with kindness and compassion." This is an example of using the crisis to grow, to transform to a higher level of being.

If as counselors we assume this view of a crisis, we are more inclined to assume a facilitative orientation than an interventive one. When individuals perceive that the values and meaning that had given direction to their lives are losing their power, there begins to arise in them a desire to change. That change can be up, down, or sideways, but it constitutes a felt need for movement, and that is a prerequisite for the growth that occurs at the center of a crisis. All crises have a future orientation. Even dying, the ultimate crisis, has a future orientation and should be understood in this way. Crises, like stepping stones, define one's life direction.

THE MEANING OF LOSS

The loss that a crisis represents is not defined by objects outside of the individual. It is not the loss of a spouse, or a job, or a part of the body, or even of oneself through death that gives meaning to the crisis, but the loss of the associated life-defining values. Any situation or set of circumstances that has the potential to upset or destroy the perceptions and values by which we identify ourselves represents a loss, without regard to the specific object of the loss. A counselor must determine the effect of a loss by understanding the meaning it has for the self-identity of the person who is experiencing it. For one person, losing a spouse does not necessarily constitute the same level of crisis as it does for another. In the same manner, counselors must know the meaning that death holds for any specific person before we can understand the level of crisis that terminal illness holds for that person.

As a result of her experience in working with terminally ill patients, Elisabeth Kubler-Ross (1969) outlined her perception of the psychological stages that dying people go through. She indicated at that time that not everyone goes through these stages, nor does every person who goes through them do so in exactly the same fashion. Yet she felt that there was enough commonality that she could develop what has become known as the loss paradigm.

Not all persons who work in the field of thanatology agree with this description of the process of dying. Shneidman (1973), for example, did not perceive these to be stages, but rather a clustering of cognitive and affective states. This difference is not one that seems to have great importance, however, in relationship to the overall understanding of the process of going through a loss. Weisman (1972) significantly expanded the aspect of denial, indicating that it is not so much a stage as a continuing issue in the whole of the dying process. In keeping with these various considerations, the position taken here is that what Kubler-Ross termed stages are important considerations in developing a counseling model for working with dying persons and that these stages form a basis for understanding the people with whom the counselor will work. They are therefore presented here as aspects of the dying process, and the questions of order and universality are considered as minimally as possible.

According to Kubler-Ross (1969), there are five stages or conditions that a person is likely to experience during a loss. These are denial, anger, bargaining, depression, and acceptance. Overt manifestations may not always occur at a given time, even though the person experiences the feelings at an unconscious level. A person may become stuck in any one of these and therefore not experience other aspects as fully. Even with these variations, however, there does seem to be a similar pattern of movement that most people experience.

STAGES OF LOSS IN TERMINAL ILLNESS

Although dying can be perceived as a single crisis, it can also be seen as a series of crises, each with its own stages or conditions. In many cases, an illness in the early stages is appropriately termed *life-threatening* because it is not known whether it will develop into a terminal illness. Even when doctors are quite certain that a disease will be terminal, the early stages are often characterized by more uncertainty, and the patient and family maintain a great amount of hope. This is also a time when there tends to be greater denial or at least an unwillingness to approach the disease as being one that is terminal.

A second stage is when the illness takes a course that is deemed by the physician to be irreversible or unstoppable. This represents a time when the disease is clearly terminal, although the length of time the person might live is often quite uncertain. During this stage, there still may be denial, but the other conditions of the loss paradigm are also likely to come into play. The third stage is when the illness begins a continuous progress toward the end point, and there is no longer hope or likelihood of remission. Again, any of the aspects of loss may occur in any or all of these stages of the overall terminal illness crisis, and this may result in a person's seeming to effectively deal with one aspect, only to later revisit it.

It is during the third stage that hospices play their most active part, yet the first and second stages are particularly important to the counselor's role. Transformational growth is a long-term process and requires considerable psychic energy. Therefore, counseling should begin in the earlier stages when the time and energy are more available. Of course, not all persons wish to become involved in counseling during these periods, but it should be readily available. It is not something that should be restricted to the period of hospice care.

ASPECTS OF LOSS

Denial

Kubler-Ross (1969) perceived denial to be the first stage that a dying person experiences. Though some do not agree with the notion of stages, there is little question that denial is a critical aspect of dying and that the way in which terminally ill persons deal with denial is of special concern. Weisman (1972) distinguished three degrees of denial. The first occurs when the person initially receives information about the illness and is unable to accept or assimilate the facts of the illness. At this point, it is the facts themselves that are being denied. The second degree is the distortion of the interpretation of the facts of the disease. The patient makes erroneous inferences about the implications of the illness. It is now not the fact of the disease but what it will mean that is being denied. The third degree of denial associated with dying is the denial of extinction, that is, denial of impending death itself.

It is this last aspect of denial that makes it special in terms of dying. There is a general process of denial that relates to any significant loss, not simply loss of life. But only in the case of dying does the denial of extinction come into play. In other losses, one can deny the impending loss of important aspects of the self, but this does not involve the loss of self altogether. Weisman pointed out that this denial of extinction is not the same as in healthy persons who believe in their own immortality but relates only to those who have come to an acceptance of their illness and its implications and still are able to deny the inevitable consequence. This is a denial that can come and go, where the reality bubbles up into consciousness momentarily and then is pushed into the unconscious again. The person who is dying may discuss the impending self-extinction in one session with a counselor, only to be in a state of denial during the next session.

As Weisman pointed out, a common purpose served by denial is coping with the threat of a jeopardized relationship with a significant key person. This leads to the dying person's denying more to some persons than others. The people who are most crucial to the person's sense of well-being are most likely to hear the most denial. This, however, is a positive aspect with regard to counseling because the counselor, at least at the outset, is less critical to the dying person than are others. The person will be more likely to let go of denial when talking to a counselor in the early stages of their relationship.

In the case of death, one of the relationships that is jeopardized is the relationship with the self; hence, a purpose is also served by denying the reality of impending extinction to oneself. Experiences that are perceived to be inconsistent with the image we have of ourselves are threatening. If these perceptions are accepted as real, they will necessitate a change in self-concept, disrupting the need for maintenance which is part of our natural tendency. The first attempt to deal with an inconsistent experience is to somehow distort it, to deny its occurrence or to alter perceptions of it in such a way as to make it fit the present concept of self so that no change is required.

One of the ways that a person may react to a crisis is by drawing more rigid boundaries around the self. This is somewhat akin to a besieged army reinforcing the defensive wall around its territory in the face of increased attack by the enemy. The first line of defense is generally to try to keep the enemy from entering, thereby protecting what is one's own. In the case of a psychological crisis, what is one's own is the self-concept, and it is this that needs to be protected. Therefore, we tend to do what we can to make the boundaries around the self less vulnerable to attack.

A crisis represents the possible loss of the values by which we define ourselves. It is an attack on one's own territory and creates the need to defend that territory. Individuals with a terminal illness may deny the threat of loss by actually not hearing the diagnosis or by telling themselves that they do not have a terminal illness (Weisman's second degree of denial). Another common strategy is to deny the terminal aspect of the illness, saying to oneself, for example, that even though the doctor says my disease is incurable, it will not kill me, it is not a "terminal" illness. In other loss situations, a man whose spouse has said she wants a divorce may deny it by believing that his wife is just saying she wants a divorce but that she won't really file for one, or a man who has been made paraplegic as a result of an accident might deny it by telling himself that the injury is not permanent and that he will walk again as soon as he has regained his strength.

Often the onset of a life-threatening, or self-concept threatening, crisis is psychologically more than a person can handle. It is necessary to push the meaning of the crisis into the unconscious, to deny that it is happening, in order to assimilate it at a slower pace. This is simply a natural way of handling significant losses and should be seen in that light. A person may have an initial reaction of outward acceptance, feeling that "we'll just take it one step at a time." Many express hope when there is little reason for it: "The doctor said 1 out of 100 people beat this disease, and I know I'm going to be one of them." Although the counselor or other helper may have an initial reaction of wanting the patient to face reality, for the patient this is reality, the only reality that can be dealt with at the present time. As long as a person is in this stage, there is no perceived need for help because the person's efforts are focused on not changing. This is a period when counselors need to show caring and concern and allow patients room to come to an awareness in their own time of the need for change. Defensiveness is not a problem to be gotten rid of but should be lived fully to discover the meaning that lies behind it. Our goal is to help terminally ill persons live their denial fully, which means allowing them their right to not accept what we might consider to be reality, yet at the same time communicating caring and concern.

It is not the denial of dying that is the question, but the denial of the loss of the self, the denial of psychological extinction. A woman in her 40s was in the terminal stage of cancer, and treatment necessitated that she remain in the hospital for extended periods of time. She was adamant that no one, not even her doctor, was to come in to see her until she had made herself presentable, which included wearing her own bedclothes and having herself made up to the standards she was used to. As her counselor, I had to make very specific appointments so that she would be ready to talk with me. This was not simply a desire to look nice but also a denial of the deterioration of her body and an attempt to maintain an image of herself as an attractive woman. This was the concept she had of herself, and she was not ready to give that up.

In such a case, it was important to allow the defensiveness. This was a period of assimilating the meaning of the crisis at an unconscious level while maintaining her sense of self at a conscious level. It was necessary to accept her reality (i.e., not to dispute it) and to show a caring and understanding attitude. It was far more important to communicate that I understood the importance to her of the perception of having an attractive appearance than it was to make her face the reality of the situation. She could only come to an acceptance of the deterioration of her body and its meaning to her after she had assimilated her experience on an unconscious level. As she experienced the understanding and caring that was communicated regardless of what was happening to her, she gradually was able to allow the experience into the conscious level of her awareness and was able to move on through the process of dealing with the loss. Attempts to make her face reality, to deny her the ability to maintain her concept of attractiveness, would simply have created a need to defend her self-concept even more rigidly.

A person must eventually acknowledge the nature of the loss and move through the stage of denial to use the crisis as a means to grow. As helpers sharing the journey with the person experiencing the loss, we counselors cannot force the person into this acknowledgment. In most cases, the counselor represents a context in which such things will be discussed, and as part of the process of denial, the dying person rejects the offer to talk to the counselor. The most positive thing we can do is to accept the reality that our patients are experiencing, even if it is significantly different from ours, and that often will amount to leaving them alone until they have worked through this initial stage on their own. We can be ready, if given the opportunity, to help or facilitate a person's movement through the denial stage, but until we are afforded the chance to help, we must allow the person to maintain the denial.

Anger

History has shown that during revolutionary times, there is typically an increase in social disruption, crime, terrorism, religious fervor, and even mental illness. These are basic human responses to the underlying anxiety and uncertainty that comes from the threat of change. The same is true on an individual basis, but it is summed up in the loss paradigm as anger. When the person comes through the stage of denying the threat and allows the reality of the loss into conscious awareness, the reaction is very often one of anger—anger at having this threat happen and perhaps at not being able to control what is occurring. The anger may be directed at the object of loss, at whomever is perceived to be responsible for the loss (perhaps God), or even at the self. The object is not so important, however, as the fact that the person is now recognizing the threat and therefore can begin to be consciously concerned with doing something about it.

Many people find fault with the stage of anger being included in the loss paradigm because they feel that it is not general enough to warrant such treatment. Their reaction often is that they have known a lot of people who were dying (or experiencing some other loss) and that many of those people didn't show anger. Sometimes individuals who are going through the loss themselves feel that they are not angry and that such a stage should not be included. Some professionals try to force "hidden" anger to the surface, certain that it is lying under the outward layer of consciousness and needs to be vented. Most likely, however, not everyone experiences anger anymore than everyone feels the need to deny the loss.

Anger is one manifestation of anxiety, yet it is only one of several possible ways that a person has of showing it. The threat of such a significant loss of self as is represented by impending death naturally gives rise to anxiety, which will be present at some level of awareness throughout the crisis. Denial is designed to manage the anxiety by keeping it suppressed, but when the denial is given up, the anxiety becomes more overtly manifest, and as Kubler-Ross (1969) pointed out, often but not always it is manifested as anger. Some people, however, show their anxiety in other ways, and so there is no universality, only a substantial generality, to the pattern of anger shown by people going through a significant loss. The second stage of the loss paradigm could be labeled "the overt manifestation of anxiety," with the understanding that this might be seen as anger or as other emotions. However, because anger is the most common emotion shown in response to the anxiety, Kubler-Ross's original model, in which anger is the second stage, seems to be a good description of the reaction of dying persons. A strong case can be made that anxiety is a universal concomitant of loss that all people go through, and that case is expanded in chapter 6.

In the facilitative model, the counselor's purpose is not to intervene in the expression of anger but to accept it, to help the person understand the meaning that it has within the context of the loss, and to allow the natural course of the anger to unfold. Though this seems easy to do, many people find it difficult in practice to allow a person to be angry (or scared or depressed), and therefore they attempt to hurry the process of working through the emotions. However, just as one's ability to hurry the process of healing a broken leg is limited, so is the ability to hurry the process of working through the anger, fear, and depression resulting from a loss. We may not be able to stop the anger, but it does afford us an opportunity to build a helping relationship. In contrast to the period of denial, when the person is likely not to want to talk to a counselor, the period of venting emotions is one in which a counselor's help is often welcome. So long as counselors do not try to deny patients the ability to engage in this expression, they are usually welcome. And being welcome to enter into the exploration of the meaning of the anger with the dying person, the counselor has an opportunity to communicate an attitude of understanding, caring, and love.

Bargaining

When a person ceases denying the reality of a loss, the emotions such as anger that have been suppressed as a part of the denial come into conscious awareness. This is the dawning of acceptance that there is, in fact, a threat to the self of the person. The rigid boundaries around the self have been broken down, and the enemy has been allowed to enter. This increases the fear or anxiety over what may happen to the self and results in the anger that often accompanies the loss. The next step then is to attempt to drive the enemy back out beyond one's own borders and reestablish the territory. This attempt is made during the stage of bargaining.

Just as it sounds, the person experiencing the loss tries to strike a bargain by which there can be a return to normal and the self-boundaries can be reestablished. In the case of the dying person, this often takes the form of beseeching God (or some other pertinent deity) to alter the course of the disease, to "give me one more chance, and I will do whatever you want." This, of course, does not work in most cases. For this reason, Kubler-Ross (1969) saw the bargaining stage resulting from terminal illness as usually being short-lived. To the extent that it is only the reversal of the illness that is being bargained for, this analysis is true. But to the extent that it is the pre-terminal illness self that the individual is attempting to recover, the bargaining may continue for a much longer period of time.

Because it is the psychological self that is being threatened, the bargaining stage takes on tremendous importance. It often represents heroic efforts to return to the preloss level, taking the form of trying to replace the lost values with others that are the same or similar. A woman who has lost her husband through death may precipitously marry a man who seems to her to be able to provide the same things that she valued in her former husband, allowing her to keep the same self. A man who has lost his job may spend considerable effort trying to get it back, even showing a willingness to take less money or do more work— all in an effort not to have to give up the self-concept that was related to his job. In the case of the dying person, the individual may try to create new activities and relationships that seem to be the same as those of the predying self.

Elaine was a woman in her early 40s who was dying of breast cancer. She had spent nearly 20 years as a career counselor, helping others find their place in the world of work. At the time she discovered she had cancer, she had a strong concept of herself as being an expert in this field, but eventually it was necessary for her to give up her job. The physical demands were too much.

Bargaining for Elaine was not a matter of trying to reverse the disease so she would not die. She had come to an acceptance of the inevitable. What she could not give up was her sense of being an expert helper to others in their search for careers and career changes. Part of her bargaining, her attempt to keep her self, took the form of volunteering her services to anyone she met who seemed to need career counseling. Much of her focus as a member of a support group was on helping others make necessary adjustments in their jobs. This wasn't simply a matter of continuing activities that she was used to but also an effort to remain as she was before the cancer.

Much of the effort in the bargaining stage is done through the process of counseling, with the person who is experiencing the loss trying to enlist the help of the counselor in returning things to normal. If a counselor accepts this role, he or she becomes an intervention worker, intervening in the loss situation to try to help return it to normal. The counselor tries to cure the injury to the self that is resulting from the loss. Such attempts might take the form of trying to help the person see that there are things that still can be done and goals that can be attained within the limited time that might be left to the individual. The counselor might try to help the dying person set short-range, personal, and worldly goals. Yet these efforts only serve to replace the former transient goals of life with other more immediate yet still transient goals. They do nothing to further the patient's movement through the stages of loss.

To help the person use the loss as a means by which movement to a higher level of self-development can be made, the counselor must choose not to intervene but to facilitate the person's movement through this stage to the point where the bargaining is given up, the fact that the loss has occurred is accepted, and movement toward restructuring of the self-concept at a higher level takes place. The counselor must allow the dying person the freedom to explore the meaning of the loss and accept that meaning without trying to stop the pain that accompanies such exploration. It is not enough simply to allow the person to accept that the precrisis self is lost and there is little hope of creating another that will have positive meaning. With the dying person, we must offer help in understanding and experiencing higher levels of existence. This is the essence of a facilitative model of counseling with the terminally ill.

Depression

Anxiety stems from the underlying fear that we will not get or be able to maintain what is crucial to our self-concept. Depression comes from a realization and acceptance that the loss has taken place. A situational depression results from values losing their power for the individual. When the values by which one defines the self are removed by loss or are voluntarily given up in the process of growing, there is a natural and invariant period of depression. Just as anxiety is natural to loss, and subsequently to growth, so is depression. As counselors, our goal must be to help the person move through these emotional states and not to intervene by blocking the pain that is a natural concomitant of them.

Depression allows the person to assimilate the change that has been brought about by the loss. It is a grieving process that cleanses, that washes out the old self-values that need to be let go of so that new ones can take their place. If this cleansing process does not take place, there will not be adequate room to build new self-values. Psychic energy that needs to be available for building a new self will instead be used in an attempt to maintain the old. Depression is the last stage of being stuck in the realm of the old self and is characterized by apathy, low vitality, melancholy, and a period when growth will not occur.

Just as in the case of anxiety, then, this is not a time to intervene. The counselor should not mask the depression with drugs or cognitive processes that attempt to reestablish the old values. It is, instead, a time to facilitate the person's movement through the depression, allowing it and all of its meaning to be freely experienced so that the person can come to the stage of accepting the loss of the old values. Following the stage of bargaining, there is a cognitive realization that the values are lost, but an experiential acceptance does not come until one has gone through the depression stage. Until depression has been experienced, there will not be the total acceptance that "I am no longer the self that I was" and then subsequently the acceptance that "I don't need to be my old self because now I can become a better self." The depression associated with dying is discussed more fully in chapter 7.

Acceptance

Acceptance can be equated with the Eastern concept of equanimity. It is a time when we have let go of the negative emotions that hold us back from growth. Kubler-Ross (1969) noted that for the dying person, acceptance may be a very short period just before death, when the period of depression has passed and there is a realization, involving the whole self, that the person is moving to a higher level of being. The acceptance of the dying person may be difficult to know because it often comes at a time when the person is no longer able to communicate its meaning to those who are near.

For persons experiencing other losses, however, acceptance is the final stage of movement from one level of development to the next. It means that the person no longer will attempt to hold on to the old self, that there is now hope for the future, and that there will be new values by which the self will be defined. It is the last stage before the transformation from one level of being to the next takes place. It represents the final letting go of the old to provide a place for the new.

In many cases, there is no need for the person not to find acceptance before the final moments of life. It should be the goal of the counselor to help the dying person reach this stage of the loss process at a time when worldly growth is still possible. If we work within a facilitative framework, having as our goal the successful movement through the stages of loss, we help our client use the final stage of life as a means of transcending the current level of consciousness and reaching a higher one. There is no reason that achievement of a higher stage cannot occur while there is still time for actualization to take place.

APPROPRIATE AND HEALTHY DEATH

There is a common process of living through a crisis that most people experience without regard to the object of the loss that is a part of the crisis. There are also special considerations that make the experience of dying different from other crises, and special needs that the dying person has. Weisman (1972) was one of the first to discuss these special needs when he talked about what constitutes an appropriate death. Foremost among the ideas he presented is that what is an appropriate death depends on the individual doing the dying. What is appropriate for one person might not be so at all for another. Counselors must listen to those who are dying and understand what they believe a good or appropriate death to be.

Weisman (1972) defined appropriate death as one that is consistent with the person's concept of self. The values and ideals that have guided the person in life should continue to operate during the final stage. There also needs to be a continuity of the individual's relationships with significant others. This is an aspect that often is not met because those who are most important to the dying person may withdraw, either physically or emotionally. This creates a disruption in the most basic of the conditions by which we know ourselves, relationships with significant others. Weisman also noted that an appropriate death is one that is peaceful and free from major conflicts. This has meaning for the nature of the counseling and support to be offered, indicating that it should not be our purpose to focus on issues that give rise to conflict. Although this may be appropriate for persons in counseling who are not dying, there are different considerations for the terminally ill person.

More recently, D. C. Smith and Maher (1993) presented their findings regarding what constitutes a healthy death. They asked caregivers to identify the attitudes that they perceived to characterize one person they believed had died a healthy death. Among the common issues expressed by the caregivers were having control, hearing painful truths, reviewing the past, maintaining a sense of humor, the presence of significant others, physical expressions of caring, and talking about spiritual issues.

Having Control

It is not easy to maintain control of oneself, one's environment, and one's circumstance during the period of dying. Very often, terminal illness takes away the ability to control one's body and functioning and, consequently, a part of one's self-concept. Also, hospitals and other care settings are not able to afford as much control as one would have at home. So in such a circumstance, providing the dying person as much control as is possible can be extremely important.

The ability to control does not reside simply in the external environment, however. Often it is a matter of perception of the circumstances one is in, and the counselor can be very helpful in this manner. Providing the opportunity to explore what is happening, how one is experiencing it, and the options one has regarding how the situation is to be perceived can be very helpful in maintaining a sense of control. Even if patients cannot control their disease, if they understand that they can control their feelings about it, that is, that they have the right to be happy or sad, mad or depressed, then the sense of losing control is lessened.

I worked with a man for several months during the time that he remained at work and in his own home. One weekend, however, he needed to go into the hospital. I stopped by to see him on Monday and found that he would be in for some time. Because we had made an appointment for the following Thursday, I asked if he would still like for me to come to see him. He checked his appointment book and told me Thursday would be fine. At the end of our session on Thursday, I asked if he would like to see me again the following Thursday. He again checked his appointment book, which, of course, was empty. He then looked at me and grinned and said Thursday would be fine. We continued that procedure during his final weeks in the hospital. Although we both knew he would always be free on Thursday, it gave him some sense of control in an environment where one generally has little if any control over the schedule. It was important that I not tell him when I would come but let him be involved in making the decision. Just the perception of having some control seemed very important to that man.

Hearing Painful Truths

Wanting to hear painful truths is at the other end of the continuum from wanting to deny, yet there comes a point for many where this is important, and counselors need to be ready to share these truths with the person who desires to hear them. Knowing what is likely to happen, and when, can be crucial to people's ability to make plans and do those things that are important to them.

A young doctor, in his first year of an oncology fellowship, told me about a young woman in her 20s who was brought into the hospital in serious condition. He said he knew she wouldn't live more than a day or two. While he was examining her, she looked at him and asked, "Am I going to die, Doctor?" I asked him how he answered her. He said he didn't have a chance, that the attending physician who was standing behind him broke in and responded, "No, we're going to do everything we can, and you're going to be all right." The fellow then told me that the woman died that evening. By not telling her the painful truth, the attending physician denied her the opportunity to say last goodbyes or in any other way prepare for what he knew was certain to come and what she wanted to know. She was denied an opportunity to reach some closure, which is a part of the dying person's need.

Reviewing the Past

Reviewing the past is a way of consolidating one's sense of self, a validation of the person one is. It can also be a dying farewell to those who will be left behind. This is a process in which counselors can be very helpful, allowing the person to explore the self in the present by remembering the relationships that created that self. Many persons who are dying also like to write journals or letters that can remain with those who have been important in their self-development. It may be difficult for the person to do the reviewing with loved ones, but by writing, they can communicate those things about their relationships that they want to share.

The term *life review* has been applied to similar processes that are of particular importance to the elderly (Butler, 1963). As persons perceive themselves changing in significant and unalterable ways, there is often a felt need to reaffirm what one has been. This is true when one is facing death as a natural consequence of age and also when one is dying of a terminal illness. "To die well one must feel a measure of self-completion—imagery of a life with connection, integrity, and movement, and of dying as a part of some immortalizing current in the vast human flow" (Lifton, 1979, p. 25). This is a feeling that many terminally ill patients have.

As with all of the other issues, it is important to let the dying person set the agenda. Reviewing the past is important to many, but there are some who do not wish to do so. It is not something that should be forced on patients so that they will die a healthy death. On the other hand, when the person indicates that this is important, the counselor should be ready to listen, and not attempt to direct the counseling in another direction.

Maintaining a Sense of Humor

A terminal illness involves considerable change, and many dying persons attempt to minimize it as much as is possible. Yet often those around the person try to thwart the efforts of the dying person to keep things as they were, as much as it is possible to do so. For example, a person who has enjoyed humor throughout life does not wish to give it up during the final period of life. To give it up is another aspect of giving up the self that the person has come to know, and as we have seen, that fight is great enough without adding to it when it is not necessary.

I was visiting a friend who was in the hospital fighting off some of the negative effects of lung cancer. He talked about wanting to get back to work, at least part time. He had been away from work since he had been diagnosed with the cancer. He was extremely weak, and the treatments were having a minimal effect, but he still held high hopes of returning to work soon. That evening he called me at home and asked if I could come in to see him the next day. I asked what the problem was. He related that the doctor had come in after I had been there, and he asked if he could go back to work at the beginning of the next month. He said the doctor told him it was time for a reality talk, that he would never be able to go back to work, and, in fact, because the treatments were having little effect, he might not even be able to go home from the hospital. My friend said that after 5 minutes of laying all this out, the doctor said he would return to see him the next morning and as the doctor walked out, he said, "Have a nice day."

In spite of the negative report, the increased anxiety that my friend was experiencing, and the overwhelming need to process what all this meant, he still saw humor in the doctor's parting words. He was able to laugh and enjoy the moment. And I laughed with him, just as we had done many times before under similar circumstances. The humor helped at a moment of devastating news. It allowed my friend to maintain at least some sense of the self he had been before the cancer.

Presence of Significant Others

One of the concerns that is often expressed by persons who are dying is that friends and sometimes even family members don't come to visit as often as they would like. There can be many reasons for this, but often it is a feeling of helplessness that causes a person to withdraw, a sense of not being able to do anything for the friend or loved one. Some patients also talk of the doctor withdrawing when there seems to be little left in the way of viable treatment. Pande (1968) pointed out that in the West, we need work to do, and when there is no longer any work that we can do with a person who is dying, there is no longer any reason to maintain the relationship. Yet just being present is important.

Many caregivers and family members have learned to sit in silence when there is no energy or desire to talk but there is a continuing need for presence. I worked with a man whose wife was in the hospital in the last stages of cancer. One day he told me his wife told him not to come every night, that once or twice a week was enough. In trying to find out the reason, we discovered that he tried to talk all evening, and she couldn't take it. In fact, she said he wasn't any good at it. I asked what things were like at home in the evenings before she had become ill. He said he watched television, and she read or sewed. I suggested that maybe he should just come to see his wife in the evenings and not talk, but just sit and watch television as he used to do at home. He began doing that and his wife was very happy to have him come every night. She needed his presence but not his misguided attempts to do something.

Talking About Spiritual Issues

Talking about spiritual issues is difficult for many persons, counselors as well as dying persons. Yet this is what many people want to do during a period of terminal illness. This is a time that brings such issues into sharper focus. Such discussion sometimes takes the form of talking about the meaning of life, particularly in regard to one's own sense of self and accomplishment. It can be a time of trying to put death into perspective with life. In fact, Levine (1982) noted that focusing on death is a means of becoming more fully alive.

It is also important for some people to discuss the afterlife. Perhaps not surprisingly, many dying persons have not thought much about an afterlife, simply taking some conception for granted. Yet at the point of consciously considering their death, the issue of afterlife becomes more relevant. Much of the discussion about spiritual issues and afterlife is not specifically religious, and many persons who do not consider themselves to be religious wish to discuss these issues.

This is one of the areas that make counseling with dying persons different from working with other clients. Most counseling sessions do not focus on spiritual issues because the clients do not perceive these to be important in the normal context of their lives. They feel a need to deal with more immediate issues. As I have indicated, however, these immediate issues become less important to a person who perceives the normal context to have a limited span, and the spiritual concerns then come into play. Counselors who choose to work with the terminally ill need to be ready to work with clients in this realm.

SUMMARY

This process of moving through a loss is the heart of understanding the dying person and of providing high quality psychospiritual palliative care. It represents the natural movement during a time of crisis, especially the crisis brought about by the threat of death. As Kubler-Ross (1969) presented it, peacefulness and freedom from negative emotions will occur only as the person reaches a level of acceptance. If there is blocking of the process at any point, with or without our help, anxiety, depression, and perhaps anger or other hindering emotions will keep the dying person from reaching acceptance. Conflicts, disruptions, and incongruencies with self-concept are more likely to result from "letting the person die peacefully" than they are from facilitating a person's struggle to use the period of dying as an opportunity to move toward greater wholeness.

Each time a person moves from one level of development to the next, there must be a loss of the old self in the interest of gaining one of a higher order. The crisis of dying is simply one more time that the self is lost, albeit the most critical one. Therefore the threat to self caused by death is one last chance for growth. Whether the crisis is one that comes as a result of natural development or one that comes from a loss forced on the individual from the outside, it is necessary to grieve the loss of the self and then move on. It is in this sense that palliative care entails helping terminally ill persons move through the stages of loss and not just allowing them to "die a peaceful death." A peaceful death will come only as a result of the person's using the crisis as the final opportunity to grow.

Chapter 3

Development of a Facilitative Model

This chapter outlines a model for helping persons who are terminally ill. That helping can best be described by the word *counseling* or, more precisely, *mental health counseling*, referring to work done by psychologists, social workers, nurses, and other professionals who work with dying persons. It is not a term that should be restricted to the work of any special group (i.e., professionally trained counselors and psychotherapists) but rather should be used more generically to describe an approach to helping that disregards the credentials of the helper.

In the West today, the most common term used to refer to what counselors do is *psychotherapy*. Some may say that psychotherapy and counseling are different functions or at least that they represent different points on a continuum of helping, but there is little value in making such a distinction. Therapy means cure or remediation and parallels the realm of medicine. The original psychotherapists were medical doctors and patterned their work after that branch of science, but this represents only a part of the work done by professional counselors. There are different focuses within the field that is known as psychotherapy or mental health counseling. Some focus their work on the physical or biological functions of the brain and body, finding the cause of psychological distress in this realm. Others focus their work on social issues and developmental relationships, and others focus on the issues of existential meaning. To one person, therapy is oriented toward psychological cure, whereas to others it is oriented toward psychological, existential, or spiritual growth. All of these persons use the terms *psychotherapy* and *counseling.*

One of the most widely accepted definitions of psychotherapy includes (a) removing, modifying, or retarding existing psychological symptoms; (b) mediating disturbed patterns of behavior; and (c) promoting positive personality growth and development (Wolberg, 1967). The first two elements clearly refer to a curative or remedial function, but the third does not. It implies what many see as the essence of counseling, if that is to be distinguished from therapy. Although in modern usage *psyche* generally refers to the functions of the mind, in its original Greek meaning it also included aspects of life principle and soul, relating to both the inner life and the life that extends beyond the earthly. *Therapy* meant to heal, not especially in the medical sense, but in a broader sense of total healing. So in spite of recent efforts, the terms *psychotherapy* and *counseling* remain confused, as do the purposes of both.

A great deal of this confusion stems from the fact that counseling is not a uniform endeavor, having developed in several distinct directions. What we know as psychotherapy and counseling, although they had their seeds in the first half of the 20th century, are primarily phenomena of the second half. Beginning in the 1950s and continuing through the 1960s, what has come to be known as humanistic psychology enjoyed a place of some dominance in the area of counseling and psychotherapy. Rogerian, Gestalt, and existential approaches are primary among these. Their focus is on the phenomenal, or perceptual, subjective world of the individual client, and their goal is to facilitate the client's movement toward fulfillment or actualization of the self. In the late 1960s, however, a reaction against these subjective, nonempirically based approaches to counseling became widespread, and since the 1970s, the primary theoretical underpinning has been cognitive–behavioral, encompassing approaches that are based on scientific, empirical methods. Behaviorism was the first force of psychology, as outlined by Sutich (1969), but its application to the counseling field did not occur in any significant degree until the 1960s. Combined with cognitive psychology, it has become the dominant force in counseling and psychotherapy.

At the same time, there has been a movement in a different direction. People who felt that the humanistic approaches that adhere to a finite, individualistic orientation to human development are too limiting and that cognitive–behavioral approaches are too reductionistic began to explore what Maslow (1971) called the farther reaches of human nature. These include aspects of development beyond that of the self or ego, into what is generally referred to as the spiritual realms. Although these approaches have not become as widespread as the resurgence of cognitive–behavioral approaches, they have developed a following that is similar in scope to those of the humanistic and psychoanalytic psychotherapies. Some of the major approaches that fall within this category are Jung's (1961) analytic psychology, Grof's (1988) holotropic breath work approach, Assogioli's (1965) psychosynthesis, and Wilber's (1977) spectrum of consciousness. It is on the last of these that the model presented in this book is most consistently based.

Many theorists and practitioners have been attempting to make counseling more scientific than it has been since its inception at the end of the 19th century, and they have based their efforts on the empiricism that characterizes medicine and the biological sciences. (Freud's original intention was to make psychotherapy scientific and therefore acceptable to the medical community out of which it grew, though paradoxically his system became increasingly anecdotal and individualistic and consequently subject to criticisms that it was, in fact, not empirical and scientific.) In their attempts to increase the scientific aspects of counseling, cognitive–behaviorists (and more recently psychobiologists) have focused on external and objective measures of psychopathology and on methods of intervention that are focused on observable behaviors. In doing so, they have been able to conduct empirical studies to measure the effectiveness of counseling.

Yet voices have also been raised in another direction. These voices question whether the same treatment is appropriate for all realms of human endeavor and suggest that the helping that comes through counseling may not be appropriate for or amenable to empirical research. It is not a question of whether cognitive–behavioral methods are effective but rather of when they are appropriate. The scientific model does not fit every aspect of the world in which humans live, and much of the concern of counseling falls within the realm of the personal, subjective, or even transpersonal.

These latter orientations to counseling encompass a broader understanding of the human psyche than do orientations that focus only on scientific empiricism and are built on a medical model. There is greater concern with intrapsychic exploration and understanding and a focus on growth and transformation. Facilitative counseling is concerned with the healing power that is within the individual and that can be brought forth through a relationship in which there is understanding and love.

When counselors work with the terminally ill, we have the same problem with terminology as when we are working with any other client. If we are involved in providing help within a palliative framework, and cure is not a question, we still use the terms *psychotherapy* and *counseling*. Although what we do may look on the surface like remedial therapy, it will be seen as transformative to the person who is dying. So we need to be careful to examine what it is that we are doing and not make assumptions based on labels.

The terms *counseling* and *psychotherapy* are used interchangeably in this book. My preference is for the former term, but references to other works necessitate that both words be used. However, each term refers simply to helping other people in their life journeys, and neither distinguishes among the persons who are offering the help in terms of their training and experience. Such distinctions are often false and are meaningful primarily to the counselors and not to the persons being helped.

APPROACHES TO COUNSELING PERSONS
WHO ARE DYING

Counseling and psychotherapy for dying persons has not received the attention that other aspects of hospice care have received. For example, two of the most widely read books in the area of death and dying and hospice care are *The Encyclopedia of Death* (Kastenbaum & Kastenbaum, 1989) and *The Hospice Movement* (Stoddard, 1992), yet neither has a section on either counseling or psychotherapy, nor is either term listed in the indexes. This seems to represent the prevailing focus in the hospice movement.

Rainey (1988) noted that there has been a tendency to focus on the psychosocial aspects of dying, with emphasis on the cognitive, affective, behavioral, and interpersonal dimensions. He went on to say that this focus seems to take precedence over other perspectives (medical, economic, demographic, and cultural) that need more attention. "To my mind, addressing the patient's psychological well-being without first providing adequate care in these other dimensions is foolhardy" (Rainey, 1988, p. 149). This gives an indication of the priority given to counseling with dying persons.

In the professional literature, there are two different focuses to helping persons who are dying. One focus is on the period of dying and the concerns and conflicts associated with that period. These approaches are generally centered on interpersonal concerns and negative symptoms. The other focus is on the intrapsychic issues of the dying person, with greater concern for the spiritual aspect of the death itself than for the final period of the person's life. Which focus is most appropriate depends primarily on the needs and desires of the person receiving the counseling.

Rando (1984) discussed processes of communication in counseling the terminally ill. She divided these into nondirective and intervention techniques. Nondirective techniques include both attending responses and responses that facilitate communication on the part of the dying person. They are predicated on the understanding that it is the client's agenda that counselors should be concerned with and that we need to allow the client to freely express that agenda. Nondirective techniques are primarily focused toward the "now" issues, those of coping with family concerns, fears about the dying process, and general emotional release.

Intervention techniques include confrontation, interpretation, and problem solving. The first two are focused on helping the person alter perceptions that are hindering full or accurate understanding of the problem. The third is an active process of working through a problem that is seen to be blocking a positive dying process. All of these ways of responding are focused primarily on the concerns, issues, and difficulties encountered in the period of dying. For the most part, these responses are psychosocial rather than intrapsychic in orientation, although that distinction is not absolute.

Shneidman (1973, 1980) has provided considerable insight into working with dying persons in a counseling or psychotherapeutic context. He has been very specific that systematically attempting to help a dying person achieve a more psychologically comfortable death is the work of a psychotherapist. Moreover, he has stated that psychotherapeutic work with dying persons is significantly different from the same type of work with persons who are not dying. Among the differences are that the goals are more finite for the dying person. Everyone dies with some incompleteness, and there is no amount of self-knowledge that defines appropriate death. Therefore, Shneidman has concluded that increasing self-knowledge, though an appropriate goal for persons who are not dying, is not necessarily an appropriate goal for a person who is dying.

Shneidman (1973, 1980) also has stated that there can be greater depth to the relationship with a dying person than is allowed with other clients. A deeper love and a more intensive transference and countertransference can be allowed because of the limits of the relationship. Counseling with a terminally ill person should focus on benign intervention and increased psychological comfort, not on working through life-long psychological problems. More than anything else, counseling should be focused on helping the person achieve a sense of peacefulness during the period of dying.

In line with this focus on comfort, Muzzin, Anderson, Figueredo, and Gudelis (1994) listed helping the patient and family maintain control and normalize everyday activity as a possible goal of counseling. Dying persons also need help with relationships and problems associated with the withdrawal of significant others. Fawzy (1994) reported that his counseling is focused on decreasing the negative symptoms of the terminal illness, such as depression, fatigue, confusion, and mood disturbances.

All of these approaches can be of help in providing some of the characteristics of an appropriate or healthy death. Maintaining control, reviewing the past, continuing positive relationships, and reducing conflicts are all aspects of the dying process that these approaches are capable of addressing. There remains, however, the issue of spiritual concerns, and it is not clear that these approaches are focused on that aspect of a healthy death.

Spirituality is that aspect of human life that transcends the personal. Full actualization of the personal self is the psychological component; transcendence of the self is the spiritual component. Each of these sides of development are a part of the unified whole, with spirituality being the second half, or transpersonal side of human development.

In recent years, there has been increasing advocacy of a focus on spirituality in counseling with dying persons. Levine (1982) pointed out that it is not the body or the physical self that dies but the sense of being a separate self. Death is a tearing away of everything one has come to know, to accept as life and self. It is through conscious dying, through consciously making ourselves aware of the impermanence of the physical and separate self that we come to a sense of peaceful death. This is a major goal of counseling with persons who are dying.

E. D. Smith, Stefanek, Joseph, and Verdieck (1993), in studying the relationship between transpersonal (spiritual) development and the psychosocial distress of cancer patients, found that the more patients explored the spiritual aspects of development, the less distress they experienced. Cohen and Mount (1992) pointed out that enhancing one's sense of personal meaning and transcendence is likely to decrease suffering in other areas and can lead to a greater sense of quality of life during the final stage of dying. In keeping with these findings, D. C. Smith (1993) presented a counseling approach to help dying persons deal with spiritual issues.

AUTHORITY IN COUNSELING

Much of the current practice in counseling and psychotherapy is to follow an authoritative model, in which the therapist is an expert directing the process of therapy or help for the client. This is true whether the focus is on helping a couple with their marriage, working with someone who has agoraphobia, or providing a counseling relationship for a person with a life-threatening illness. Shortly before his death, Carl Rogers responded to a question put to him at a major conference regarding what he perceived to be some of the significant directions in the field of counseling today. He noted the growing schism between therapists following a medical model (an authoritative "do-to-the-client" approach) and therapists who favor a more person-centered model (one in which the client is perceived to be most knowledgeable about him or herself and the therapist is the facilitator). There is a belief that although Buber's (1970) *I–Thou* relationships or encounters are commendable, they do not constitute therapy. A therapist must be doing something to the patient to bring about desired changes.

The counselor of today may feel that clients are likely to misinterpret their own inner, subjective world to serve neurotic needs and therefore that an authority is highly recommended to do an objective and correct analysis. Such authoritative views tend to find favor with many counselors and therapists working in the field because their experience often tells them that such an approach is more effective. Moreover, it is perceived to be effective because the clients with whom they work are more receptive to, and perhaps more demanding of, such an approach. If one doesn't satisfy the clients, there will soon be no more clients.

In hospice care, one of the concerns is to allow dying persons to retain as much control of their lives as is possible. Patients decide whether they want pain medication (and possible negative side effects), whether they wish to have efforts made to resuscitate them if their heart stops, and whether they want the help of a cleric, social worker, or counselor. Current discussions regarding physician-assisted suicide attest to an increasing advocacy for the patient's right to decision-making power in the most critical area of all. Based on the premise that patients should have responsibility for their own lives to the very end, all of these aspects of care indicate a trend away from the authoritative treatment model that has characterized the field of medicine. The question therefore must be raised as to why the person with whom we work should not have at least equal rights in the area of counseling. Is there any compelling reason for a counselor to assume that he or she knows what is best for a dying person?

The approaches to helping the dying person described at the beginning of the chapter advocate this same orientation to authority. Shneidman (1973) made it very clear that counseling with the terminally ill is very individual and that it is the client who is to set the pace and the agenda. He stated that the relationship between a counselor and a terminally ill person is very much an *I–Thou* relationship, not one of authority. Rando (1984), with her stress on nondirective procedures, also advocated an approach focused not on authority but on working with dying persons in ways that they deem appropriate and in whatever direction they desire.

THE MEANING OF PROFESSIONAL

As a corollary to the need to be authoritative, the concept and practice of licensing has increased during the past several years. Licensing in and of itself may not be a problem, but conceptually it separates the therapist from the client in a way that hinders the growth that most of us would like to see result from counseling. Regardless of what other factors are critical to therapeutic success, a significant and meaningful relationship is at the top of the list. (Support for this contention is provided in the later chapters of this book.) When we view ourselves as licensed professionals, we tend to perceive the therapist–client relationship as a business proposition, with the therapist assuming responsibility for making the patient well to earn a fee and be viewed as a professional. This is an especially critical issue in working with persons in the final stage of life, when their concerns are far more with experiencing the connectedness that alleviates death anxiety than they are with solving the interpersonal conflicts of the present world.

Many persons are reluctant to accept help from a psychologist, a social worker, or a cleric because they have a perception (often misperception) of the role that is carried out by each of these professionals. When we establish ourselves as licensed professionals, we create boundaries, or at least an illusion of boundaries, between so-called expert helpers and those whom we wish to help, and these boundaries are difficult to overcome during the depths of a crisis such as comes during the period of dying. Hospice patients cannot see us as a friend or fellow human being who wants to share the journey with them but instead perceive us as additional treatment experts that they do not have the emotional energy to deal with. When told by a nurse or physician that such an expert is available in the hospice program, the response is often, "Oh, that's nice, but I really don't think I need their help." There is little understanding of what a counselor can offer from a facilitative point of view.

This orientation also leads to a reliance on diagnosis and labeling by psychotherapists, a phenomenon that has become much more evident in hospice care since insurance reimbursements were introduced in the United States in 1982. Licensing and third-party payments are two sides of the same coin. If insurance companies are going to pay for services, they want to have those services provided by experts. Licensing is one evidence of expertise, and the ability to make diagnoses based on standardized criteria is another. This causes counselors to look at clients very differently than phenomenologists like Carl Rogers and R. D. Laing envisioned, however. No matter how hard one tries, when a diagnosis has to be made, the client is seen as an external entity, and empathic understanding suffers. Insurance reimbursements require external assessments and treatment plans, contributing to the lessening of a person-centered orientation. The payer wants proof that the help we are offering is valid, and this is not perceived to be forthcoming through paraprofessional, nonauthoritative helpers. When the effect of counseling is evaluated by the person receiving the help, experiential criteria can be used. When a third party evaluates the effectiveness, however, procedures must be quantified.

There is a dearth of research related to the comparative successs of licensed and unlicensed counselors. Consequently, we do not know if licensing makes one more effective in working with dying persons, or even if formally educated counselors are more effective than those prepared through hospice training programs. Indeed, many hospice patients may feel more comfortable talking to volunteers than they do talking to the professional social workers or counselors. This is not to say that we should do away with professionally trained counselors in the hospice program, but rather that we need to clarify our purpose, our process, and the nature of our relationship with the dying person to offer the help that is most beneficial. Many hospices started with volunteers as their core prior to the inception of Medicare certification. They were organizations of people helping people, in which relationship was the most critical aspect. Although many benefits have been gained with insurance reimbursements, much of this original concept has been lost. Providing high quality facilitative counseling to dying persons is an effective way of recapturing this lost emphasis.

Shneidman (1973, 1980) has made it very clear that what we are talking about is psychotherapy and that it is professional. He noted, however, that this role can be taken on by a psychotherapist or by someone acting in the role of psychotherapist, leaving open the possibility that a person other than a trained professional may be the counselor. The important thing is how the person responds to the patient. Shneidman distinguished between ordinary talk or conversation and a psychotherapeutic exchange, the latter placing more emphasis on the underlying significance of what the client is saying and its meaning in the context of the client's perception of self and the world. There is a way of responding to a client that is professional, but it is not dependent on externals such as licensing and insurance certification.

TECHNIQUE OR PROCESS?

An additional aspect of the status of counseling is that counselors continually and progressively move toward being technicians, with the conduct of counseling being a matter of proficiency in the use of techniques. Over 30 years ago, Rollo May (1958) warned that psychotherapy was becoming highly technique oriented and was losing the sense of the phenomenal meaning that lay at the core of therapeutic relationships. His warning appears not to have been taken seriously, for the years since the publication of his book have seen an increase in processes that appear to be unreal or unrelated to the authentic relationship between counselor and client. Indeed, empathy itself is often viewed merely as a technique rather than the way of being that was such an integral part of Rogers' counseling.

At a recent conference on psychotherapy, the syllabus was full of these kinds of objectives: "To underscore specific treatments of choice . . ."; "How to precipitate a symbolic experience"; "To learn three techniques for improving assertiveness"; "To learn therapeutic technique for. . ."; "To learn six strategies for integrating family. . ."; "To describe and be able to use some of the most popular techniques of RET"; "How to use metaphor and fantasy." Many techniques had labels, such as the *method of injunctive communication.* So integral were techniques to the conference that on the last day, in protest, one of the participants virtually shouted, "Psychotherapy is soul searching, not technique."

Certainly counselors need procedures, or techniques, for relating to clients, but the point is a matter of emphasis. Techniques must be means, not ends. On several occasions Rogers was heard to bemoan the fact that his approach to counseling was referred to as a technique—the nondirective technique. His concern was with creating a therapeutic relationship, and any procedure that could be shown to further that goal was appropriate from his point of view. But far too often counseling is defined primarily or solely by its techniques.

In attempting to follow the model set by the medical profession, counselors have been lulled into a reductionistic point of view, reducing the problems of our clients to the most well-defined symptom we can. By doing so, we can then apply the most effective technique for removing that symptom and thereby parallel the medical doctor who treats symptoms. There are those who, with some justification, say that such an approach is a worthy endeavor, but it certainly is a long way from the soul searching that a transformative approach to counseling entails. To be of significant help to the hospice patient and family, counselors must zealously guard against using techniques and instead focus on creating a helping relationship.

Sheldon Kopp (1977) maintained that the process of therapy is a folk art not well taught in universities. If this is so, then good therapy may be more effectively developed through open awareness of experience than through understanding of theoretical formulations. Each of us develops our own ideas about what therapy is and what it should be as we experience life in general and counseling in particular. Learning to become a good counselor comes not from adopting theoretical orientations but from understanding the experiences of other counselors and measuring that understanding against one's own experience.

We need to be persons, not treatment experts, when we work with the terminally ill. Our help should be filled with understanding, compassion, and love of humanity. We are not therapists and clients, but human beings who have the opportunity to be near to each other and yet who often remain distant. In the final hours of an individual's life, when another human being experiences anguish and despair, when the need for loving and care manifests itself, even in obscure ways, we must be willing to share the journey. Treatments and interventions will no longer serve us well.

FACILITATION AS PURPOSE

In the process of determining the appropriate model for counseling the dying person, the meaning and purpose of hospice needs to be reiterated and the concept of whole-person care recaptured. MacDonald (1991) stated that hospices have allowed the larger health care system to push them into relinquishing their mission of change and force them into being an ancillary service. This is as true of the psychological, social, and spiritual dimensions of helping as it is of the medical. We have allowed the health care system to mold us into a medical model that is alien to the needs of the dying person. In this process, we have failed to appreciate that suffering has multiple causes, resulting from a threat to any part of the person's self. When our intervention is directed solely at disease and symptom control, no matter how technically good it may be, we will not only fail to relieve suffering, but we may even be its cause (Johanson, 1991).

Although many theorists and practitioners, in accepting an authoritative posture, have been attempting to make counseling more scientific, based on the empiricism that characterizes medicine and the biological sciences, other theorists and practitioners question whether the same treatment is appropriate for all realms of human endeavor, and they suggest that we must seriously question whether the helping that comes through counseling is appropriate for quantification and empirical research. Much that is positive in human relationships cannot be reduced to basic elements and examined in such a light. The scientific model does not fit every aspect of the world in which we live.

A COMPARATIVE VIEW

As psychotherapy is primarily a Western phenomenon, we could well pay attention to a perspective raised in a different environment. Pande (1968) pointed out several cultural differences between East and West that are manifested in our work as therapists and that relate specifically to how we help persons who are dying. In our Western perspective, we focus on the need to be working, producing, getting something done. To establish a relationship with another person simply for the sake of the relationship is not acceptable—it must be related to a task. Because the United States is a life-affirming society, we cannot afford to stand still. We must come to grips with our problems, and this is especially true for those who work with dying persons. There is a last remaining need to use the time productively, and if the counselor cannot find work that is appropriate for the client in this last stage of life, then there is a perception that therapy is at an end. To establish a relationship in counseling is only acceptable as a means to the end of producing something, but it cannot stand on its own. The Western world does not run on relationships, it runs on products and completed tasks.

A second perspective of the West that is different from that of the East is the focus on self-reliance, power, achievement, and sexual fulfillment. In short, the focus is on fulfillment of the individual person, whereas in the East focus is on interdependence and one's role as a member of a group. In the West there is a focus on goals and destinations, on "getting there" rather than being in the present moment. Empiricism makes one see life from a directional and linear attitude, always pressing toward the future. Along the way we forget to enjoy the scenery.

Counselors are preoccupied with content in psychotherapy because we are traditionally interested in objects of consciousness rather than in consciousness or awareness itself. We are bound by our encapsulated individual selves, and we favor the concrete symptoms and problems that can be managed and manipulated. The Eastern orientation is to focus on the person as the subject of consciousness, that is, to see consciousness as a phenomenon to be studied and understood in its own right. Western humanistic approaches have attempted to follow this orientation, but the voices of the empirically oriented cognitive–behavioral psychologists have been stronger.

Finally, we in Western society are enamored with the idea that rational thought is the highest level of functioning that we can achieve. From this perspective, we view our clients through theoretical frameworks to be able to analyze their personal dynamics in a reasoned manner, to make correct interpretations, and to give them insight into their problems and neuroses. Approaches that are not based on this high level of reasoning are seen as less than first rate because they do not function at the highest level of human endeavor.

We need to see counseling and psychotherapy from a different perspective. This does not mean that we need another theory. What we need is a different perspective from which to see what we are already doing and what we already know. The empirical scientific way of viewing the world is only one possibility, and we need to open ourselves and our counseling to other orientations.

TOWARD A FACILITATIVE MODEL OF COUNSELING THE TERMINALLY ILL

The model of counseling presented in this book is especially focused on the concerns of the dying person. This model can become as integral a part of care for the terminally ill as is medical care. The model is focused on helping persons become aware of the meaning that death has for them. It is grounded in all modes of knowing and is large enough to encompass the whole spectrum of human consciousness. It is based on the following principles:

1 Counseling should be designed to enable the client to move toward wholeness, overcoming the dualities within that lead to pain and anxiety. It should not be designed to cure illnesses or solve problems, although this may occur as a part of the content of counseling. The overall intention should be to help the client reach a higher level of consciousness, to be a soul seeker. For the person who is terminally ill, this is a crucial opportunity to focus inward and find the meaning that not only life but also imminent death has.

2 All counseling focuses around a crisis, and all crises have a future orientation. Even death, which is the ultimate crisis, has a future orientation and should be perceived as the individual's last opportunity for growth. Crises, like stepping stones, define the direction of life. We can help clients use the crisis of dying as the basis for understanding themselves at whatever level they are living and to use that understanding to move to greater health.

3 Successful movement through a crisis involves letting go of the old self and moving onto a new level of self-development. The individual must redefine the self in terms of values that are appropriate to the new level of development. This requires integrating the remaining old values and the new ones into a new self.

4 There is a natural flow of energy within each person that needs to be allowed and encouraged. It is not external agents that cause pathology but a blocking of the transformations that characterize positive movement. We each have a vital force or energy that is the body and mind's own healing power, and any blocking of this energy through procedures of intervention will hinder our ability to heal ourselves or grow in the most positive manner.

5 The experience of the client should be valued for its own sake. We should not assume that there is an external reality with which the person needs to become congruent. Many of a person's beliefs may in fact be illusions, but contrary to an intervention approach, which attempts to block such beliefs through cognitive reorientation, the facilitative approach encourages the client to continue with the chosen path in the expectation that the beliefs will be discovered to be an illusion and that the person will then be able to integrate the beliefs into some meaningful relationship to the self.

6 The experience of pain and depression must be accepted rather than suppressed or avoided. Unfinished psychological processes need to be completed. Interruption or blocking of feelings of anger or depression,

or of integrating experiences that are inconsistent with currently held values, can obviously lead to a reluctance or lack of preparation for moving from one life stage to the next. Part of the facilitative approach is to encourage clients to acknowledge and accept values, feelings, and meanings that they might otherwise suppress or deny. The counselor should encourage the natural flow of feelings and experiences but should not take an initiating role in bringing these feelings and experiences to the surface.

7   Denial is not a problem to be gotten rid of but a characteristic present within the individual that needs to be lived fully so that the denial is understood and accepted in its relationship to the client's self. It must not be blocked or cut off where it can remain a stumbling block to the process of transformation. We cannot force clients to let loose of the boundaries by which they protect the self, however; we can only create an atmosphere of freedom in which they can choose to do so of their own accord.

8   Theoretical assumptions and techniques tend to get in the way of counseling. Sometimes simple is best, but we convince ourselves that we need to make the process more complex and difficult. We must enter the counseling relationship free of preconceptions and free from the need to use specific techniques.

9   Being is more important than knowing. Change, particularly transformative change, does not come from knowing but results from allowing the total person to experience a dissatisfaction with life and to accept the need to move on. As counselors, we must focus more on the way we are and be less concerned with what we know.

10   Relationship removes the need to defend and maintain the self in its current state. When the counselor and client see each other as separate selves, this hinders transformation. To work through a crisis, there must be a sense of sharing. Transference equals corrective parenting, a restructuring of development. Encounter equals a mature sharing of one's journey through life.

11   The therapist must have intuitive, psychic, or causal knowing of the client. The teacher points the way, but the guru is the way. We should add to that saying that the counselor facilitates the way. Counselors must be fully functioning and self-actualizing, high on the spectrum of consciousness. We cannot facilitate a way that is unknown to us.

SUMMARY

Persons who are facing a terminal illness have concerns that are often different from those of clients we may see in other circumstances. These concerns include those of a spiritual nature and are often focused on transformative growth. A counseling approach that is designed for persons who are dying needs to be cognizant of these concerns and needs. It should be one that is focused on facilitating exploration of the meaning of life and death, and one that helps the person move to a higher level of consciousness. Counseling with terminally ill persons should be aimed at helping them to use this final crisis as an opportunity to grow in a transformative direction.

There are different approaches to counseling and psychotherapy—some are oriented toward a cognitive, empirical understanding of human development; some are focused on existential meaning and self-actualization; and others follow a transpersonal orientation. Though each of these approaches has validity, an approach that accounts for both the psychological and the spiritual aspects of development is most likely to meet the particular needs of a person who is dying. For this reason, the model presented in this book is based on the third of these general orientations, particularly on the approach offered by Wilber (1977), who described development as occurring within a hierarchy of personal and transpersonal levels.

Chapter 4

Psychological Underpinnings

Counseling has been defined as helping people handle crises and conflicts having to do with existential, developmental, interpersonal, and social strains (Browning, 1976). It is a one-to-one relationship with another person that is designed to help that person become psychologically healthier. Its focus is primarily intrapersonal; its method is primarily introspective and self-explorative.

There are a number of different approaches to counseling. These can be divided into the major categories or forces presented by Sutich (1968, 1969): (a) *Cognitive–behavioral* approaches focus on the empirical mode of gathering data and therefore limit counseling to experiences that can be validated by empirical evidence; (b) *psychoanalytic* approaches stress the personal unconscious and are concerned primarily with the development of the ego and self through the early stages of life; (c) *humanistic* approaches focus on phenomenal, subjective experience and the full validity of that experience and perceive the full actualization of the personal self to be the ultimate goal of counseling and life in general; and (d) *transpersonal* approaches see development as continuing beyond, or transcending, the full validity of personal human experience and are not limited to the beliefs of any particular tradition or philosophy.

The model presented here is predicated on the assumption that facilitating a client's transpersonal, or transformative, growth is an essential and integral part of counseling. Transpersonal psychology, at its inception, was defined primarily by activities, contents, and techniques. The definition presented by Sutich (1969) in the first issue of *The Journal of Transpersonal Psychology* is as follows:

> Transpersonal (or "fourth force") Psychology is the title given to an emerging force in the psychology field by a group of psychologists and professional men and women from other fields who are interested in those *ultimate* human capacities and potentialities that have no systematic place in positivistic or behavioristic ("first force"), classical psychoanalytic theory ("second force"), or humanistic psychology ("third force"). The emerging Transpersonal Psychology ("fourth force") is concerned specifically with the *empirical,* scientific study of, and responsible implementation of the findings relevant to, becoming, individual and species-wide meta-needs, ultimate values, unitive consciousness, peak experiences, B-values, ecstasy, mystical experience, awe, being, self-actualization, essence, bliss, wonder, ultimate meaning, transcendence of the self, spirit, oneness, cosmic awareness, individual and species-wide synergy, maximal interpersonal encounter, sacralization of everyday life, transcendental phenomena, cosmic self-humor and playfulness, maximal sensory awareness, responsiveness and expression; and related concepts, experiences and activities. As a definition, this formulation is to be understood as subject to *optional* individual or group interpretations, either wholly or in part, with regard to the acceptance of its content as essentially naturalistic, theistic, supernaturalistic, or any other designated classification. (pp. 15–16. Reprinted from Sutich, 1969 with permission of Transpersonal Institute, © 1976.)

This definition has proved to be quite cumbersome because it includes activities that do not differentiate it from humanistic psychology (self-actualization, ultimate meaning, and maximal interpersonal encounter, for example) and because it does not adequately separate itself from the first force (empirical, scientific study). For this reason, professionals committed to the transpersonal have attempted a number of revisions over the years. Lajoie and Shapiro (1992) reviewed all the definitions they were able to uncover from 1968 to 1991. In doing so, they presented a picture of the developing nature of the field and a consensus of the current thinking. After presenting the various definitions of transpersonal psychology (40 in all), Lajoie and Shapiro presented the predominant themes in these definitions, and based on these themes, offered their own contemporary definition. The themes are various states of consciousness, highest or ultimate potential, beyond ego or personal self, transcendence, and spiritual. The definition that they offer is as follows:

> Transpersonal psychology is concerned with the study of humanity's highest potential, and with the recognition, understanding, and realization of unitive, spiritual, and transcendent states of consciousness. (Lajoie & Shapiro, 1992, p. 91)

PSYCHOLOGY AND SPIRITUALITY

Counseling, whether or not it involves working with terminally ill persons, needs to be based on an understanding of human growth and development. In addition, it should encompass both psychological and spiritual development in a unified whole. Such a contention is predicated on a definition of spirituality that comes from one of the oldest traditions, that which understands reality to be multidimensional along the "great chain of being" (Lovejoy, 1964; Wilber, 1993). Although the number of stages and the specific names of the stages are described differently by different authors, the most commonly accepted schema is "matter to body to mind to soul to spirit." It is within this concept that my definition of spirituality lies: Spirituality is the highest level of reality, or consciousness, that is known, and represents the completion of the hierarchical evolution of humanity.

This conceptualization of spirituality is not an outcome of modern psychology and philosophy, nor is it restricted to American or even Western culture. It is at the heart of what is referred to as the perennial philosophy, the world view that the greater number of the subtler speculative minds and great religious teachers have, in their various fashions, been engaged in describing (Lovejoy, 1964). Watts (1968) noted that individuals get so tied up in their own world orientations that they lose sight of the fact that there has been a single philosophical consensus of universal extent. This was expounded by Huxley (1970) in his book, *The Perennial Philosophy*. Wilber (1993) stated that this world view is either the single greatest intellectual error to ever appear in human history or else it is the single most accurate reflection of reality yet to appear. He went on to translate the principles of this view into what he referred to as the *perennial psychology*, aspects of which undergird the model presented herein.

The great chain of being is central to the perennial psychology, although the psychology itself is broader than this one concept. It is the chain with which I am most concerned, however, because it provides the meaning of *spiritual* that serves as the basis for my discussion of counseling with dying persons. The great chain of being describes reality as being not one-dimensional but composed of several different but continuous dimensions. Moreover, these levels of reality are holistic, in the sense that each higher level encompasses the lesser levels. Imagine a series of concentric circles, where each circle represents a level of consciousness or reality. The smaller the circle, the lower the level that is represented. As these are concentric circles, each is an integral part of the succeeding circle, meaning that a higher level of reality is greater than the lower because it both adds to it and includes it. In this sense, spirit is not wholly other than mind. It adds something to mind but also integrates all the reality of mind into the level of spirit. Mind and spirit do not then form a duality but an integrated hierarchy.

Such a hierarchical ordering describes development of the person, with each succeeding stage being more developed than the previous one. Each succeeding stage emerges later than the preceding ones, knows and encompasses the earlier stages, and yet possesses characteristics and abilities that were not present in the preceding stage. In this sense, spirituality is a more developed stage than is mind, which is more developed than is body. In fact, spirituality is the highest stage to which humans can evolve, according to this system. It must be noted, however, that this is an evolutionary sequence, which is not the same as a value hierarchy. A later, or higher, stage is not necessarily better than an earlier one; it is just more developed. Therefore, work that is done in the realm of spirituality is not necessarily better or more admirable than work done in the realm of the mind, or psychology, but work done in the realm of spirituality is of a higher, or more developed, nature.

In terms of counseling, questions of spirituality versus religion and spirituality versus psychology take on a new meaning within this framework. Browning (1987) implied that these are separate issues when he raised the question of whether Western culture will be oriented to inherited religious traditions or whether it will increasingly assume the orientation, especially with regard to the inner life, of modern psychology. The *or* in this question strongly implies an either/or orientation.

Within the context of the great chain of being, however, religion, psychology, and spirituality are all part of the same hierarchy of reality. Where a counselor focuses attention is dictated by where an individual is on the developmental spectrum or at what level a crisis occurs (e.g., is it a psychological or spiritual crisis?). Just as a young man of 14 is the same person at 24, but manifests his personhood differently, so an individual dealing with psychological issues is the same person when the focus is on spiritual issues. There is no duality, just different manifestations of the same holistic entity.

The orientation known as the *spectrum of consciousness*, set forth by Wilber (1977, 1979, 1980, 1983, 1991, 1993), is based on the perennial psychology and serves as the theoretical underpinning for counseling with terminally ill persons as described in this book. Two critical aspects of this approach are set out here as a preparatory statement.

The spectrum of consciousness is not an approach that is set out against other existing approaches. As the name implies, all of human development is perceived to fall on a spectrum, which Wilber (1993) referred to as a *holoarchy*. This means that there are different levels of consciousness (i.e., different ways that we perceive and understand ourselves, our environment, and our relationships) and that these levels build on each other. Each succeeding level encompasses and integrates the preceding levels but also goes beyond, meaning that each level is higher than the preceding one.

Moreover, Wilber (1986) stated that positive development, psychopathologies, and therapeutic treatments occur at all of the levels and that counseling can only be complete and successful if it addresses the level at which the pathology develops. For problems that arise at the level of early personal development, when the characteristic way of understanding the world is through concrete operational thought, cognitive–behavioral approaches may be most appropriate because the person is not yet able to work through problems in a self-reflective and introspective way, which is characteristic of humanistic psychologies. In short, the consciousness level of the therapy must match the level at which the client is living. For problems at the early personal level, cognitive–behavioral approaches are most appropriate, but for problems at a higher personal level, humanistic approaches are most likely to be successful. It is not a question of one approach being better than the other but rather of matching the level of therapy to the level of the client's consciousness.

This aspect alone does not differentiate a spectrum from any eclectic approach that modifies treatment to the needs of the client, however. It only provides the basis for the second critical aspect of the system, which is that the purpose of counseling is not to focus on the content, or problem, or pathology of clients at whatever level they are living but to facilitate movement up the spectrum of consciousness. The problem represents an opportunity for transformation. Successful counseling, then, does not rest in solving the problem, in instilling moral behaviors, or in altering a person's behavior. It rests in helping the person to move to the next level of consciousness.

The spectrum of consciousness posits up to 20 or more different stages, from the prepersonal through the personal into the transpersonal. The transpersonal involves those levels in which the ego or self is gradually transcended. However, most persons who come for counseling do so within the personal realm of the spectrum, and they will continue within that broad range during and after counseling. If counseling is successful, they will move to a higher level within the personal realm as a result of the experience. This approach is called transpersonal not because clients start out or end up in the transpersonal levels but because an understanding and acceptance of the spectrum of consciousness underlies the approach and because the purpose of counseling is derived from the direction of development inherent in the approach.

MODES OF KNOWING

There are different ways of approaching work with dying persons. Much of the current emphasis in the field of counseling is on models that have an empirical basis. However, different modes of knowing have been discussed throughout the history of humanity, and to be of the most help to the terminally ill, counselors must be willing to look at more than their own traditional way of perceiving the world. These different ways of knowing are the major distinguishing characteristics of the various levels that define human development and ultimately the way each of us perceives the meaning of death.

The current predominant way of perceiving the world, which has come about since the beginning of the scientific revolution, has in many cases become too narrow. There are some who want to limit knowledge to that which can be proved by experimental investigation. Knowledge that is based on logical operations, intuitive perception, or introspective understanding is not acceptable to those who believe that the empirical or scientific is the only valid mode of thinking. Empiricists believe that if we can divide all of human endeavor into its smallest parts, we can make it more measurable and manageable. As counselors, we may want to reduce the terminally ill patient to a pain to be treated, a tumor to be controlled, a body to be buried, an anger to be vented. We want to perceive the person in terms that can be measured and controlled and to ignore the spiritual and existential meanings that do not conform to empirically based techniques.

With the Copernican revolution, our perception of the world changed from one that was teleologically oriented to one in which the universe is conceived of as a closed entity (Harman, 1988). This is in line with the Aristotelian view that the senses are the source of all knowledge and therefore what cannot be known empirically is knowledge of a lesser sort. Death represents the end of sensory functioning, and therefore death is the end of everything. As counselors, such a perception forces us to focus on the process of dying and to ignore the meaning that death has for the individual. It causes us to see little hope for further growth in our patients and causes us to be concerned only with making them comfortable while they die. Yet a different perception of the world tells us that ignoring the meaning of death precludes any significant sense of comfort during this final stage of life. When we widen our perception of the world to include modes of knowing beyond the scientific and empirical, we realize that ignoring the meaning of death keeps us from providing help that facilitates our clients' transformative movement through the stages of development.

Huston Smith (1982) said that four kinds of knowledge are excluded by the modern scientific position because science is unable to deal with them. These are purposes, intrinsic and normative values, global and existential meanings, and questions of intrinsic quality (H. Smith, 1982, pp. 66–67). He pointed out that one way of viewing the impact of the scientific revolution on society is to note the shift in the sort of knowledge that is valued. If questions could not be answered by the paradigm that science was developing, then it was judged that the questions were irrelevant. To the scientists, knowledge that could not be verified by empirical experiments was not knowledge at all. As Harman (1988) pointed out, behavioral scientists who hold to a rigid point of view insist that it is impossible to build a reliable science based on self-reports of inner, subjective experience. He noted that this is exactly what the phenomenological psychologists have tried to do, and they have been rejected for it. This is very likely a major reason so many counselors seek the cognitive–behavioral approaches to counseling. These approaches are more acceptable in a world that values so highly the scientific over the phenomenological.

Many followers of the empirical model have drawn their boundaries tightly around observable sensory data, and knowledge that does not fit that mold is ignored. In this sense, science has actually restricted rather than broadened our knowledge and understanding of our world. One of the most pervasive directions that our understanding of the human condition is presently taking is an increasing focus on trying to determine the biological causes of our psychological and spiritual being. Psychobiologists operate on the assumptions that all mental illness is a function of faulty physiology or brain chemistry and that as we increase our knowledge of the specific causes of these faults, we can treat them with drugs. They believe that a person's inability to find answers to such existential questions as the meaning of life and the unalterable alienation of impending death cannot account for the despair that that person experiences. To them, the declining potency of self-defining values that accompanies significant loss is not an adequate reason for anxiety or depression. To the empiricism of the psychobiologist, these are not experimentally verifiable propositions, and therefore they can hold little truth. We must find our answers in the observable world that only the senses can know. Yet according to Sperry (cited by Harman, 1988, p. 11), "Current concepts of the mind–brain relation involve a direct break with the long-established materialist and behaviorist doctrine that has dominated neuroscience for many decades. Instead of renouncing or ignoring consciousness, the new interpretation gives full recognition to the primacy of inner conscious awareness as a causal reality." A recapturing of the perennial psychology with its emphasis on successive levels of knowing reasserts the primacy of the spiritual levels of consciousness rather than relegating them to the realm of magical or mythic thinking.

In the face of such restricted thinking, we must assume that there is a difference between life and consciousness. Life is the continuity of the physical self, whereas consciousness is that which transcends the world of the senses and the material. This is not a concept that will be accepted by materialists who accept the empirical as the only valid mode of thinking. Yet during the 20th century, there has come to our awareness a paradox that brings a strictly empirical view into question. As science has been reducing all of what we know, including our consciousness, to the smallest particles of matter, it also has come to the conclusion that such reduction is impossible and that the predictability that was being sought is not within the realm of possibility.

Wilber (1977), in discussing the new knowledge that has come to us through the world of science, said that we have available to us two basic ways of knowing ourselves and the world around us. The first of these is the symbolic or inferential knowledge of the sensory world, and the other is what has been called intimate, direct, or nondual knowledge. This is the understanding of knowledge that has come to us not only through the writings of the mystics and members of esoteric religions but also more recently through the work of scientists such as Edington, Schroedinger, and Heisenberg (Wilber, 1983). Speaking of this second, intimate kind of knowledge, Edington pointed out that it will not submit to codification or analysis. As soon as we try to dissect it to find its meaning, it in fact loses its intimacy and meaning, to be replaced by the first, symbolic kind of reasoning.

St. Bonaventure taught that humanity has three modes of thinking (Wilber, 1983). The first is the way of the flesh, which is the empirical, scientific way based on sensory apperception of the world. The second is the way of reason, in which we use logic and inferential thought and which is the realm of the philosopher and psychologist. The third way is that of contemplation, which is a direct knowing of the realities that transcend the material world. The concept of these three ways of knowing has been part of the perennial philosophy, with similar ideas being found in all major traditions (Wilber, 1983). The wording is somewhat different—the gross (flesh and material), the subtle (mental and animic), and the causal (transcendent and contemplative)—but the concept is the same. The point is that such views of the realms of knowledge preceded the scientific revolution. They are not an expansion of the scientific revolution but an attempt to recapture a broader view that has not simply been refined by Western empiricism but has become restricted by it.

If the knowing that comes through the senses (the eye of the flesh) is the mode of knowing that is pertinent to the world of empirical science, then it also belongs to the world of behavioral and cognitive psychology. The eye of the mind is that of Western philosophy and also of the world of phenomenological psychology (humanistic and existential approaches). The eye of contemplation is that of religion and the Eastern traditions, but as of yet it has found little significant base in Western approaches to psychotherapy. It is this third way of knowing, however, that may be most pertinent to the dying person.

THE QUESTION OF REALITY

Western philosophy comes, by and large, from Greek philosophy, and Greek philosophy is the philosophy of dualisms. "Rutted firmly in these dualisms, Western thought throughout its history has continued to generate those of its own: instinct vs. intellect, wave vs. particle, positivism vs. idealism, matter vs. energy, thesis vs. antithesis, mind vs. body, behaviorism vs. vitalism, fate vs. free will, space vs. time—the list is endless" (Wilber, 1977, p. 30). Kelsey (1973) lamented that we have segmented our selves into the body (worldly) and the soul (heavenly). Having done so, we have determined that the church's realm is with the social and moral aspects of the self and with the worldly, and we leave the soul for later because it is not a question for this world. The point is that not only is there knowledge beyond the bounds of traditional science and the Aristotelian perspective, but that knowledge is a whole that is much greater than its parts and can be fully understood only as a whole and not as the individual parts. It is not a question of behavior *or* mind, or of mind *or* spirituality, but of transcending the dichotomous thinking that currently prevails in Western psychology.

Counselors have different starting points for understanding clients. We can begin with the behaviors that can be observed and verified with experimentation; we can begin with self-determined truths of the mind (values, beliefs, attitudes) that are known only by understanding the reasons (reasoning) of the client; and we can begin with a client's revelatory insights (understanding that comes from direct apprehension), which can be understood by the counselor only on the basis of acceptance. No one of these is better or preferable than the others. The point is that all three are superior to any one or two as a means of knowing the client and being of the greatest help.

/ Much of counseling talks of reality—what reality is and how to get our clients to accept it. There are three ways of perceiving reality: what reality is like, what reality is not, and how to reach reality (Wilber, 1977). None of these, however, tells us what reality is. The empirical approach tells us what reality is like, but it does not tell us what reality is for our clients. Humanistic approaches attempt to tell us how to reach reality, but again, they cannot tell us what reality is. Consciousness is not the end product of our material evolution, but rather, consciousness was here first and is what gives us our understanding of the material world of reality (Harman, 1988). Reality is only a perception that comes to us from our consciousness. For a counselor to assume an external reality for a client, to assume to know what reality is, is to miss the point completely.

To understand the terminally ill person—both the personal and worldly concerns of dying, as well as the esoteric and transpersonal levels—it is necessary to use all modes of knowledge and not restrict ourselves to the level of the empirical. To understand dying persons in their wholeness, to have a true sense of empathy from which to facilitate their growth during this final stage, we must be able to work at all levels of the spectrum of knowledge and consciousness. "A 'transcendental paradigm,' meaning an *overall* knowledge quest that would include not only the 'hardware' of physical sciences but also the 'soft ware' of philosophy and psychology and the 'transcendental ware' of mystical–spiritual religion" (Wilber, 1983, p. 1) is necessary if we are to develop ways of helping people that encompass the entire range of the great chain of being.

Joseph Campbell (1988) said that people talk about seeking meaning in life. Yet what we are really seeking is an experience of being alive, so that our life experiences on the purely physical plane will have resonances within our own innermost being and reality. To be segmented in our knowledge and understanding of self and world, as well as the transcendent aspects of our universe, is to deny ourselves the opportunity to feel alive. It is to shut out our innermost being and to live a reality based only on externals. We need to move beyond the dualities that Western science has created for us—to move beyond the limits of a single way of thinking and learn to live and know life as a unity.

A SPECTRUM APPROACH TO DEVELOPMENT

Our understanding of human development, both positive and negative, is seen through different "eyes," just as our general understanding of the world comes to us through different modes of thinking. Using only one eye is akin to seeing the elephant from only one perspective. We cannot see the whole picture. Wilber (1982) has provided us with a holistic view of the human spectrum of consciousness, that which enables us to see the elephant in its wholeness. Having intensely studied both Eastern and Western psychologies, he said that he could not bring himself to believe that any of the geniuses behind these various approaches to understanding humankind could be all right or all wrong, but that somehow there must be significant truth to all of them. This led him to study traditions and psychologies of both East and West and to come to an understanding and acceptance of the great chain of being. This led to the development of his concept of a spectrum of consciousness, a structure and stage development approach to understanding how one grows from birth to the ultimate level of human endeavor that is well beyond the confines of a healthy self (Wilber, 1977, 1979, 1980, 1982, 1983).

The various stages of the spectrum are universal and cross-cultural and begin with the undifferentiated fusion state of birth and end with the state of ultimate or unity consciousness—the level of full transcendence of the self. In between are the gross categories Wilber labeled *prepersonal, personal,* and *transpersonal,* and there are numerous other stages within these categories. Each of these stages of development builds on the preceding one and constitutes a basic structure of the person. At each stage, specific transition tasks are required for the person to have an adequate basis for moving to the next stage. Successful movement through these tasks provides a foundation for the person to transcend the current stage, whereas unsuccessful negotiation of the tasks will cause a person to remain stuck and growth to be limited.

Wilber used the term *outward arc* to refer to the levels of development in the first half of the spectrum of consciousness (from birth to the development of a complete and unique self), and he used *inward arc* to refer to the stages between self-development and unity consciousness (the transpersonal half of the spectrum). This inward arc contains the more advanced levels, building on the lower levels of self-development. Although this scheme describes the total realm of human development, experience shows that most people reach only a certain level, often far short of the highest level of the outward arc. The spectrum of consciousness maps the direction of human growth, but not everyone reaches the final destination.

The meaning that the various levels have for the way we perceive ourselves and the world depends on the level of the spectrum at which we are living. The spectrum also defines the direction of our lives and the process by which we grow from one level of consciousness to the next. This is the essence of our growth and therefore must be the basis on which we formulate our approach to providing counseling care for the terminally ill.

DIFFERENTIATION AND INDIVIDUATION

The spectrum of consciousness is different from other developmental approaches in at least three significant ways: First, rather than setting itself against other developmental schemes, the spectrum incorporates other major approaches to create a megatheory. It shows how different systems, focusing on different aspects of development (cognitive, self, moral, consciousness) all fit into a single directional pattern, paralleling rather than denying each other. Second, the spectrum approach not only includes the stages of development but also shows how the structures of each stage emerge, and it describes the self-system that coordinates movement through the various stages. Most stage theories focus on only one aspect of the developmental ladder. Third, the spectrum includes both the personal and the transpersonal, the psychological and the spiritual levels of development, whereas other models of development concern themselves with one or the other.

The first half of the spectrum is that of the development of the self—its emergence from the ground unconsciousness and the conflicts, fears, anxieties, and rewards that accompany that process. This emergence involves differentiation and separation, creating feelings of alienation, and it involves growth and individuation (Wilber, 1980). The second half of the spectrum is that which occurs beyond the self and is the psychology of eternity. The first half examined alone is psychological in nature, the second is spiritual. Both together can be called *psychospiritual.* An example is shown through the story of Buddha, who became dissatisfied with the suffering of the personal world and found enlightenment in the transpersonal realm. This story is part of the perennial psychology.

A person comes into the world as a totally undifferentiated being, fused with mother and the surrounding world. The tasks of the early life of the child involve the beginning of the process of developing, out of this state of total fusion, the sense of being an individual self. Psychoanalysts have divided this period into two parts: the development of a self that is perceived as being physically other than the rest of the world and the development of a perception of being an emotionally separate self. Beyond this the child must also develop a sense of being a mental being, having for the first time a mental concept of self. With successful completion of these early, prepersonal stages, the child has differentiated a self that he or she knows to be physically, emotionally, and mentally different and separate from the rest of the world. The child is now a distinct person.

Moving on to the personal realm, the child must now begin fitting that distinct self into some relationship with other separate persons. This first involves acquiring a sense of membership in the personal world, satisfying what Maslow (1968) called the need for belonging. The person seeks the acceptance of others and develops an awareness of being an integral part of a society, culture, or other human groups. It is a stage characterized by "shoulds" and "oughts," by conformance to the ways of the group. The sense of belonging and connectedness keeps the person from feeling alienated and alone and makes it possible to keep the anxiety of separation at a manageable level.

Having come to at least a minimal level of satisfaction of the need to belong and feel connected, the individual then needs to focus on developing a sense of self-esteem and perceptions of worth and success. This process involves what Snygg and Combs (1959) called the *enhancement of the self* and can be equated to Erikson's (1963) *stage of generativity,* which includes most of adult life. It is during this time that the individual strives to establish him- or herself as a distinct human being through the works that he or she generates, developing a self that is separate and different from others.

Beyond this level, the individual develops an ability to be self-reflective, to think in the abstract, to understand higher principles of human endeavor. He or she moves from a reliance on others in determining the quality of the self to an ability to make such evaluations from within. The conforming self is now set aside in favor of one that can be developed on the basis of reasoned principles, a self determined by an internal evaluation of the world rather than evaluations imposed from the outside. The self of the previous stage no longer serves the person well and must be given up for the new self to have room to develop.

The final level of development within the personal realm is characterized by actualizing the potential that is inherent within the person. The need for a sense of worth and belonging has been satisfied to at least a minimal extent and now must be let go. The person must turn to becoming the best self that he or she can be. If this potential and drive toward self-actualization is not fulfilled, the person will fall into a state of despair.

In this process of differentiation, boundaries develop. Some aspects of the emerging self will be appropriate to what the person wants to be and will produce feelings of esteem and belonging, and other aspects will run counter to these goals. What the person comes to perceive to be the real self (the persona) on the basis of needing to belong and to be accepted will be separated from that which is unacceptable and therefore repressed (the shadow). A second major boundary develops between the self and all aspects of the world that are considered to be not-self. As seen earlier, it is the self that is the heart of modern psychology and is the focus of counseling and psychotherapy. Therefore, these boundaries become crucial to the work of the counselor. When one understands the mind and spirit, the psychological and spiritual, to be a dichotomy, however, counseling tends to be concerned with helping the person dissolve the boundary between persona and shadow, ignoring the boundary between self and other. In the last analysis, though, these are inseparable, and if it is to be complete, counseling should facilitate a person's movement through the successive stages of the chain of being.

Each of the prepersonal and personal stages involves successive steps of differentiating self from other, thereby causing perceptions of more and more separateness. In this process, different and higher ways of seeing the world—new levels of consciousness—come into being for the individual. This development includes moving from an external to an internal locus of evaluation. It necessitates shedding the outward-oriented needs of security, belonging, and self-esteem and moving toward inward-oriented self-actualization. It leads the person to a level where morals and ethics are based on a deep reflective process rather than an externally dictated one. The early stages of development are characterized by an empirical and sensory mode of knowing the self, but as the person moves into the higher personal realm, a self based solely on this way of knowing must be given up and new ways of thinking must be integrated into the self-perception. The eye of reason must be used to develop a self-consciousness at the highest levels of personal development.

This is the end of the story for the traditionally oriented forces of Western psychology, but it is not the end of the spectrum of consciousness. Full development does not culminate with self-actualization, and it does not necessitate giving up the formal reflective, self-actualizing self to make room for a new self. It requires giving up the self altogether. As we move through the personal realm, giving up our other-oriented needs of belonging and self-esteem, we gradually move away from strictly self-oriented concerns. There is movement toward principled social contracts instead of purely self-gratifying ones. There is an increasing concern for the good of the whole of society without continually measuring one's own needs. We become more pluralistic and universal in outlook and begin to allow the self to become subordinate to higher principles. This is the first level of transcending the self.

Beyond the personal is the realm of the third eye of knowing—contemplation. As the person moves beyond the reasoning mind of the personal realm, there is an entrance into the eye of direct knowing, called *gnosis* in many traditions. At this level, the person apprehends the limits of rational thought and the way that such thinking distorts the reality of the world. Higher truths, such as the *ideas* in Platonic thought and the *archetypes* of Jungian psychology, gradually begin to replace those of the lower levels. Having spent all of his or her life to this point developing a strong and healthy sense of a separate self, the person now begins to see the interconnectedness of all beings and the illusion of that separate self. This is a stage that cannot be known through the eye of reason but must be understood by moving to the higher realm of contemplative thought.

This is a brief and simple description of the process of differentiation, separation, and individuation in the prepersonal, personal, and transpersonal levels of the spectrum of consciousness. Wilber and others have delineated many more substages in the process of development, but my purpose here is only to give an indication of the direction the spectrum takes. I want to describe the basic direction inherent in our lives, which I believe is defined by progression along the spectrum. At each stage and substage, we are inherently pulled to the next level on the path to what, at the end of the spectrum, is called *unity consciousness—* where there are no longer any separate selves, only the interconnectedness of the consciousness that underlies us all.

What, then, makes the transpersonal level of development superior to the existential and humanistic level or the egoic and behavioral level? Why should facilitation of the person toward this level of the spectrum form the purpose of counseling?

The first consideration lies within the assumption that there is a teleological pull toward the transpersonal or spiritual as defined by the great chain of being. Admittedly, this philosophical assumption is not accepted by all, but it is a significant underpinning of transpersonal psychology. In accepting this position, one accepts the proposition that full human development is more than that defined by the existentialists and that to satisfy oneself with less than full development is to create a sense of dissatisfaction. This is the sense of despair set forth by Erikson (1963).

Second, the transpersonal approach is not set against the egoic or existential approaches but encompasses them. Therefore, all that is good within these lower levels is incorporated into the higher levels and remains as a part of the person. A person who is loving, just, and altruistic at the existential level of development maintains those same qualities at the higher levels but adds to those characteristics qualities of the transpersonal, for example, empathic understanding, unconditional love and forgiveness, and a greater openness to experience.

The difference between the personal and the transpersonal is a loosening of the attachments by which we define ourselves. We give up not the definition itself but our need to hold on to that definition. It is not specific behaviors that determine whether a Gandhi or Martin Luther King, Jr., is at an existential or transpersonal level development but the degree to which they are or are not free to respond to the needs of the moment without first evaluating their own needs. One who lives beyond the existential does loving acts because that is what the moment and relationship calls for. One whose development is still within the egoic or existential realm does loving acts, at least to some extent, because the needs of the self will be met by such acts. The acts themselves may look the same and the consequences may be the same, but the egoic or existential person is more separated from the ground of being than the person acting from a transpersonal level of consciousness.

In this sense, then, we can say that the highest social actions can occur at the highest realm of the personal—the humanistic and existential. Being incorporated into the early levels of the transpersonal realm, they will also occur there, but added to these self-defining actions will be a lessening of self-related needs and consequently a beginning of movement toward greater unity.

Life after death is not an issue here. When transpersonal psychology talks of death and rebirth, it is not a physical death being described but the death of the individual self and a rebirth (within this life) at a higher level of universal self. Moreover, this is not a one-time occurrence but one that takes place in many lesser stages. At each level along the spectrum, one gives up (dies to) the self of that level and is reborn at a higher level. One dies to the egoic self and is reborn to an existential self. The transpersonal realm is a long series of levels or stages in which, at each stage, there is a lessening of identification with the self and a consequent rebirth at a level closer to the ultimate level of universal self. With each death and rebirth, the person expands consciousness by incorporating the earlier structures into the present level, thereby moving toward greater wholeness because the whole is defined as the total of all consciousness, or all stages, which ends in unity consciousness.

THE QUESTION OF PROOF

This presentation of the great chain of being, or the spectrum of consciousness, can be criticized on the basis that it is theoretical and has little substantiation in the real world. Yet when one makes such a criticism, the real world tends to mean the world of concrete, empirical proof. In fact, such proof is hard to come by. The problem is that because such a system cannot be proved by empirical means, it is perceived to be either untrue or irrelevant. A similar criticism holds true if one attempts to prove the system on a logical, reasoned basis. As logical as it may seem, it has little tangible proof.

Certain principles hold true for any process of validation (Wilber, 1983). First, there must be data. There must be a way of gathering that which is to be measured or validated. The process takes the form of "If you want to know this, do this." This is a primary ingredient of experimental research. Second, the information must be processed. The point here is that the evaluation of the data must match the collection process. To count and classify data gathered with the eye of the flesh, the empirical mode is appropriate, but to attempt to quantify or classify data that is gathered through the eye of reason makes no sense. It is comparing apples and oranges, or as the scientists would say, a category error. Third, there must be some communal agreement on what has been found and processed. If 500 people can gather data by empirical means, process it mathematically, and come up with the same numerical conclusion, the proof of the proposition has been enhanced. The same holds true for the other modes of knowing.

When we want to prove something in the realm of the transpersonal or spiritual, the eye of the flesh is inappropriate. To put such issues to experimental study is to perform a category error. Data must be gathered in a mode appropriate for the subject, and in this case the eye of contemplation is the appropriate mode. In fact, over many centuries and in many locations, sages and saints have gathered such data by such means—meditation and contemplation. Moreover, there has been a communal sharing of the data and a consensual agreement on the findings. This is the only way to establish the truth of a system such as is represented by the higher levels of the chain of being. To attempt to prove or disprove direct, intuitive, or revelatory knowledge with the tools of empirical science is to make a gross category error and to end up knowing nothing more than when the project began. It is not justified for an empiricist or a philosopher to reject the knowledge of the contemplative unless the data has been gathered with the eye of contemplation and submitted to validation appropriate to that realm of consciousness. Such methods are, of course, available to anyone.

There is a widespread tendency among empiricists, philosophers, and contemplatives to focus on one side of the spectrum, either the outward or inward arc, and to assume that that one side represents the whole picture. For example, the empiricist or philosopher who believes only in the personal side of human development will see reason as the highest order of cognitive processing. In this case, anything other than high-level reasoning must be lesser because reasoning is as high as one can go. Processes such as intuitive thought, the psychic channeling that characterizes shamanic episodes, and the direct knowing of gnostics is not reason and is therefore of a lower order. This leads empiricists to apply such labels as *hallucination, narcissistic neurosis, regression,* and the like to cognitive processes that very well may be further developed than rational thought. On the other side, contemplatives tend to see an emphasis on rational thinking and sensory endeavors as childish, immature, and regressive. There is little understanding of the integration and connectedness of the continuous developmental aspect of humanity.

So what constitutes evidence? How can one establish the validity of the transpersonal realm? The first part of the answer is that validity cannot be established through the means of the empirical, scientific eye. Although this is the superior means of establishing validity within the realm of the concrete world that can be known through the senses, it is not appropriate for determining those aspects of the world that can be known only through reason or revelation. For example, one cannot establish empirically that it would have been better not to kill 6 million Jews in the Holocaust or that genocide should not be committed in some African country. This is a question within the humanistic and existential realm, and it can only be answered through the eye of the mind.

Nor can validity be established simply by adding up the number of people who favor one action over the other. As Wilber (1983) pointed out, data must be gathered, but it must be gathered through the eye of the mind, through reasoning and logic. When data is gathered in that manner it must be processed through the eye of the mind, not the eye of the flesh, which holds no method for dealing with such questions. For example, the use of dialectics to process this data would be an appropriate method because it is designed for this purpose. Finally, there must be a consensus on what is found or determined to be valid with these methods of data gathering and processing. If we cannot use these methods, then, as was pointed out by H. Smith (1982), we are restricted to data that is compatible with empirical scientific methods.

In the same manner, proof in the transpersonal area must be obtained with appropriate methods, and a consensus must be reached on what these methods tell us. The primary methods advocated over the years are meditation and contemplation. It is through these methods that intuitive, psychic, and revelatory data can be gathered. There are clear rules for conducting this type of data gathering to provide for consistency over time and place, which is necessary for any validation procedure, be it empirical, rational, or transpersonal. Once data is gathered with these methods, it must be processed within the realm of the transpersonal. Methods of reasoning do not work because the transpersonal is by definition beyond reasoning. Yet when data is gathered in this way, and it is shared with others who are gathering data in the same way, a consensual agreement can be reached regarding the validity of the data.

Difficulty arises in this area of consciousness because most of us in the West are well acquainted with the realms of the empirical and of reason but not with the realm of the transpersonal. The term *gnosis* is used to broadly define at least some aspects of processing within the transpersonal realm, but this is not empirical or reasonable. Therefore, if we reject this data on the basis of scientific experiment or logic, we are making a category error. To follow the procedure fully, we must subject ourselves to the strict rules of meditation and contemplation, and only then can we adequately judge the data. The great majority of persons who reject transpersonal data do so without having followed the appropriate rules of data gathering. In fact, few meditators and contemplatives who have been trained in these methods reject the validity of such data.

SUMMARY

Transpersonal counseling attempts to join the traditional Western approaches of psychoanalytic, cognitive–behavioral, and humanistic psychology with the perennial psychology that is a part of other traditions. Wittine (1993, p. 166) set forth five principles that undergird such a system. These are (a) the need for healing and growth on all levels of the spectrum of identity—egoic, existential, and transpersonal; (b) therapists' unfolding awareness of the self, or deep center of being, and their spiritual perspective on life as central to the therapeutic process; (c) the process of awakening from a lesser to a greater identity; (d) the healing, restorative nature of inner awareness and intuition; and (e) the transformative potential in the therapeutic relationship not only for the client but also the therapist.

The assumption underlying transpersonal approaches is that the egoic and existential (i.e., the behavioral, cognitive, and humanistic levels of consciousness and of counseling) are valid and worthwhile, but that there is more. To move toward more complete wholeness, levels of consciousness that transcend the self must be added. Good is not necessarily good enough.

Knowledge of certain aspects of the spectrum of consciousness can help in fully understanding the terminally ill person and the way in which the process of dying affords a final opportunity for growth. The meaning that the various levels have for the way we perceive ourselves and the world depends on the level of the spectrum at which we are living. The spectrum also defines the direction of our lives and the process by which we grow from one level of consciousness to the next. This is the essence of our growth and therefore should be the basis on which we formulate our approach to providing counseling care for the dying person.

Chapter 5

The Meaning of Life and Death

Awareness of what is going on within someone who is dying and an understanding of how to help that person would be much easier to attain if we all had the same conception of the meaning of death. Moreover, it would be helpful if our conscious understanding of the meaning of death were, in all cases, the same as our unconscious beliefs about death. Yet experience tells us that this is not so. As in other circumstances of human endeavor, people's behavior and emotions often belie their overt rationalizations.

What death means to a person who is dying is an important consideration in the process of counseling. Yet the meaning of death cannot be explored as a concept that is distinct from the meaning of life. If death is anything other than the complete cessation of the individual being, the total discontinuity of that which I call myself, then it must find at least a part of its meaning in the experience of the life that leads to it. On the other hand, if the meaning of death is the complete end of existence in any realm, that, too, affects the meaning that life has. The meaning of one cannot be fully considered in the absence of understanding the meaning of the other.

Sogyal Rinpoche (1992) said we can use our lives to prepare for death. If we can find meaning in our lives now, we are not condemned to meet death unprepared. It is impossible to understand the meaning of death if we cannot first understand the meaning of life, yet so few of us seriously attempt to do either.

GROWTH AND LIFE DIRECTION

The basic direction in life is one of achieving successively higher levels of knowledge, awareness, or consciousness. We tend to believe that once we have reached the level of a highly developed, healthy self-concept, we have gone as far as we can go—we have become all that we can be. Death is the ultimate threat to this sense of self, and hence there are feelings of loss, helplessness, and depression surrounding the event. We are threatened with losing all that we have become, and no one can help us turn back the tide.

There are levels beyond the self, however, that remain hidden to most of us throughout our lives. We are so focused on the external world, on what is clearly other than ourselves that the idea of unity beyond the self-and-other duality is incomprehensible. Yet the threat of loss of the physical self, the being that in our minds has become differentiated from, and therefore separate from the rest of the world, not only can create feelings of loss and helplessness but also can free us from the bonds of the self–other duality and allow us to see that there are levels of being beyond the self. If we can keep from getting stuck in the mourning process of our own death, then the opportunity for moving to a level beyond the self is possible. This is the final stage of growth during this lifetime.

A life-threatening illness does not raise the question of death or not death. Even if there is remission or cure, the person will at some point die of some-thing. The issue is, "Can we use this crisis of living with a terminal illness as an impetus toward increased emotional and spiritual growth, toward a transforma-tion of the personal worldly self?" This is the true healing associated with dying.

The behavioristic framework, in which what we become in life is deter-mined solely on the basis of our experiences in the world, represents what is perhaps the predominant Western view of the direction of life for human beings. In this view, no essential characteristic of the person exists prior to birth. The direction of life is determined simply by the way the environment impinges on the individual. People become whatever the environment makes of them. Be-havioristic theories view the person as an entity whose boundaries are birth and death and who comes into the world as a blank tablet on which experiences are written. It is these experiences alone that make us what we are, without regard to any underlying direction.

Other theorists believe that there is an essence to each of us that is present at birth and that defines our human nature. Human development, regardless of race or culture, time and place, is posited to follow a basic direction. Carl Rogers (1951) said that we all have an inherent capacity and tendency toward positive growth. Carl Jung (O'Connor, 1985) defined the direction of life through his concept of the Self, the ultimate level of being toward which we all move. The spectrum of consciousness is perhaps the most comprehensive description of the basic direction of life for all people.

When working with persons who are experiencing a crisis, a counselor must become aware that there is something beyond the contents of the problems that clients bring to counseling. There appears to be a universal striving for a basic direction or orientation to life. There is a teleological pull, in the development of the individual as well as in evolution as a whole, toward increased awareness, complexity, freedom of choice, and integration that shows we are going somewhere, that there is a preferred direction in our development. It is this pull, this need to be "going somewhere" that is at the heart of counseling.

According to the major philosophical traditions throughout history, described by Huxley (1970) as the perennial philosophy, the rediscovery of this infinite and eternal wholeness is a person's greatest need, and it is what moves a person forward in life. Transcendence beyond the self follows the stage of self-actualization in Maslow's needs hierarchy. The first five stages as presented by Maslow constitute the egoic realm and define the path of self-development. The sixth stage transcends the personal in search of the nondual level of realization called unity consciousness. It is the point at which the selves of all the personal levels have been released, and there is no longer a need for a separate identity.

"If we include persons from all walks of life and the numberless directions in which their hopes and thoughts extend, we can only conclude what has become a truism: that no comprehensive vision, no concerted sense of reality, informs our age" (H. Smith, 1982, p. 3). Such a vision is perhaps precluded by our inability or unwillingness to look squarely at death and probe its meaning. We know that from birth we are pulled to this inevitable worldly conclusion, yet we orient ourselves to life as if death were not going to come. We see death as the ultimate of the dualities that characterize our lives: We are either dead or alive; we are, or we are not. Perceiving a healthy separate self to be the ultimate development, we fear the destruction of that self through death.

When we have no awareness of such a vision, we have no awareness of where we are going in our lives. When self alone becomes our vision, we lose all sense of continuity, of connectedness to something beyond the separate being we have come to know as "myself." We must have a vision that transcends the personal self. If we can view life's direction as continuing beyond the self, transcending the dualities of the outward arc, we begin to see that death represents not a final dichotomizing of our self and the world but a major step in moving toward an integration of the dualities, toward unity consciousness. We then begin to feel a pull beyond the closed boundaries of an earthly reality.

We are not the *tabula rasa* that Locke would have us believe, nor does our existence totally precede our essence as the existentialists profess. There is a basic direction to life, inherent in all of us, that forms the comprehensive vision.

Given the appropriate growing environment, a tree will grow of its own accord in a positive direction that is inherent within its structure. In the same way, human beings, given the appropriate conditions, will also grow in a direction that is inherently defined and is positive. Our goal as helpers is to provide that positive climate.

THE PERSONAL SELF

We progress through life by transforming our selves from one level of consciousness to the next, continually becoming more differentiated and individualized persons. The first half of the spectrum of consciousness is characterized by this development of the individual, separate self. Though many theories of human development have been offered over the years, they can be categorized into four major classes, representing different levels of the spectrum of consciousness. As described in chapter 4, these four major divisions of psychology are psychoanalytic, cognitive–behavioral, humanistic, and transpersonal. Although there are many differences among the theories that fall into these broad categories, there is at least one common thread—they all include the concept that the process of differentiation and individuation that leads to the development of a healthy self is common to all humans. Psychoanalytic theories have developed the most well-defined description of self-development, in which the focus is on the dynamic interaction of instincts and the ego. Out of this interaction and based on relationships with others, there is a continuing definition of one's self as a separate entity. Erikson (1968) placed primary stress on his fifth stage of psychosocial development, the identity of the self, with each of the prior stages being preparatory to it.

Although cognitive–behavioral approaches tend to ignore unconscious dynamic processes and are even reluctant to accept unobservable concepts like *self*, they do describe thoroughly the process of learning by which one develops patterns of behavior that come to be considered the essence of the unique self. Out of the mass of possible responses that we can make to our environment, we differentiate those that prove to be satisfactory and those that do not, and each of us builds a separate pattern of behaving (including emotional or feeling responses) that becomes descriptive of who we are. Whatever terms are used by theorists, this is certainly a process of differentiation and individuation on the way to becoming a unique person.

Self-concept has been a central part of humanistic psychology from its inception. Rogers (1951) stated that the self develops out of evaluational interaction with other persons in the environment, becoming a fluid but consistent pattern of perceptions that each of us considers to be the self. This self then becomes the center of our experiencing of the world, with those experiences that are threatening to the self being distorted so that they fit the self-concept. Here, again, is a process of continually making more precise differentiations between what is self and what is other than self. Just as with the psychoanalytic and cognitive–behavioral approaches, we are posited to begin life as an undifferentiated mass and continually develop toward existence as clearly distinct and separate individuals.

Common to each of these three approaches is a belief that the development of a strong, differentiated self is the ultimate goal of human development. One simply can go no further. Some Western theorists in the 1960s, however, were aware of levels of development beyond the self, and they were led to suggest that there is a fourth "force" in psychology, which should be called *transpersonal.* Theories in this realm perceive human development, in its most complete form, as involving growth beyond the personal self and propose stages of growth that transcend the pinnacle of traditional Western thought. Hence, the term *trans*personal. Although these approaches go beyond the traditional level of development of the self, they do not disagree with the position that the development of a healthy self is essential to positive growth; they simply do not perceive that the path of human development ends at that point.

If as counselors we accept that human development follows a basic inherent direction and we believe that that direction is characterized by differentiation of the self at successively higher and more complex levels, then to be of the most help to the persons with whom we work, we must understand the process by which these self-definitions come about. It is the process of moving through these successive stages that creates the life crises that are the center of counseling, the ultimate crisis being that which occurs when death is imminent. To understand the terminally ill person, we need to be aware of the process of self-development and self-transcendence, and we should know the nature of the crises that such development and transcendence creates.

There is no *self* inherent in human beings. The structures of humanity that constitute the stages of consciousness do not include anything that could be described as the ego, the identity, or the self of the individual. It is only as we experience the world that we develop a *perception* that comes to be called self. Through evaluational interactions with other people in the world, we gradually develop a sense of self, a conceptualization of all the perceptions about who we are (Rogers, 1951). This is, for all practical purposes, the same process of development described by theorists who have focused on the self as an integral part of psychological growth.

Self-concept, then, is defined as a unified consistent whole of all the perceptions that we have of ourselves and the values attached to those perceptions. This is what we identify ourselves to be, what we consider to be *me* or *I.* The perceptions themselves and the values attached to the perceptions create two important ways of looking at the self: the way we see ourselves to be, and the way we would like to be. This distinction creates not only a self but also an ideal self, the latter defining the direction of growth and enhancement that we have chosen for ourselves. In normal circumstances, we strive to let go of aspects of the self that we consider to be negative, and we try to become more like our ideal self.

Many of the values attached to self-perceptions are specific to the stage of development at which we find ourselves, however, and must be replaced with new values when we move to a higher stage. As we move through the structural stages of growth, each stage creates new needs and new ways of acquiring perceptions from people in the world who are important to the development of our self-concept. As this happens, the ideal self continually changes toward increased sophistication and complexity. The self that is valued by a child of 10, who is most likely focused on the need to belong, who is a concrete operational thinker, whose moral development is of a law-and-order level, and whose most pressing psychosocial task is to develop a sense of industry, is quite different from the self that is valued by a more developed person who is a formal operations thinker, who is concerned about self-esteem, whose moral development is oriented toward social contracts, and whose task of greatest concern is developing a sense of intimacy.

If replacing values of one stage with those of the succeeding stage were all there is to self-development, there would be little to keep us from continually moving toward the ideal self and progressing positively through life. However, although there is a drive to enhance the self by moving closer to the ideal, we also have a need to maintain ourselves as we are. As Maslow (1968) indicated, there is a need for security, which in part translates as a need for sameness. Even though we may not like ourselves, or all aspects of ourselves, at least we know how the world behaves toward the self that each of us is, and there is security in that. We may want to be different (better or enhanced), but we do not know how the world will relate to the new self, and this creates anxiety. Therefore, there is the tendency to defend against the forward movement. The need for maintenance of the self in the interest of psychological security causes us to develop boundaries around the self. Life is a continual process of building these boundaries, then realizing their inadequacies and recognizing the need to transcend them to reach a new level, where the building of boundaries begins all over again. Rogers (1951) said that the positive self-concept must be consistent but fluid, meaning that there must be enough structure to provide for a strong self-image, but there must also be enough openness to one's experiences to allow new perceptions in, thereby providing the basis for growth. Moving from one level of self-development to the next constitutes a crisis created by the need to give up one self to make room for a new one. Only as we feel secure will we have the courage to move forward toward a new self. As will be seen in chapter 10, the creation of a climate of security is a major factor in facilitating a person's movement toward growth during a period of crisis.

When a person feels secure enough to move to a higher stage of self-development, positive growth will occur. Throughout the outward arc of the spectrum of consciousness, we must continually define ourselves at higher levels of existence. Movement through life is one of continually giving up the self of one stage to move on and develop a self appropriate to the next level. As the ways that the person has of perceiving the world become more sophisticated, the self too becomes more sophisticated. In many ways, the self also becomes progressively more difficult to give up.

Having spent so much of our psychic energy developing a healthy concept of self, it is natural that any threat to that self-concept is going to precipitate a crisis. We see the self differently at each of these stages, and in order to grow, we must give up (lose) the self of one stage to replace it with the self of the next stage. For example, in moving from the last of the prepersonal stages to the first of the personal stages, the child must give up a self that is determined and evaluated from the outside, one that can be viewed as good on the basis of external judgments received from the world the child lives in. To move to the next level and the next mode of knowing, the child must begin to look inward to determine the goodness and badness of the self. There can no longer be satisfaction with the external determination because the child's consciousness has been opened up to new ways, self-reflective ways of viewing the self. The self of the prepersonal must be given up and replaced with the new. In this process of reforming the self from a new perspective, there is the danger that the person might not like the self that emerges and therefore be inclined to hang on to the old familiar self.

One aspect of the spectrum of consciousness is that each successive level incorporates the preceding levels. As a person moves to a new level of development, the self identifies with that level. This means that all of the emotional and mental characteristics of that stage become integrated into the individual self-concept of the person. The psychological needs, the moral phase, the sense of self that are relevant to that stage are incorporated into the identity of the person. However, the knowledge and experience gained at earlier levels continue to be a part of the person and are now integrated into more sophisticated conceptualizations. We do not understand the workings and dynamics at levels beyond our own personal development, however, and therefore conceptualizations particular to higher levels remain outside the realm of our consciousness, appearing as untruths or simply as folly.

At this point, it appears to us that the stage at which we are currently living is the highest level of development. Aspects of earlier stages are remembered and brought into the new stage as appropriate, but those of succeeding stages are either not known or not understood. We assume our identity by integrating and consolidating into the self the characteristics demanded by the present stage. We then begin a process of preserving the self in relation to these stage characteristics. Seeing the stage as the highest level of development, and consequently the self as having achieved a high level of sophistication, we go about the business of making sure that the self of this stage is not lost or that we do not regress to an earlier, less complete stage. Perceiving the current level as the highest, we cannot perceive of change as being progress. The assumption is therefore that change must be regression, and, of course, that is to be guarded against.

After adequate consolidation, however, and a period of time of living the stage and successfully negotiating all of the appropriate substages, there begins to surface a pull toward an even higher level. Initially, what that level and its characteristics are is hidden. There are only the early proddings that tell the person there is more to life. Snygg and Combs (1959) pointed out that the driving force within the individual is singular, although it involves three parts: maintenance, enhancement, and actualization. It is singular in the sense that all of these three are operating at once within the individual. Upon first achieving a given stage, the person focuses psychological attention on maintaining the self within that stage through consolidation of perceptions, while turning attention toward enhancement of the self within the transition boundaries of the stage. However, the pull toward actualizing the potential of the self occurs throughout the stage, and that eventually will necessitate transformation. So the person is continually trying to maintain the self within the stage, trying to achieve enhancement, and yet looking to grow beyond the stage.

THE ANXIETY OF TRANSFORMATION

Moving from one stage to another, often called a transformation, involves a pattern of starts and stops, of beginning to move forward and then pulling back and going forward again until the boundary is finally transcended. At the beginning of this process, there is a point at which the old begins to seem inadequate, when there is an increasing sense of wanting and needing to move on. This leads the individual to make several attempts to cross over into the next level, with each attempt involving more anxiety over the potential loss of the self as it is defined at the present stage. Finally, the crossover becomes complete in the sense that the individual is more in the next stage than the last one. At this point there begins a period of integration of new perceptions about the self and a time when there is satisfaction with being in this stage. Anxiety is returned to a manageable level until the person begins to perceive the new level as inadequate, and the process of transformation begins again. These transformations continue throughout life, which involves in its most complete form movement through all the stages of self-development and then movement through the stages beyond the self, the transpersonal stages.

This process of successive transformations does not come easily, however. Imagine that you have only $100 to your name, and a man offers to give you $120 *if* you will first go and give your $100 to a charitable organization. Your first reaction will probably be to suggest to the person that he give you the $120, and then you will give your $100 away. But the answer is "No, you must give up your $100 first." Such a choice creates anxiety because the desire to have the greater amount of money conflicts with the fear of giving up the money already in hand without a guarantee that it will be replaced with an amount that is better. Transformation to a higher level of development is like that. You must give up your self of the present level before you can begin to develop the self of the next stage. As much as you would like to hang on to the old self until you see what the new one is like and whether or not it is adequate and satisfactory, you cannot do it. You must let go of the old self first, and therefore you must face the anxiety of giving up what you have without any guarantee about the nature and quality of the self with which you will replace it.

The process of transformation is always associated with new anxieties, for we are leaving a stage where there has been a comfortable sense of knowing who we are, and we are attempting to move to one where that sense can only be surmised. This is the tendency toward maintenance and enhancement, to keep things as they comfortably are while at the same time wanting to move forward to the next stage, to grow and enhance the self. It is the process in which the needs of the present stage must be minimally satisfied before psychological energy is available to move on. The anxiety of the present stage must be within the bounds appropriate for moving on to the next level of development. It is when this anxiety is not within appropriate bounds, when the current needs are not satisfied to a minimal extent, that the anxiety associated with movement is too great and blocking of the transformation occurs.

The heart of Erikson's (1968) system of psychosocial development is the fifth stage—developing a sense of identity. The key to positive growth through this stage is the ability to work through a crisis and commit oneself to the values that will define the new self that emerges at the other end. When one is in a crisis situation, that is, a situation that calls for choices to be made in some area of major significance, that need creates anxiety. The term *significance* denotes that the choice relates to some critical desire, with the possibility of making a choice that will not achieve the desire or of making one that will achieve the desire; hence, the anxiety over not getting what one wants. If we have the choice made for us or in any other way are relieved of the pressure to make the choice (external locus of evaluation), then we suffer a foreclosure, an aborted opportunity for developing our own self, and though anxiety is averted, growth is foreclosed. This results in a condition known as *learned helplessness,* whereby an individual is taught to be dependent on others for psychological security, definition, and esteem. It is this condition that creates anxiety so great as to block transformations because the need for maintenance is greater than the need for enhancement. The ability to reach out and move forward on one's own has been stunted.

When we are denied the opportunity to make the choices that will eventually define our person, we do not develop a sense of how to become aware of ourselves or, particularly, how to go about the process of redefinition that is necessitated by a crisis. We have not been a part of making decisions about the values and beliefs by which we now identify ourselves, and therefore we are even more afraid of facing the next crisis without someone to make the decisions and define our self. We maintain an external locus of control and evaluation, continuing to rely on external sources for our identity. We come to the place where we lack confidence in ourselves to work through a crisis, to seek awareness and to accept ourselves, and to make the necessary decisions for transformation. When we as counselors become a part of this process of leading the client to choices, we become a party to the process of foreclosure and create in our client an unnecessary and unhealthy dependence on others for self-definition.

Many of our institutions—religious, political, educational, and family—teach this pattern of other-directedness, introjection, and learned helplessness. We create hierarchies by which the rightness of all values and behaviors are determined at the top and are passed down to the people at the lower levels of the hierarchy. This develops an external locus of control and forecloses movement to internal control, which characterizes the higher levels of the spectrum. This pattern is seen in all systems that attempt to dictate from the outside what one should be and do, utilizing the basic anxiety of alienation to maintain this pattern. As seen earlier, there needs to be freedom to move from one stage to the next, a freedom brought about by satisfaction of the needs at the present stage. This involves a belief, and communication of that belief, that the individual is ready and capable of moving on to a greater degree of self-determination. To communicate the opposite is to tell the individual that we will not accept the person if he or she moves beyond the present stage, especially if the movement is beyond a dependence on others to define values and behaviors. This threat of loss of acceptance can create a separation anxiety so great as to foreclose any possibility of movement. Such foreclosure is carried on by parents, teachers, peers, and many other significant sources.

Given the anxiety inherent in a crisis and the process of transformation through the life stages, there are obviously many points at which the process of transformation can be blocked by the individual. External agents do not cause what we refer to as psychopathology, but rather a blocking from within of the transformations that characterize positive movement along the direction of life. For this reason, intervention procedures are inappropriate as a means of helping the person through the crisis because they encourage the blocking process. As counselors, we need to facilitate the individual in moving through the period of loss.

CONTINUITY OF PERSONHOOD

What is the meaning of death? Carse (1980) discussed the many different conceptualizations of death and its meanings, and he pointed out that one of the significant elements of the various belief systems is whether or not they hold that there is a life beyond the bodily one that we know on earth, and if so, what the form of that afterlife is. There are three main options for contemplating death: complete extinction, preservation of the personality, and the continuing rebirth of the soul (John Hick, cited in Carse, 1980). Although there are many variations of the explanations of these options, in the final analysis, they must all come down to one of these options. It is in this context that we work with persons who are dying, trying to help them focus on the specific meaning that death has for them.

The fact that there is a direction to life means that there is a continuity, a history. The structures of the self build on each other, creating an ever greater degree of complexity to the self. We add experiences on experiences in relationship with others and we build perceptions, identities, and images of who we are out of these experiences. At any moment in time, we perceive ourselves to be the sum of all these perceptions, identities, and images. There is a continuity to our lives and to who we are. The issue, then, is whether that continuity ends at one's death or continues on in some form in a different realm.

Carse (1980) talked of the web of connectedness we develop with other people during our lives. The self is a direct result of interactions and relationships with other people. We have no conception of being a person in the absence of those connections. Death threatens to destroy those connections and signals the end of the worldly continuity of our lives. It means the end of the self that is dependent on interaction with others, who will no longer be with us when we die. It is this idea of no-self that is most difficult to deal with (Maezumi, 1993).

Yet it is only as we realize the inevitable end to the worldly continuity that we can find positive meaning in death. Carse (1980) pointed out that we must find a higher continuity in the face of death, one that is beyond the temporal continuity that is restricted to a worldly life. "Death, perceived as discontinuity, is not that which robs life of its meaning, but that which makes life's meaningfulness possible" (Carse, 1980, p. 9). He went on to discuss 10 major conceptions of death, Eastern and Western, showing that they each have a different way of conceiving how our continuity is threatened and the means of establishing a more inclusive continuity. Still, in all the conceptions, the issue is that death destroys our web of worldly connections and ends the temporal continuity that we call life. However an individual person interprets the meaning of death, it will be within the context of the possible end of the continuity of personhood.

WESTERN CONCEPTIONS OF DEATH

Although it is impossible to explore here all the possible conceptions of death, I will describe the two major orientations that prevail in the West. Some believe that philosophy and religion have no answer at all to the basic question of death and that death is final extinction of the individual self. Others opt for a continuation of the individual person in some form and in some place.

Modern science has done significant damage to many of the conceptualizations upon which the traditional religions of the West have been based, and with the passing of the influence of such concepts, the ability of religion to provide solace in the face of death has also waned. Much of current Western thought is the legacy of the Aristotelian orientation. The philosophy of Aristotle includes a conceptualization that knowledge arises from the senses and is solely dependent on them (Carse, 1980). Aristotle rejected the dualism of Plato, in which true knowledge transcends the material world. The belief about death based on this philosophical orientation was put forth by Epicurus, Aristotle's student: Because knowledge is based on the senses, and the senses end with bodily death, life must also cease to exist when the physical body dies. The empirical orientation of Western science basically leads to the same conclusions that Epicurus drew. Death is the discontinuing of all that provides us with consciousness, knowing, and any sense of being. It is the end.

This view of final extinction takes two different directions, the first of which is congruent with the view that there is no direction to life, that we are simply the sum of environmental influences. In such a view, life is inherently meaningless, and the primary life goal becomes one of need and wish satisfaction. To those who follow this view, there is no inherent good in life, no ultimate consequence relating to how one lives, and purpose becomes one of immediate momentary pleasure, whatever leads to satisfying consequences. Death is simply the end of this hedonistic life.

There are also those who view death as extinction of the person, both the body and the self, but who take a different view of the purpose of life. The belief that there is no afterlife or continuation of the self does not preclude the possibility of an inherent direction in life. Such a direction has been described by humanistic psychologists as actualization of the self (e.g., Maslow, 1968, 1971; Rogers, 1951, 1961). Within this context, movement toward the greatest use of one's inherent potential defines the nature of the person. Even though death finally puts an end to movement toward this goal of self-actualization, this inherent pull overrides the hedonistic self-gratification that comes in the absence of any perceived direction to life.

Only as we face death and openly explore its meaning do we have the freedom to fully actualize the self. If the meaning of death is, most of all, the discontinuity of worldly connections, then for a person with terminal illness, the threat of this severing of ties becomes immediate. Grief, according to Carse (1980), comes when we perceive the continuity in our lives to be destroyed. It is "our refusal to recognize the fact that death has not taken away our freedom to reconstitute the continuities it has destroyed" (Carse, 1980, p. 8). Yet, for the dying person who views the world from the scientific empirical model, that freedom is a limited one, because continuities, old or new, continue to have the limits of worldly existence placed on them. Within this context, however, we can make efforts to help the person replace connections whose power is future oriented with connections that are more present centered. We can help the person focus on continuities whose limits are within the scope of a more strictly bounded time. Such focuses might take the form of "dying a good death" or finishing business with friends and loved ones. We might try to help the dying person be a more effective communicator with family members during this final time together. Those concerns discussed earlier as constituting an appropriate or healthy death include aspects that are significant in their ability to help a person move toward greater self-actualization.

Although the spectrum of consciousness in its entirety moves through the personal into the transpersonal, those who reject the transpersonal are still able to see the validity of the personal side and its implied inherent direction from the prepersonal to the ultimate level of self-actualization. A counselor who accepts the whole of the spectrum is not thereby limited to dealing only with those who also accept the transpersonal. The period of dying allows for continued growth within the personal side even for those who perceive death to result in complete extinction.

PRESERVATION OF THE SELF

The second major orientation in current Western thought about the meaning of death and the consequence of the discontinuity of the temporal life is that which comes from the Judeo–Christian heritage. There are variations in this heritage (see Kastenbaum & Kastenbaum, 1989) that are too extensive to discuss here, yet must be considered on an individual basis in one's counseling. The purpose here is simply to present the conceptualization in its global form in contrast to the view of extinction, as well as in contrast to the third view, rebirth of the soul, a number of variations of which are becoming more numerous in Western culture.

The premise of Christianity is faith in the resurrection of Christ and consequently the possibility of personal resurrection for all believers. There remain some forms of Christianity that believe in bodily resurrection, that is, that at some point in time all believers will be resurrected in the same form as they have known on earth. Such a view runs directly into conflict with a modern scientific understanding of the world and the nature of the physical body. Other believers of the Christian tradition, understanding the paradox of bodily resurrection, see the resurrection of followers of Christ to be a spiritual one in which the person remains the same distinct individual in a different, more spiritual form. Regardless of these differences, however, the Christian view is that there is a continuity of the self, or personhood, after worldly death.

A second issue within the Christian tradition is what happens to the self after death. The range of thought is greater here, ranging from an eternal hell or damnation to an ultimate reunion with Christ in a heavenly realm. Such beliefs, of course, have a tremendous effect on how an individual approaches impending death, and these beliefs must be understood by the counselor if significant help is to be provided. These beliefs have an important effect on a person's fears and anxieties surrounding death, which are discussed in greater detail in chapter 6.

These views can provide both the basis for a dying person to want to enter into a counseling relationship and the basis for seeing no need for it. I once approached a woman in the final stages of life, who was referred to me by an oncologist. She was very polite and told me she appreciated that I would offer my services but that she already had a counselor. In stating this, she pointed to her Bible.

On the other hand, there are those who see the time of dying as an opportunity to more fully explore their beliefs and understanding about death. Although we say that dying is the final stage of growth, that means only that it is the final opportunity in this life. It can also be seen as a time of preparation for growth beyond the worldly.

THE THIRD VIEW OF DEATH

Although the two orientations to death just discussed represent the predominant views in the West, there seems to be an increasing interest in the third view, one that is equated more with Eastern views of death. This is the conceptualization of a rebirth of the soul.

Sogyal (1992) pointed out that reincarnation and a belief in an afterlife have been a part of most religions and that it was a part of traditional Christian belief for several centuries after the death of Christ. Indeed, according to a poll conducted in 1982, nearly one fourth of Americans believe in reincarnation today (Gallup, 1983). There has been an increasing interest in past-life regressions, indication such beliefs represent a significant part of Americans' concept of the meaning of death.

The basis for belief in rebirth, or reincarnation, is that there is a continuity of mind, or consciousness (Sogyal, 1992). In this view, what provides the continuity is not the body or physical self but the subtle levels of consciousness. There is, then, a continuity of the self, but it is spiritual rather than physical. This can be compared with the Christian view that resurrection is of the soul, not the body. The spiritual self remains even if the body is lost.

The major difference between resurrection and reincarnation is that the former is in another realm, whereas reincarnation is in this world. The mind continues in this realm, albeit in a different body. Yet in each conception, there is a transformation. Even if there is a continuity of the self, it is a self of a different nature. When Jesus talked of his followers needing to die to be saved, he was alluding to a metaphorical death (Borg, 1987). It was a dying to the self as the center of one's concern, which will lead to a transformation to a higher level of consciousness. Even though the notion of successive lives and deaths is primarily an Eastern tradition, the concept of continually dying to the self is basic to Christian scriptures.

Both Hinduism and Buddhism accept the concept of *karma*, which is the idea that whatever we do in any life has consequences for the next (Sogyal, 1992). There is a continuity of effect as well as consciousness that characterizes rebirth. This is different from the Christian concept of sin, in which one must answer for acts that violate divine laws or injunctions (Carse, 1980). Karma is, on the other hand, the existential consequences, the result of the actions of one life carrying into the next. Negative effects of karma are not the result of punishment by God but the result of not fully transforming oneself to higher levels of consciousness.

This is a very brief discussion of just the major concepts surrounding the meaning of death. Yet on the basis of an understanding that there is a basic direction to life that stems from the development and continuity of self, it is important to be aware of the meaning that the potential end of that continuity has for a person who is dying. It is an understanding and acceptance of death as discontinuity that allows for the meaningfulness of life, even within the confines of terminal illness. Whatever the dying person's understanding is, it will most likely come from one of the major conceptions just discussed.

SUMMARY

The meaning of life is found in the meaning of death and vice versa. There is a continuity to life, an underlying direction that is inherent in all humans. It involves the development of a strong sense of being an individual self—one that is separate from the rest of the world in terms of the way we perceive ourselves, the way we feel, and the way we think. Traditional Western psychology accepts that the development and actualization of the personal self is the highest level of human development of which we are capable. Death threatens to destroy this self, this sense of being an individual person.

We find meaning for this ultimate and invariable threat through the ways in which we conceive of death. If death represents the end of all that I am, then development of the self serves no other purpose than guiding my life on earth; it has no use beyond that. If the separate self continues beyond this life, however, then the basic direction of life is one that continues after the death of the body. My development as a human is preparatory to a continued existence after death. In each of these broad conceptualizations, the meaning of death influences my perception of life and the meaning that I give to it.

Understanding the meaning that death has for any particular dying person is essential to understanding how the crisis is perceived and how growth might occur. Such an understanding can come only from being open and listening to the experience of the person as he or she is willing to express it.

Chapter 6

Death Anxiety

Research and theoretical positions on death anxiety account for a significant amount of the literature in the field of thanatology. Neimeyer (1989) found 528 published articles on the topic through 1985. An even greater number have been published since. Even so, there remains considerable disagreement regarding the definition and nature of death anxiety and the means for alleviating it (Neimeyer, 1994). In this chapter, I explore some of the discussion and findings regarding this aspect of dying and consider the concept of death anxiety within the parameters of the model of counseling that is being presented.

WHAT IS DEATH ANXIETY?

An inability to develop a consensus on what death anxiety is has hindered efforts to effectively deal with the phenomenon. First, there are terminology problems: the difference between fear and anxiety and the difference between fear of dying and fear of death. With regard to the first two terms, *fear* has traditionally been used as a term for which the object is known, whereas *anxiety* surrounds unknown objects or causes (Schulz, 1979). This distinction has been made in specific relation to death and dying (e.g., Kalish, 1987), but Neimeyer (1989) pointed out that in the construction of instruments and therefore the measurement and research on death anxiety, little distinction has been made between fear and anxiety. There appears to be a discrepancy between theory and practice in this area.

The terms *fear of dying* and *fear of death* also present some confusion. There are fears associated with the process of dying that are unrelated to fears regarding discontinuity or annihilation of the person. Being afraid of unmanageable pain, deterioration of the body, and withdrawal of support are often realistic fears about the process of dying. Weisman (1972) said that the fear of dying is "associated with autonomic symptoms, and usually conveys a preemptive conviction that collapse is at hand" (p. 14). He distinguished this from fear of death, which he said is not an immediate event but a reflection of one's helplessness. Lonetto and Templer (1986) referred to death anxiety as that which surrounds the thoughts of one's own death, which could be construed as involving both thoughts associated with the process of dying and thoughts associated with death itself. Although the meaning of these terms remains in conflict, within the context of this book the fear of dying will be distinguished from death anxiety.

In addition to the confusion regarding the definition of death anxiety, there is also disagreement as to whether it is an inherent or learned phenomenon. Kastenbaum (1989) noted the contrasting theories of Freud and Becker, which characterize much of the thinking on death anxiety. Freud believed the fears surrounding death stemmed from unresolved psychological conflicts from childhood, meaning that they are not inherent, but learned. What is expressed as a fear of dying is in reality a transfer of a different fear onto the subject of death. The alleviation of the anxiety then comes through discovering and resolving the original source of conflict.

Behavioral theory also supports the position that death anxiety is not inherent. As one interacts with the environment, there are threats of all kinds, and one learns or does not learn to effectively cope with these threats. The fears and coping procedures are transferred to the experience of death, in the same way that all responses to life are learned. The means of alleviating fear or anxiety surrounding death is through learning new, more appropriate responses.

On the other side, Becker (1973) contended that death anxiety is the most basic driving force for an individual. He also discussed the psychoanalytic position, which he termed the "healthy minded" argument, one that says that fear of death is not natural to humans. Instead, fear of death is posited to result from a repression of life and the naturalness of our being, which creates shame, guilt, and self-hatred. Within this conception, children who have bad early experiences will likely become fixated on anxiety of separation and anxiety of death.

In contrast to this view is what Becker called the "morbidly minded" argument, which supports the idea that the fear of death is natural and present in everyone. This is the point that Becker accepted and expounded in his book. This point of view is also accepted by other thanatologists. Shneidman (1973) said that death is universally feared: "Over the ages death has been the source of fear, the focus of taboo, the occasion for poetry, the stimulus for philosophy—and remains the ultimate mystery in the life of each man" (p. 3). Weisman (1974) pointed out that even though we recognize and cope with various conflicts and crises associated with dying, and although we face death with different levels of acceptance and denial, still "none of us is entirely free of a deep fear of death, or exempt from dread of annihilation" (p. 2). Rando (1984) said that death threatens us with negation of ourselves and all that we value. Many of our everyday occurrences remind us of this fact: losses, illnesses, separations. All of these add up to a continuing realization that at some point there will be no future, which leads to a natural state of anxiety.

I have already discussed denial as a part of the process of dying. It is a part of Kubler-Ross's (1969) stages of dying, and it is the subject of two widely used books, Becker's (1973) *The Denial of Death* and Weisman's (1972) *On Dying and Denying*. In all of these, denial is a result of anxiety, an inability to face or accept the inevitable consequence of annihilation, or nonbeing. This is more than fear of alienation or separation, in which one would continue to exist as an individual being, albeit cut off from the sources of emotional support. Annihilation means total absence of self or existence and is a concept that is difficult, if not impossible, for most of us to comprehend. Yet the fact that we have to deny is support for the contention that we are filled with anxiety which, at least for the moment, is beyond our ability to handle. The presence of denial means the presence of anxiety. So although there is some discrepancy with this issue, the majority of thanatologists appear to side with the idea that death anxiety is inherent in being human, and that is the position on which this model of counseling is based.

DEATH ANXIETY RESEARCH

The fact that a number of measures of death anxiety have been created and published may perhaps account for the reason that death anxiety is one of the most discussed and researched topics in thanatology (Kastenbaum & Kastenbaum, 1989). Whatever the reason, there is a considerable body of research available to better help counselors understand the phenomenon.

The great majority of research on this subject has involved questionnaires, which elicit conscious and willing-to-be-expressed attitudes. Some attempts to establish unconscious attitudes through the use of projective techniques have been made, but these have yielded questionable findings (Neimeyer, 1989). Therefore, although some interpretations can be made from research, one must guard against drawing conclusions about unconscious attitudes and fears.

Neimeyer (1989) presented an overview of findings regarding death anxiety, and though much of the research is inconclusive, some general indications of correlations with personal factors can be found. Only a few that are especially relevant to the model presented here are discussed.

Gender and age seem to be at least minimally correlated with death anxiety, with women expressing slightly more anxiety than men, and younger persons expressing greater anxiety than older persons. Interpretation of these findings is difficult, however. It is not known from the research whether women have more anxiety or are simply willing to express it to a greater extent than are men. Perhaps men are as anxious or even more anxious than women but are able to repress or deny their anxiety more effectively.

The same questions can be raised with regard to findings that age is negatively correlated with death anxiety. Neimeyer (1989), for example, pointed out that the lesser degree of anxiety expressed among older persons may be a result of deteriorating health, greater religiosity or spirituality, or greater experience with death and opportunity to work through related fears. As many questions remain as are answered by the research on death anxiety.

Another area of research pertinent to this model of counseling is related to attempts to alleviate death anxiety. Studies examining the impact of death education courses, counseling, hypnosis, and behavior therapy have produced inconclusive results (Neimeyer, 1989). In some studies, the amount of anxiety expressed on various measures increased. Such a finding is not totally unexpected because these interventions may serve the purpose of increasing people's awareness of their own mortality; that is, they destroy denial to some extent, and the consequence is increased feelings of anxiety. Whatever the explanation, a great deal remains to be learned about the nature and alleviation of death anxiety.

THE NATURE OF ANXIETY

In the absence of any conclusive research findings on the subject of death anxiety, and given the disagreement surrounding its cause and nature, it is necessary to present a discussion of the premise on which my model for counseling is based.

Anxiety is a universal concomitant of psychological crises, and therefore it is also a natural and invariant characteristic of terminal illness. Although not everyone goes through a period of denial or feel anger over a loss, and although for many people the stage of bargaining may be very short, every person facing a significant loss does experience anxiety. It is a part of the journey of dying, and the counselor's help should be focused toward facilitating dying persons in the process of working through their anxiety.

Experience has proved to psychologists that anxiety is at the heart of counseling. It is at the center of all growth and all psychospiritual concerns; it is the most prominent mental characteristic of human civilization, whether we live in the East or the West. Anxiety is the life force and has been described in various ways—the angst of existentialism, Selye's stress, the neurotic anxiety of psychoanalysis, the suffering of Buddhism. It is an essential part of loss, and along with pain, despair, and depression it is what a terminally ill person has to live with.

As hospice care has developed, there has been an increasing focus on the control of pain as the central aspect of providing quality palliative care. Without attempting to diminish the importance of this concern, we must look at the possibility that the anxiety associated with death is a more universal and important characteristic of dying. Indeed, pain has been found to be a significantly lesser concern in persons who are dying of causes other than cancer (Seale & Addington-Hall, 1994), whereas anxiety is part of the deep structure of being human. To provide the most effective care for the terminally ill person, then, counselors must be as concerned with helping the person deal with anxiety as we are with managing the pain.

Agreement on the cause of anxiety is not complete, but there does appear to be a general consensus in the writings of psychology. On the basis of this consensus, it is possible to say that, in the most simple sense, anxiety stems from wanting something that is perceived as being crucial to one's sense of self. If we want something, there is the possibility that we might not achieve it, and this fear of not getting it is translated as anxiety. If, for example, a young man wants to get a college degree (he values himself as a college-educated person), there exists the possibility that he might not achieve that goal. There is the possibility that he will not be the person that he values, and it is this possibility that creates anxiety. This fear of not getting the degree is what propels him forward, what keeps him studying, taking courses, and worrying about term papers and tests. It is in this sense that anxiety is the life force. As seen earlier, however, if the threat of loss is too great for the person to handle, there may be a period of maintenance, of restructuring the boundaries around the self to ward off the threat. Only as the person works through perceived danger to the self will there be freedom to use the anxiety to move forward.

The extent of the anxiety depends on how much the young man wants to get the degree and how realistic he perceives the goal to be. If the whole matter stays on the surface, that is, if the man is consciously aware of why he wants the degree, what it means to his self-concept, and the likelihood of achieving the goal, we would probably label the characteristic as stress because it stems from a known source. But if the source of wanting the degree is more hidden, coming perhaps from an early introjected value from the young man's parents, then the fear has a lesser known cause and would be translated as anxiety. The terminology, however, is not as important as the process of using the stress or anxiety as a growth force.

This is a fairly straightforward and simple description of the cause and experience of anxiety, yet it is a process that occurs in all times and places and among all cultures and that is seen at any level of development and at all levels of complexity. When we speak of the anxiety as being a part of a crisis and the process of moving through a loss, we understand that the something that we want is our self; we want to maintain ourselves as separate persons with specific identities. It is the threat of losing this self that creates anxiety, and in the case of dying, the loss of self is the most complete that we can imagine. Therefore, the greatest anxiety is likely that which occurs during a crisis created by facing death.

Earlier, I made a distinction between the fear of dying and death anxiety. There certainly are many reasons to feel anxiety over what will occur during the final stages of life. Separation from friends and loved ones and the fear of losing parts of the world that are critical to one's sense of self and well-being can give rise to anxiety. This is different from deep-structure death anxiety, however, which is an inherent fear of nonbeing, of total alienation from one's roots. Acknowledgment of this fear is found in most major religious and spiritual traditions throughout the ages, where explanations of salvation and continued existence are posited as a part of the cosmic scheme. Although these take many different forms (Carse, 1980), they have a common purpose and that is to help people deal with the anxiety of death: the fear of being dead, of not being.

Existentialists point out that wherever there is a separate self, there is suffering; the terror of being, and at the same time, the terror of death (Wilber, 1982). According to Boss, "the essential, basic arch-anxiety is innate to all isolated, individual forms of human existence. In the basic anxiety, human existence is afraid *of* as well as anxious *about* its 'being-in-the-world'" (cited in Becker, 1973, p. 208). But the anxiety of nonbeing is not only an existential concept. Psychoanalysis teaches that anxiety causes us to repress much of our experience, which limits our freedom to make life choices, and conscious awareness and acknowledgment of death is the primary aspect of our selves that we repress (Becker, 1973). In the Eastern traditions, the separated self is seen as the source of suffering, what we in the West refer to as death anxiety. For example, the Upanishads, the sacred writings of the Hindus, teach that wherever there is other, there is fear (Wilber, 1982).

Pascal (cited by May, 1950) talked about humans finding themselves in a world that they do not understand, not knowing how they got there, and not knowing what will happen to them when they die. He likened this to a man being carried during sleep to a deserted isle, not knowing how he got there or how he will leave, alone in a world that he cannot understand. The marvel is that we do not totally despair in such circumstances. But Pascal went on to point out that we do not despair because we plunge ourselves into a morass of worldly diversions, creating a sense of meaning and connectedness through relationships that must inherently be temporary. This is our only way to avoid the anxiety and despair of being alone in an alien world.

As soon as we begin to shed the security of our worldly diversions, which help us deal with the surface, or learned, anxiety, the deep-structure anxiety returns in its fullness, forcing us to acknowledge again the despair of being human. Having grown beyond dependence on others to allay the anxiety of losing our selves, we find ourselves alone and afraid of being alienated from the source of our being. The inward arc of the spectrum of consciousness is the long process that leads to finally transcending ego entirely in the attempt to return to the source. This defines the direction of life, with variations depending on whose orientation one studies. Assogioli (1965) distinguished between the personal and spiritual realms of existence, and Jung (1971) distinguished between the personal and the collective unconscious. At each level, there is the basic anxiety, surface and deep structure, that is the concern of counseling, growth, and transpersonal transformations.

MEMBERSHIP ANXIETY

The creation of a separate self results in the establishment of boundaries, and the life of boundaries is a life of battles. When we draw a boundary, the purpose is to differentiate outside from inside. If the distinction is important enough for us to create the boundary, then it is important enough to fight for. Although there are many ways to fight battles, the first strategy we choose tends to be developing strong barriers around that which we wish to protect. If we can keep others out, we can protect what is ours. By keeping nonself things from invading our boundary of self, we can keep the self pure and intact. If it is invaded from the outside, then it will become polluted, and in the end will be something other than the self that we have come to know and now want to protect. When a crisis occurs, there is a fear that the boundaries will be invaded and that the "territory" by which we define ourselves will be violated. We will lose the self. Suffering and anxiety are precipitated by a recognition that our boundaries are not forever and are not secure from invasion and change.

There are differences in the psychological needs that characterize the self at the various points along the spectrum of human growth, and these differences lead to the different ways that a person draws boundaries around the self. In this sense, loss has different characteristics depending on the level of the person's development. In the stages that constitute the prepersonal level of development, when the child is developing a sense of a separate physical self, a separate emotional self, and finally a separate mental self, the needs are of the lowest level. According to Erikson (1963), they are the need to have a sense of trust in the environment, to become an autonomous person, and to have the freedom to try new roles. These are what Wilber (1986) has called the transitional aspects of the spectrum of consciousness, those that come into being at a given point along the spectrum and then lose their emphasis as the person moves on to new stages.

The earliest stage defined by Erikson is *trust versus mistrust*, describing the time when children need to develop a sense that they can trust the environment to take care of their needs. This stage occurs at a time when they cannot take care of their needs themselves and must depend on others to satisfy them. When their needs are satisfied from the outside, children learn that the environment is structured in such a way that their "self," which at this point is only beginning to emerge, is not unduly threatened and will be allowed to remain intact. Whatever is necessary for maintaining that self is being provided at a time when the children cannot take care of it for themselves.

If, however, the self is threatened because the environment is not trustworthy, then children have such a high level of anxiety over the prospect of losing the self that they withdraw from contact. A child whose consciousness is at the sensoriphysical level has little course other than to psychologically shut out all nonself aspects of the environment to secure his or her boundaries. In doing this, the child cuts off the possibility of moving beyond this level of earliest self-development and forecloses growth. Self-development never has a chance to reach mature levels of the spectrum.

It is easy enough to imagine a child in this stage of prepersonal development who has the security of a trusting environment stripped away by the loss of his or her mother. Being the primary force in providing an atmosphere of trust, the mother is the key figure in helping the child differentiate him- or herself (physical, emotional, and then mental) from the original perception of fusion that characterizes the world view at birth. The loss occurs at a time when the child is beginning to develop a crude definition of him- or herself as separate, loved, and able to do things independently. The mother is the object through which much of this definition comes, and the loss of that object means the destruction of the values by which the child is learning to define the self. This is the earliest stage at which the emerging self can be lost, yet the pattern of grieving will be the same as for any significant loss that might occur at later stages. The initial reaction is to deny—to draw the boundaries rigidly around the self, shutting out the world so that the separate self that has so far emerged can be maintained.

When one observes a young child who has experienced a loss of this sort, the other stages of the loss paradigm can also often be detected. After an initial period of withdrawal (the child's form of denial), anger may be manifested in what we consider to be negative and destructive behaviors. One might then see bargaining through the process of trying to adopt a substitute mother so that the self can be maintained. We also may notice a period of apathy, an "I don't care" attitude that is indicative of depression. Even at this most elementary level, the loss of self-defining values and the consequent grieving period can be seen to follow the consensual pattern.

This process of defending boundaries occurs at all levels in the outward arc of the spectrum of consciousness, whenever there is unmanageable anxiety resulting from a threat of losing self-identity. The cause of the threat is different at each stage because it is created by needs specific to each stage, and different methods are used to reinforce the self, depending on the mode of cognitive processing appropriate for each level. In all cases, however, the source of the anxiety is consistent, stemming from a perceived threat of losing the self.

Maslow's (1968) needs hierarchy provides a good description of the transitional aspects of the spectrum of consciousness and thus shows the differing ways that the self is threatened at different stages. In much the same way as Erikson, Maslow stated that at the prepersonal level of the spectrum, we pass through the stage of dependence on others for our livelihood. During this period, if a child is provided with a psychologically healthy environment, one that satisfies the physiological and security needs, anxiety will remain within manageable bounds. As the child develops the ability to be physically independent from others and free from the need for security, however, the anxiety that was created through a fear of physical separation now becomes focused on psychological dependence. The need to be psychologically connected to others through feelings of belonging and self-esteem is, at the personal level, the process by which the person defines the self. It is defined through identification as an accepted part of another person or group. A fear of not being able to fulfill these needs now becomes as anxiety producing as was the fear of an inability to fulfill the physical needs of the earlier stage.

Many of the people counselors work with during a period of terminal illness are at a stage of development that is still characterized by the need for belonging or self-esteem. These persons may feel that they belong and are esteemed, but these needs have not been satisfied enough to allow them to move to the level of self-actualization. Death will remove the belonging or esteemed self that has been the focus of their needs. What they are threatened with losing, then, is not only their individual self but also a particular kind of self. The loss of an esteemed self is a crisis at a different level than the loss of a physical or mental self or the loss of a self-actualizing or psychic self.

For a person faced with loss of a belonging self, there may be a period of bargaining, in which the person attempts to reinforce relationships with the people who are the focus of the belonging. In the case of esteem, a dying person might attempt to produce more of the works or deeds that have previously led to a sense of accomplishment and worth. Having moved through the denial and anger stages, the person might explore whatever options are available for maintaining the present self. If this self is defined by belonging and esteem, then this is where the person will attempt to create a semblance of maintenance. This is where the boundaries are drawn and where the person will now fight. The critical point is that if as counselors we can facilitate a person's movement through the bargaining stage, he or she can come to a place where acceptance of the loss of the belonging or esteemed self is possible and can then move to a stage of actualization or perhaps even beyond to the transpersonal realm of the spectrum of consciousness.

EXISTENTIAL ANXIETY

Wilber (1980) called the stages characterized by Maslow's (1968) belonging and esteem needs the membership and egoic levels. During these periods, the anxiety of separation is managed by psychologically allying oneself with others in the worldly environment. The fear is of being abandoned, of being left without any self-defining values. This could happen if the person were to lose the connections and relationships that provide a sense of belonging and self-esteem. But we must differentiate this fear from the anxiety that comes simply from being a person in the world. When our self-reflective mode of knowing emerges, we become aware that the security of belonging and self-esteem is illusory, appropriate only for the lower levels of consciousness. There is a dawning awareness that there is nothing we can do to alleviate the anxiety because simply being a separate self *is* anxiety. As counselors, we must not try to understand dying persons who are experiencing existential anxiety as if they were having a problem with separation anxiety. This would be to miss the point completely.

When the needs for belonging and esteem are adequately met, the person is freed to move on to the next level of self-development, where psychological energy is focused on actualizing inherent human potential. Such movement, in the healthy developing individual, represents the attainment of a level where gratification no longer depends on others but must come from within. In the stages preceding this level, definition of the self is very much dependent on relationships with others, and the loss of these others creates a loss of self-identity. Now, however, the person has moved to a stage where the self is defined through self-reflection and inner directedness.

Fromm (1941) argued that the modern individual's struggle for freedom—that is, the freedom to think for oneself and to express oneself unhindered—is by necessity anxiety producing and even frightening, for it involves a confrontation with one's ultimate aloneness in the world. Such anxiety keeps us from engaging in the battle; instead we seek to escape from this freedom by reaching out in an other-directed way. We refuse to move forward, and instead, we draw the boundaries more tightly around our other-directed selves. Life follows a pattern of separation from the source of our being at birth, which is followed by an attempt to deal with that separation by connecting to others in the world (the development of the ego). To grow beyond that to a point where we can stand alone in an inner-directed way (self-actualization), we need to engage in the battle. We need to let go of our boundaries and go out seeking a higher self.

In assuming transpersonal levels of the spectrum of human development, we accept that we have a relationship or connection with a consciousness that is beyond what we normally know within the world. Moreover, we accept that it is out of this consciousness that we derive our existence, and therefore we can refer to it as the source of our being. The original separation creates a deep-structure anxiety, a fear that we will not be able to return to this ultimate source. We refer to it as a deep structure because it is not learned but is inherent in being a human in the world. We mask this anxiety by focusing on the development of a personal self and all the meanings that entails, which as already seen, creates its own anxiety of separation and loss of self.

DEEP-STRUCTURE ANXIETY

There are common characteristics of humanity that appear throughout the philosophical and theological writings of the ages, defined as the perennial philosophy by Huxley (1970). In the area of psychology, however, there has been little work in the delineation of such common characteristics or basic structures. One characteristic that does stand out, however, is the concept of death anxiety. Throughout the ages, in essays that could be classified as psychological, this is one characteristic that can clearly be termed perennial.

The most basic aspect of being human is that inherent within each of us is a fear of death, a deep-structure anxiety that is a continual focus of attention, either conscious or unconscious. Wilber (1979, p. 80) asked, "What pushes man away from his centaur, his total organism?" He then provided the answer: that humanity is still in flight from death. We see death not as a return to unity but as total alienation. We therefore create a self that will allow us to continue to belong in the world even after bodily death.

If there is a spiritual side to psychology, by definition it must be characterized by deep structures in the entities we call human beings. These are structures that are present without regard to time, place, or culture but are part of the essence of being human. They must appear as a part of all psychologies throughout the history of humanity, not just those characterizing the 20th century or those based on an understanding of the American population. They must be universal, perceived by scholars as being present in all ages and in all cultures. They are what Jung called archetypes and Plato called *anamnesis,* structures that are *known* and must be brought forth or remembered, as opposed to surface structures, which are *learned* through worldly experience.

While science has been telling us that knowledge is based on our senses, psychology has been telling us that the development of a strong healthy self is the pinnacle of human development. Even though this self is a worldly phenomenon, based on interactions with others in this life, and science tells us that there can be no continuation of the personal self after physical death, we have been so focused on the development of our sense of identity that it becomes virtually impossible to think of giving it up. Even in the face of our knowledge of science, we continue to seek some answer that will allow our self to continue its existence even after death. In this search, we most often turn to religion.

The inherent fear of separation that we call death anxiety is the core of all philosophical, psychological, and religious exploration; it is an attempt to find an answer to the question of how to face nonbeing. These attempts find expressions at various levels along the spectrum of consciousness because the people seeking the answers view life from different perspectives. In the Christian religion, for example, the answer is sought at one level in an understanding of the bodily resurrection of Jesus Christ and a return to the kingdom of God, which is seen as something "out there." At a totally different level, however, the kingdom of God is understood to be within the individual seeker and the resurrection of Jesus to be symbolic of the need to die to one's worldly self. These conceptions represent in a simple fashion only two of the possible levels at which the meaning of death can be understood by a Christian, and there are many more, as attested to by the writings of many Christian mystics. The same multilevel explanations of death and its meaning can be found in other traditions.

The anxiety of death is the fear of alienation from the greater unity, with life being a struggle to return to that unity. This has been described metaphorically in Judaism through the concept of the wilderness, where the Jews wandered (alienated) for 40 years, and it is described in Christianity as Jesus' attempt to return to the Father. It is described in Buddhism as the suffering that comes from desire, from attachment to worldly things, which separates one from awareness of one's own Buddha nature. To the extent that one can accept the concept that alienation from the source of one's being is characteristic of a worldly life, one can then accept that wanting to return to that source and the consequent fear that it might not be achieved is the cause of the basic, universal, deep-structure anxiety of life.

Death anxiety is a teleological fear, a fear of where we are going and what may happen, not a fear of what has happened. The anxiety that comes from *eros,* the life force, is a fear of moving forward in the process of becoming a higher level individual; the anxiety that comes from *thanatos,* the death force, is the fear of losing one's individuality and of not being reconnected to the unity from which that individuality developed. The perennial philosophy says that the capacity to suffer (have anxiety) arises when there is imperfection, disunity, and separation from an embracing totality. For persons who achieve unity within their own organism and union with the divine source of their being, there is an end to suffering. This has been taught throughout the centuries in all philosophical and religious traditions.

SUMMARY

The direction of life, then, is characterized by an initial separation from the source of one's being, which gives rise to a basic deep-structure anxiety. This anxiety is managed by looking to others in the world, creating in our minds attachments to these others. These attachments, in turn, give rise to surface, or learned, anxiety (the fear of not being accepted, not belonging, not having a positive sense of self in relation to others). As we come to the place in our development where we can transcend the need for belonging and worldly attachments, we become actualizing persons, but this transcendence unmasks the original alienation. While the surface-structure anxiety subsides, deep-structure anxiety returns to consciousness. We are now not afraid of being separated from worldly sources, but we are once again aware of our fear of not being able to return to the original source. This is the anxiety of existence, which arises simply from awareness of being a separate self, and the only remedy for this anxiety is to give up the separate self altogether. This crisis introduces us to the inward arc and the journey of return to the source of being, which has been termed *Atman, God consciousness,* or *unity consciousness* (Wilber, 1980). The essential quality of the self is that it is both the source and the goal, the beginning and the end. In the inherent direction of life, we strive to be what we were, which can only be accomplished by not being.

The crisis of death is characterized by the renewal of deep-structure anxiety, a fear of alienation. The need for connection takes form at both the mythic and transcendent levels, which is seen in Chinese folk religion and formal Buddhist religion and in Christian charismatic religion and mystic Christianity. Ancestor worship, intercession by mediums, and fortune-telling are mythic means of trying to reestablish the transcendent connection. Such concepts as the rapture, reunion with Jesus, and membership in the body of Christ are the mythic Christian counterparts to these Chinese beliefs. At all levels of the spectrum of consciousness, we see the attempt to ward off the archetypal anxiety that arises from fear of alienation.

The development or conceptualization of an "other" God, a father God, is the development of a surface structure to satisfy the need to belong. God loves and accepts me, Jesus loves and accepts me. To ancestor worshipers, my ancestors love and accept me, and so it is with other religions, all of which have their beginnings and development in the world of learned meanings. The church plays on this surface structure by inserting itself between God and humans as the surface source of the belonging. Perhaps the great attraction of evangelical Christianity is that it teaches that the love and belonging given by Jesus on behalf of God is direct, not needing the intermediary of the church fathers. This concept is also true of Eastern traditions, where the source can be directly known through meditation, and no intermediary is necessary.

The church structure that keeps people at the level of surface anxiety by serving as an intermediary is very much like a counselor who intervenes when a person is in the process of moving through the anxiety of a loss. By trying to make things okay, we cut off the possibility of growth. Yet that growth is the purpose of life and must be the essence of psychospiritual care of the dying person. We must facilitate individuals in seeking their own way through the loss and not insert ourselves as intermediaries ready to interpret the meaning of their experience and provide direction for their journey.

Chapter 7

Pain, Anxiety, and Depression

Terminal illness is often accompanied by pain. One of the primary motivating forces in the development of hospice programs has been to provide freedom from pain in the final stages of a person's life. As counselors in such programs, we stress the control of pain, but not merely its physical aspects. We must be concerned with total pain, including that which has its source in the social, psychological, and spiritual spheres of the person's life (Rhymes, 1990). We should not consider pain to be only a physical problem to be managed with medical procedures. Although in many cases this is the nature of the pain and the only consideration, in many other cases pain is more than or even other than a physical problem. Therefore we must have a broad understanding of the cause of all pain that is related to terminal illness and the methods of its alleviation. In this chapter, pain, anxiety, and depression are described as related to each other in an integrative manner and as occurring on more than one level. Each aspect is important to the focus of palliative care.

There are certainly times when pain is quite straightforward, with the direct and sole cause being a physical problem. Pain is nothing other than a symptomatic manifestation of a physical body that is not working as well as it should. This does not mean that the pain does not affect the emotional outlook of the person or that it cannot be controlled through psychological rather than physical means. It's just that there is no need to look for underlying or hidden causes.

There are times, however, when pain may have a different source or when the level of the pain may be affected significantly by factors other than the physical condition of the body. Some persons find it easier or more acceptable to express their fears through pain than through more common manifestations of anxiety. For many terminally ill persons, pain is integrally associated in their minds with dying, and in some cases the pain, or at least the level of the pain, is affected by this knowledge more than by the tumor or the deterioration of the body.

Regardless of its source, pain is not an entity that stands by itself. It gives rise to anxiety and depression, especially in the persons who are dying. The pain may remind them that they have a life-threatening illness and that it may very well be getting worse. This causes a continual awareness of the threat of losing one's self, a condition that invariably creates anxiety. In turn, however, the anxiety is also likely to increase the pain by creating physical stress at its source and perhaps by reducing the body's own resources for managing the pain. The relationship between pain and anxiety becomes circular, with the pain increasing the anxiety and the anxiety increasing the pain.

In the same way, pain creates depression and, in turn, depression worsens the pain. Anxiety arises from the threat of loss, whereas depression occurs when the loss is perceived as inevitable. When it is no longer only a possibility or even a probability that the values of self-definition are going to lose their potency, but instead is accepted as fact, then the force that has been the motivation for maintaining and enhancing the self is gone. The values that have provided the person with an individual direction of growth and enhancement no longer will serve that purpose.

Common characteristics of depression are apathy, withdrawal, fatigue, and sadness, and these characteristics are descriptive of persons who have temporarily lost their forward movement. When dying persons assimilate into their experience the knowledge that death is inevitable and imminent, all of the values related to belonging and worldly self-esteem immediately become meaningless. All of the activities and relationships by which the individual has learned to satisfy these needs are about to disappear, and there is little if any way of replacing them. The needs can no longer be satisfied, and therefore the way by which the self is defined is lost.

We noted earlier that in the *Phaedo* (Plato, 1952), Socrates told his friends that when people have thought about death all their lives, it cannot be frightening when it comes. Just the opposite holds true for most people living in the Western world today, however. We do not think about death, in fact we zealously avoid it, and when it comes we are not prepared. Not having thought about it, we are at first frightened, beset by the anxiety of separation and alienation. With the realization of the lost values, the fear turns to depression.

Depression is a natural stage in mourning—the fourth stage of the loss paradigm. Within this context, it is a temporary condition of moving from one level of being to the next. It is a time when the spirits are low and there is little vitality as the person takes the time necessary to come to an acceptance of the loss. This is different from despair, however, which is characterized by an abandoning of hope. The period of terminal illness is often described as one of hopelessness and despair, yet this implies that there is no future. There is no cure for the condition of grief. The point is, however, that if we can facilitate movement of dying persons through the period of depression and help them to not despair or lose hope, growth can and will occur. The illness may not be cured, but there may be a curing of the spirit.

It is also important to understand that even though we can describe anxiety and depression as occurring in a linear fashion, that is, the anxiety comes when there is fear of loss and *then* when the loss occurs there is depression, in actuality they occur simultaneously. The fear, or the hope that there will not be a loss, does not suddenly go away and then the depression begins, but rather, in the process of working through the grief, realization comes slowly, allowing times when there are signs of depression yet still signs of anxiety. Each affects the other in this process, too, with the depression increasing anxiety surrounding the remaining vestiges of hope, and the anxiety keeping in the person's consciousness the reality of the impending loss, which increases the periods of depression. And, of course, this process will increase the negative effects of pain and in some cases, even create it.

The interrelationship among pain, anxiety, and depression is both positive and negative. Though one of these conditions may have a negative effect on the cause and intensity of the others, the three are also positively integrated. If dying persons are able to lower their anxiety, they are likely to find that the intensity of their pain decreases. In the same way, persons who are not depressed are not likely to feel as much pain. Humans are integrated beings, and this calls for a holistic approach to helping.

LEVELS OF PAIN, ANXIETY, AND DEPRESSION

When pain, anxiety, and depression are viewed as an integrated syndrome, their cause and meaning must be perceived as a whole rather than as three separate problems or symptoms. Although there are symptoms or overt behaviors by which we can know that the person is experiencing pain, anxiety, or depression, the meaning of the syndrome can occur at different levels and is not always so easy to see or understand. If we intervene by treating the symptoms without any effort to help the person explore their meaning, we will only be working on one level and our help will be considerably less than it could be. We must attempt to understand the complete relationship of the pain, anxiety, and depression and work with the person to facilitate movement through all three.

Several levels of this syndrome can be delineated, paralleling those of the spectrum of consciousness discussed earlier. First, the syndrome may have its meaning at the level of the prepersonal, where the person is primarily afraid of losing the physical or emotional self. People who have identified with the physical body and conceive of nothing surviving the demise of that body fear losing the concrete, tangible evidence that they are persons. The psychological concerns that are attached to the self are of little importance because the person has not yet arrived at a place where there is a sense of being that transcends just the physical aspect of existence. Note that many adults continue to operate with this world view because they did not satisfactorily complete the prepersonal stage in their early years. They look in many ways just like other adults, but their viewpoint and their level of consciousness is still characteristic of the prepersonal child view.

The experience of Mike provides an example. He was a 63-year-old man with testicular cancer that had spread to his bones. The cancer was creating particular problems in the ribs on the left side of his body, and there was certainly little question that the deterioration of the bone was a primary source of pain. There was also little question that the physical pain detracted strongly from the quality of Mike's life. His ability to carry on the simple pleasures of walking around the neighborhood and puttering in his garage had decreased to the point that on most days these activities were impossible.

Mike's problem appeared to be a matter of symptom management. We had worked together for several weeks before the pain became significantly debilitating. As the bones deteriorated, the pain increased, and the physician prescribed medication. Quite possibly, if Mike had taken the medication and reduced the pain to what he considered to be manageable bounds, little else might have occurred. Because we had been working together, however, and had established a relationship, Mike had also begun to talk about what the loss of his self meant to him. We both knew that he was beset by considerable anxiety as well as periods of depression, manifestations of both a fear and a realization of what was happening.

The doctor had told Mike that the medication would decrease his alertness and energy, especially as his need for the drugs increased. I asked Mike if he would like to try using imagery procedures as an alternative, and he accepted the suggestion. Using this method of control, he was able to keep the pain within manageable bounds for several weeks, until finally it became so severe that he needed to use the medication. During this period, however, we had the opportunity to talk about the pain and what meaning it had for him. We talked about why he was anxious and what sense he was able to make out of the feelings that he was experiencing, especially those related to his dying.

Mike had lived what he considered to be a rather ordinary and routine life. He said there had been no great joys or thrills, yet it had not been a bad life. He did not have any regrets. At the same time, there were many simple satisfactions that he would miss. He still enjoyed life, and given the choice, he would choose not to die. He accepted that this was not a choice he could make, however, and that his death was imminent.

All of this does not sound like the makings of great anxiety, yet we need to understand that these are only conscious expressions. Underneath this, Mike had a fear of not existing, of having what was for him a very elementary level of self wiped out by his death. The ceasing of the physical body meant a ceasing of existence for Mike, and he could not come to an easy reconciliation of that aspect of the loss. As we talked, however, Mike brought into consciousness the significance that the death of the physical body would have for him, and he was gradually able to discuss it at an overt level and to see that there was not so much to fear as there seemed when the significance remained hidden in his unconscious. He came to an understanding that he would, in fact, cease to exist from the perspective of a physical entity, but he found when he examined that, that it was not really so frightening. As he came to this understanding, the pain lost its power as a signal of his dying and was reduced only to the power it had as a physical source of discomfort.

Mike's story is not much different from many others in that he was afraid of dying and he was mourning the loss of those things in life that he liked and would no longer be able to enjoy. Even though the pain was real and had an easily explainable physical source, it also had a meaning that could only be known by Mike. This meaning was not especially complex, nor was it deeply hidden, but neither did it manifest itself without Mike's making significant efforts to explore that meaning. As we looked into these meanings, and their significance came into his consciousness, the symptoms of Mike's anxiety and depression also lessened, and this naturally had a positive effect on the pain.

If we had treated the pain only as a symptom to be controlled with medication, Mike's pain would have been well controlled during the final stages of his life, but he would have missed the opportunity to use the time for growth. This opportunity was one that Mike freely chose to exploit; the exploration was not forced on him. If he had instead chosen not to avail himself of the help of a counselor, that choice would have been honored. The important thing is to clearly make the opportunity available.

THE LEVEL OF THE EGO

A second level of the pain, anxiety, and depression syndrome is one in which underlying psychological concerns manifest themselves outwardly through physical symptoms. The concerns at this level are egoic rather than physical or emotional. It is not just a physically distinct entity that is going to be lost but a psychologically distinct entity. At this level, pain or anxiety serve to cover up a feeling of inadequacy, a basic lack of trust in oneself or others, or an underdeveloped pattern of socialization. Such symptoms often represent a way for the person to avoid dealing with repressions, such as those associated with sex, self-responsibility, or introjected values. As counselors, we must remember that the map is not the territory, and at this second level, pain, anxiety, and depression are only part of the map—the territory is the unconscious. It is here that we may need to help people focus their attention.

As seen earlier, the level of the ego is one where the person is concerned with belonging and self-esteem needs and therefore sees him- or herself, in the positive sense, as a belonging or esteemed self. It is this self that will be lost through death. Marty was a woman with lung cancer, married to the same man for 28 years, and the mother of three grown children, two married and one divorced. She was a very religious person and regularly attended church services, as well as other church activities during the week. She defined herself primarily through her family and the church. She belonged in the world through her relationships with these people. If the church, her husband, or one of her children had been taken away from her, it would have represented a significant loss of values by which she defined herself. In the case of her own death, however, it was the complete belonging self that was in danger of being lost.

Lung cancer often causes significant pain. In Marty's case, however, there was reason to believe that the pain was, at least to some extent, caused by the fear of loss. She had been taught as a young girl to suppress emotions and therefore found the symptoms of anxiety unacceptable. She also knew that lung cancer was responsible for pain and that it would be more in keeping with her concept of self to attribute the negative feelings resulting from her anxiety to the discomfort of pain. To protect her standing as a member of the family and the church, she needed to maintain the self that had been successful in gaining membership, and that self did not express emotions. To have pain would not threaten her belonging so long as she did not deal with it in an emotional way. Therefore, to treat the pain with medication would have been to mask the underlying cause and foreclose the opportunity to explore its meaning, and it probably would have been less than totally successful. When pain has a cause other than simple physical condition, medication is often less effective. The cause, which is the psychological need for the pain, is stronger than the effects of the drugs.

Death for Marty meant that she would no longer be a member of her family or church and therefore that she would no longer exist, because this was the way she defined herself. When she stopped being a member of these relationships, she would, in her own mind, no longer be a definable being, and there was nothing a doctor, counselor, or anyone else could do to stop the loss. What we could do was create an atmosphere in which Marty felt free to explore the meaning that her death would have for her, thereby allowing her to come to an acceptance of that loss.

In the same way that Mike had to give up his physical body, or more exactly, his attachment to that body, Marty needed to be able to give up her attachment to her memberships. As with a developmental crisis, she needed to be able to give up the self that was defined by these relationships so that she could move to the next level. The difference, as I have pointed out before, was that she had no choice in the matter of giving up the self because death was going to forcibly take it away. Efforts to maintain the self by drawing the boundaries more rigidly would only lead to frustration and despair, the feelings of hopelessness that come when there is perceived to be no way through the loss.

As Marty explored the meaning that death had for her, she experienced many of the stages of loss. The stage of bargaining lasted over a year and was characterized, first of all, by increased activity centered around the family and church, in what seemed like an attempt to make the relationships stronger. At one point, she also joined several other religious groups to expand the number of places where she could perceive herself to belong. Yet through all this, there was a continuing sense of dissatisfaction; she knew that this was not getting the job done. Although Marty did not admit to being bothered by anxiety, her outward behaviors indicated that the anxiety continued to get worse, and she complained of increased pain.

Toward the end of her illness, however, she began a process of distancing herself from her family, which was accompanied by such statements as "I just don't seem to have the energy anymore" and "It just doesn't seem to be as important as it used to." As these experiences increased in number, Marty complained less of her pain. When asked about the pain, she would say that it was about the same, without any elaboration. According to the doctor, she used what he considered to be very light amounts of medication for pain control, and she used nothing for anxiety or depression management. Her period of disease was surprisingly drug free.

At the end, less than 2 weeks before she died, Marty said that she felt at peace, that her family could get along fine without her, and that she was ready to die. She did, in fact, seem to me to be at peace, not the uptight woman I had worked with for the majority of our time together. She seemed to let go of the self that she had been and accept that that self was not necessary any more.

If Marty had been treated with amounts of medication large enough to manage the pain that she was experiencing in the first weeks of our relationship, or if she had been given tranquilizers to manage the anxiety that she never felt but that seemed obvious to an outsider, the force that moved her to explore the meaning of her relationships would have been masked. To have viewed her pain as a single entity, caused only by the physical condition of her lung, would have been to significantly restrict the opportunity for her to use the crisis to grow.

THE EXISTENTIAL LEVEL

There are deeper levels of meaning of the pain, anxiety, and depression syndrome, levels where the pain is a surface manifestation of spiritual suffering, and anxiety is the angst of being a separate self. It is the point where the only forward movement left is that which goes beyond the self. It is difficult for us as humans to comprehend that we can achieve this level of being if we have no self with which to move forward. In the West, we have become so centered on our concept of self that we do not see a possibility of nonself existence. We live by the empirical belief that matter gives rise to consciousness and that without a material body, there will be no consciousness. So we fear that with the ultimate loss of self we will be forever separated from the source of our being and that there will be no transcendent connectedness. This is the meaning of death anxiety.

The deeper levels of meaning of the outward arc are understood through a consciousness that has moved beyond the outer-directed orientation of concrete thinking and is based on self-reflective and abstract knowledge. Persons at this level have been able to transcend the need for esteem and are in the process of becoming self-actualizing. When they look at death, they do not have the need to defend their psychological selves, even though they are still in the grip of its anxiety. Rob was a man whose consciousness appeared to be at this stage. He was in his early 40s when he was diagnosed as having acute leukemia. The doctors told him that the likelihood of his living more than a year was very slim. Rob and I started working together about 3 weeks after the diagnosis was made, while he was in the midst of his initial chemotherapy.

Rob achieved a period of remission, although there was a series of ups and downs—times when things went well for him, but also many times when he was in the hospital because of infections and other complications of the disease. Almost from the beginning of our relationship, he began to talk with me of his life, what had been good about it and what had not been so good. Rob's life was characterized by a long and difficult struggle to separate himself emotionally as well as physically from his mother. He had continued to live with her until he was 26, at which time he left to get married and establish his own home. The marriage lasted only 2 years, however, and he went through what he described as a difficult and bitter struggle, aided by a long period of counseling, to maintain the independence that he had gained from his mother. He finally decided to leave the town where he and his mother lived, separating himself physically from her and, with considerable effort, finally separating himself emotionally.

For 10 years after that, he made significant strides forward in his career and began to feel positive about himself. He said that prior to finding out he had cancer, he had considered himself to be successful and was happy with his life. He felt he had finally been able to move beyond the confines of needing to satisfy his mother with what and who he was and that he had had a period of tremendous satisfaction with his accomplishments, which he described as being his own and not something he had done for someone else. The leukemia had proved a real threat to the sense of self he had achieved during this time.

Economic considerations and the availability of medical expertise had brought Rob back to his original home for chemotherapy treatment. Because the effects of the treatment prohibited him from returning to work, he had chosen to stay rather than return to the town where he worked, and this brought a renewal of the conflicts with his mother. She attempted to take over the direction of his battle with the cancer and his life in general, and he used much of his energy to fight this.

Faced with the crisis of death, Rob appeared to be, first of all, struggling not to regress to an earlier stage of development, one characterized by the dependency and other-directedness of his relationship with his mother. (He went through the same resistance to regression during the crisis created by his divorce.) It was only as he worked through this issue that he was able to focus his energy on using the crisis to grow.

Dying persons usually attempt to maintain the current self in the face of the impending loss, and this was true with Rob. We spent many hours discussing whether he would be able to return to his work, what it would mean to him if he didn't, his need to return to friends, and the strong possibility that he never would. He explored possibilities both in the direction of a long remission and in that of a fairly early death. He seemed to honestly try to understand what all of that meant to him. Many times he would say that he was ready to die; if that was what was going to happen, he could accept it. Yet he never seemed satisfied with this. He continued to explore ways that he could have an impact on others, things he could do that would be meaningful during what time he had left. Even though he consciously faced death, Rob still struggled unconsciously to keep from losing his being.

The cancer eventually took a downward course, and the treatments were not able to stop its progression. Over a period of several days, Rob became more withdrawn and less friendly with the nurses. At one point, he refused to get out of bed and told the nurses he did not want to talk to anyone except the counselor. I visited with him several days in a row, sitting by his bed and talking about much of what he had previously told me, particularly the meanings he had attributed to the various aspects of his life. I received very little communication from Rob during these sessions, usually nothing more than a one- or two-word response to what I said. I checked several times to see if he wanted to continue, if he wanted me to leave, or if he preferred I stay but just remain quiet. He always told me that he wanted me to stay, and that what I was doing was fine. After 4 days of remaining in bed and talking to virtually no one, Rob got up and returned to the outside world.

Rob's recovery from the depression seemed to many to be dramatic, yet it follows closely the pattern of growth we have been discussing. Rob went through the stages of loss to the point where he realized that death, and consequently the loss of his worldly self, was inevitable. This led very naturally to a period of depression, a grieving of that lost self. The symptoms of depression were severe enough that medication was prescribed, but Rob declined to accept it. He knew that he had to live through the depression and that the drugs would only cover up his ability to take that opportunity. Because he had been exploring the meaning that death would have for him during the period when it was still only a threat, the assimilation of the loss came relatively fast. He had gone through his bargaining, both the part of resisting a regression to an earlier state of dependence and that of wanting to be able to keep his present self. He had effectively dealt with any anger that may have been a part of his experiencing of the threat and he was therefore ready to move on. He only needed enough time to assimilate the loss during the period of depression.

Beginning work with a person when he or she is in a depressed stage makes facilitation very difficult. The nature of depression causes a person to be non-communicative, and communication is essential to establishing a counseling relationship. Having come to an understanding prior to the depression of what was going on within Rob, however, and having created a relationship that he felt was very important to him, I was able to facilitate his continuing the movement that had been going on for several months. Compared with other instances of depression, Rob's movement through it did indeed appear very quick and dramatic, but it is understandable when perceived from a facilitative point of view.

Although I discuss the process by which one facilitates movement through a crisis later in this book (see chapters 9–12), two comments should be made here with regard to the three cases just presented. First, I have attempted only to describe my perceptions, reporting primarily feelings and attributions that came from the people themselves. Describing Marty as having an underlying need to belong, for example, is not intended to be diagnostic, but simply to succinctly describe the way that she expressed her experience and how I understood that experience.

Second, I have made no attempt to relate changes in the patients' progress to specific actions taken by me, the doctors, or the patients themselves. This is a description of my relationships with them and how I understood those relationships to have unfolded. Whether Rob changed himself, for example, or whether I did something that caused Rob to change is irrelevant. I had the opportunity to share his journey with him, a relationship that was desired by both Rob and myself, and whether I caused any changes is not the issue.

PSYCHOSPIRITUAL PALLIATIVE CARE

When we work with persons who are terminally ill, we need to be careful not to fall into the easy trap of inhibiting the person's growth by using methods of intervention when they are not warranted. The relationship between pain and anxiety control and success in hospice care is not absolute. Although intervening may relieve symptoms of anxiety or pain, it also causes people to remain stuck at their present level of awareness, covering up the deeper meaning that the anxiety or pain may have in relation to the process of growth.

The pain, anxiety, and depression syndrome has different levels of meaning, and therefore as counselors we must be concerned about where we draw the boundaries and at what level we choose to work. Where we draw the boundaries determines where and how the battle will be waged. If we draw the boundary at the point of symptoms, this is where we will fight the battle, and we will fight it with symptom control procedures. When this is the level of the person's hurting, we will be helpful, but if the hurt comes from a deeper level, our help will be minimal at best. Rather than draw boundaries, we can be of more help if we simply provide clients with a facilitative climate and allow them to draw their own boundaries.

There is a dichotomy in counseling between reductionistic and holistic approaches. Reductionism gets its name because its proponents attempt to reduce the pathology of a person to its smallest part, be that a chemical imbalance, a lesion, or a behavior. Once this smallest part, which is seen to be the source of the problem, is established, then that part is attacked through some intervention to effect a cure. Among psychiatrists, drugs, electric shock treatments, and surgery are the most common forms of treatment, whereas counselors use such methods as aversive therapy (in which one tries to stop the behavior by creating a negative consequence), cognitive therapy (in which the counselor tries to stop, or correct, negative thoughts), and confrontive therapy (in which one attempts to verbally intervene in the individual's feeling processes). Whatever the method, reductionism is based on the concept that the problem, or illness, needs to be corrected. Blocking or intervention of the symptom is the appropriate mode because the problem is believed to be caused by an agent that is external to the will of the individual.

Holism, however, sees the individual as an integrated unit in which all the parts operate together and consistently. When referring to humans, it means unified individuals who are greater than the simple sum of their parts. They are greater because of the interdependence and integration of the parts, and it is these qualities that tend to be missing in the orientations that subscribe to a reductionistic view. The term *synergistic* might even be more appropriate because it refers to the integrated action of two or more parts of the self to achieve an effect of which each is individually incapable. There is now considerable evidence that the mind is a key controlling factor in disease (Harman, 1988), and this leads to acceptance of the notion that treatment most effectively originates from within rather than without. Individuals often have the resources necessary to cure themselves and, in such cases, need facilitation, not intervention, as an external aid. This is a major precept in dealing with pain, anxiety, and depression within a palliative care context.

The emotional, the physical, and the spiritual parts of a person are integrated. Psychospiritual support not only supplements medical treatment in an additive way but can also have an integrative effect on the treatment. In offering palliative care, counselors can choose from three basic viewpoints: (a) *reductionist*—medication can help relieve symptoms, and cognitive–behavioral interventions can be used to increase compliance; (b) *interdisciplinary*—psychological procedures can be offered in addition to medication so that we attack the problem from two or three different angles; and (c) *holistic*—a phenomenological understanding of the integrated nature of the pain, anxiety, and depression can be used to facilitate the patient's utilization of all resources. From the holistic viewpoint, symptoms are only a map of the territory, a symbol of the meaning death holds. When pain is not viewed as an entity in itself but as a partial indication of a whole that includes suffering, despair, and angst, then an integrated holistic approach to helping the patient is most appropriate.

The control of pain through drugs is oriented toward intervention. We must be careful that by intervening we do not leave the patient with unfinished business. When pain is a manifestation of psychospiritual suffering, a facilitative approach to helping may lead to a positive resolution of the personal loss. In contrast, pain control with drugs can interfere with the process of exploration and transformation, leaving that business unfinished. Contrary to the beliefs of some, the blocking of pain and anxiety through drugs does not free the person to deal with the issues for which the symptoms are an overt manifestation. Rather, it causes the person to no longer be driven to search for the underlying meaning of the pain and anxiety. Therefore, differentiation of physical symptoms from suffering is essential and addresses, in part, the question of what kind of help is most appropriate.

Caregivers establish priorities for patients' goals according to what they know and do best. What many doctors and nurses know best is the level of symptoms, and the management of these symptoms occurs most effectively with drugs. What many social workers and psychologists know best is the level of the ego, and so they manage the depression of a dying person through cognitive revision of goal-setting behavior. However, each of these strategies is counterproductive for patients whose pain, anxiety, and depression is symptomatic of deeper concerns. For those patients, facilitating their process of moving beyond worldly goals and attachments is most appropriate.

To some it may seem unfeeling or even inhumane not to provide medication for a patient who has severe pain. If persons are physically hurting, should we not do what we can to relieve the pain? Why should we allow them to suffer unnecessarily? The answer is not an easy one. For example, if a 5-year-old boy is afraid of going to school for the first time, should we relieve that pain by allowing him to stay home? Of course not, because doing so would restrict growth. The same is true with the dying person, except that we must respect the right of the patient to determine whether to take medication or explore the meaning that the pain, anxiety, and depression holds for them.

Neither the counselor nor the doctor should choose the course of action for the patient. It is not our role to deny persons medication if that is their choice, and it certainly is not our role to force them into an exploration of the hidden meanings of the pain. Nevertheless, complete alleviation of the pain, anxiety, and depression comes from thinking about the meaning of death, not in hiding from it. To offer the highest quality palliative care, we must strive to give the dying person options. Rather than offer only medication, we should offer the most effective facilitative climate we can and then let the patient choose his or her own direction. The choice to move or not move *must* be that of the dying person.

SUMMARY

Shamanism is a practice found throughout the ages that connects humans with nature and the cosmos. Through a trance or state of ecstasy, the shaman serves as an intermediary between the transcendent being and the persons of the world. But it is not the shamanic state of consciousness that heals; that is simply the vehicle. In the same way, hypnotic trance and guided imagery do not heal, nor does the psychological climate that counselors create. The healing comes through connectedness, which removes the barriers that block healing.

The passing of shamanism in the West occurred, at least to some extent, because the Church would not allow its authority to be undermined. We need to seriously consider whether or not medicine has taken over that posture in our modern world. Allowing dying persons to heal themselves through compassion and understanding instead of drugs has the capacity to undermine much of what the medical model stands for. Counseling is not corrective surgery, nor is it therapy or cure, but rather it is facilitation of the natural processes of the individual. External agents do not cause spiritual pain and anxiety but rather a blocking of the transformations that characterize positive movement through the spectrum of consciousness. As counselors we are needed because clients seek help in moving along this path, help in overcoming the blocking of the transformations. Unlike medical doctors, who make diagnoses and perform treatments, we serve as helpers to people in the process of becoming soul seekers and living life more fully.

Moustakas (1961) spoke of two kinds of loneliness. The first comes from avoiding the crucial questions of the meaning of life and death by seeking the company of others and keeping busy or, in other words, by belonging and gaining self-esteem. The other, according to Moustakas, comes from the reality of being human and an awareness of the intrinsic loneliness that comes from being a self alienated from the source of our being, the consciousness that is beyond personal.

Loneliness is often the cause of pain and anxiety, and connectedness is the antidote. The willingness to share the journey with someone else in their suffering and thereby establish a sense of transpersonal connectedness may be the best medicine we can offer. Life is a series of developing boundaries, and "the life of boundaries is a life of battles—of fear, anxiety, pain, and finally death" (Wilber, 1979, p. 86). When we live a life of boundaries, we perceive of death as the final boundary, separating us from the source of our being. It is only as we recognize the falseness of our boundaries that we can transcend the separateness we have created.

Chapter 8

Facilitation of Growth

What is the meaning of healing? How does one facilitate the growth of a person who is dying if there is no self beyond the death of the worldly body? What is left to grow? The answer lies in understanding that there are levels of knowing beyond reason, even though the rational mind is not aware of them. There is a world of existence beyond the senses, *which can be known prior to death* and which does not depend on faith. Even though some persons may not attain this level of consciousness, such knowledge is still a part of them in the deep-structure unconscious. It is the potential that is available to awareness through the process of unfolding and which provides the direction of our growth.

Healing comes through transformation, not through the curing of illnesses. Levine (1990) noted that some people get cured of a life-threatening illness but are less healed than ever. The power of healing is in moving forward; it does not involve restructuring oneself at the present level of growth, which simply results in drawing the boundaries around the self more rigidly. This is true for any developing person, and it is certainly true for the person facing imminent death.

Knowledge of impending death does not change the deep-structure direction of one's life, it only makes one conscious of it in a different way. Life is a paradox of continually striving to get better, yet knowing all the time that life and growth will suddenly stop. Most of us do not know when that is, but we do know that it will be the conclusion to our lives. The difference between most of us and those who are terminally ill is that they are likely to have a greater conscious awareness of this ultimate fate.

The period of terminal illness is a continuation of the basic process of moving toward wholeness, and if we expect dying persons to give up, to quit growing simply because they are dying, then we should expect everyone to give up and quit growing. Turned around the other way, we should all continue to grow until we die, and this is irrespective of whether or not we have a terminal illness. Camus (1955) asked this very question in his philosophy of the absurd. If we are destined to die, why prolong the struggle we call life? Why not just commit suicide and end it now? The answer is found in the meaning of existence. Our basic nature, the direction of life, the potential of the unconscious is transformation to increasingly higher and more complex levels of consciousness. We proceed from relative fusion and lack of differentiation to increasing articulation and hierarchical integration, and there is no point at which this drive stops. Certainly it does not end with a diagnosis of terminal illness, nor does it end with enrollment in a hospice program.

Rokeach (1960) said that people are psychologically fragmented in that while the conscious mind is making one set of choices, parts of the mind that are outside consciousness are making other choices. Moving toward wholeness involves bringing these fragments of self into relationship with each other. This is the process of healing we undertake when we are born, not the process of keeping the physical body going forever. Healing among the Navahos is not directed toward symptoms or the body but is focused on bringing the psyche into harmony with all of the natural and supernatural forces around it (Sandner, 1979). We must use whatever opportunities we have to achieve as much harmony in our lives as we can, and the period of terminal illness provides one last opportunity to do that.

As seen in chapter 7, Mike was a person whose most basic boundary was the skin; that is, he defined himself by the values associated with his physical body. The passing from existence of his body meant, to Mike, the end of who he was, the loss of his total self, and, of course, this was frightening. One can ask, "If Mike's body had been cured of this illness, would Mike have been healed?" He would have been the same person, limited to the same physical self, waiting for the next crisis. Is that healing? Another question follows, "Why not just have given Mike medication to control the pain and let him die in peace?"

If, as healers, we cure just the body or we simply allow a person to die in physical comfort, we have done nothing to help that person grow or to achieve a higher level of consciousness. This is as negligent as a teacher who does not facilitate students in learning and growth, an employer who doesn't provide an atmosphere in which employees can improve, or a physically healthy young adult who chooses to do nothing in life to move toward transformation. The intentional foreclosure of opportunity for actualization, whether that foreclosure comes from within or outside of the individual, will lead to dissatisfaction with life. Letting Mike die (or curing his physical illness) without helping him to use the crisis to grow would have left him dissatisfied with himself.

As Mike struggled toward increased self-understanding and movement beyond his body-oriented self, he demonstrated an obvious sense of satisfaction and accomplishment. He brought into the open various perceptions and values he had about his physical being, for example, that he was a good fisherman and a strong worker. One by one he accepted that those values were losing their power, and he struggled to assimilate that into his conscious mind. He began to ask himself what his death would mean to his family, his friends, or to anyone else, and he began to perceive, in a different light, the meaning that he had invested in his self. As he gradually realized the loss of the meaning of that physical self, he began to see himself from the perspective of other people and to examine his values from that vantage point, a level of consciousness that he had not reached before. He used the crisis as an opportunity to look squarely at who he was and to accept that that self was lost. Where he ended up is not the issue; his concept of himself was still quite elementary. But he continued to move toward wholeness, to satisfy the underlying teleological pull that is part of our nature, and that is what gave quality to the last stage of his life.

Movement from one level of growth to the next replaces one way of defining the self with a higher level definition. Mike gave up his physical self to replace it with the beginnings of a psychological self. Marty replaced her belonging self with an esteemed self. Both Mike and Marty still had a self, which is binding to this world. This is the nature of normal developmental movement through the spectrum of consciousness. A person may not achieve a high level of self or even enter the realm of the transpersonal, but the struggle for movement and transcendence even in the period of dying is positive.

Often as counselors we see persons who appear to have transcended their current level of consciousness, but we are not able to determine the level at which they have arrived. We see the outward manifestations of acceptance, such as peacefulness and tranquility, and we can infer that the process of movement has relieved the person's anxiety and pain and led to psychospiritual comfort. We can also hypothesize that at least in some cases, in the transcendence that comes at the time of death, the person is able to move to a level at which there is acceptance of not being a self at all.

THE PURPOSE OF COUNSELING

In the past several years there has been an increase in individual and group counseling programs designed specifically for persons who are living with a terminal illness and for those who support them. It is hoped that these programs are able to help individuals assume greater control of their lives, both physically and psychologically. Although many of the issues that dying persons bring to counseling are similar to those brought by persons who are not faced with a life-threatening illness, dying persons also often have unique concerns, though they may not be clearly expressed.

During the past quarter century, counseling and psychotherapy have been characterized by a proliferation of theories and techniques. A number of approaches carry distinct titles and claim to be different from the others. The literature abounds with studies and essays that attempt to establish the success for a given approach, sometimes implying that the approach discussed is the only successful approach. This is an irrelevant issue, however.

Theories of counseling and psychotherapy may no longer serve us well. The purpose of theory is to provide a framework into which all of our observations and experiences can fit in a meaningful unified whole. But as Wilber (1982) pointed out, many theories of counseling and psychotherapy are focused primarily at one level of human development, and phenomena that fall outside the scope of a theory are ignored or distorted to fit the theory, rather than the theory being altered to include the phenomena. This has resulted in less productive communication among theorists, thereby hindering the growth of knowledge about counseling.

Whenever we enter into a counseling relationship, we must first ask ourselves what our purpose is and what we hope to accomplish. The answer to this question leads us to our determination of how to proceed and how to evaluate our effectiveness. It is because counselors have different answers to this question that there are so many different interpretations of what counseling is and so many different theoretical orientations to the methods by which we try to help others.

It is my position, however, that the primary purpose of counseling is to help a client in the transformation through the stages of the spectrum of consciousness. Other goals that underpin theoretical approaches should be considered as subgoals and should be subordinated to this primary purpose. Counselors are not therapists in the sense of curing people but in the sense of promoting growth that has been temporarily arrested and needs facilitation to follow its natural path. Problems, symptoms, and neuroses are only the content that helps us in this process, and their solution must not be considered the end point of counseling.

The idea of karma is, to some, too deterministic or even fatalistic to be acceptable. It has been referred to as "the hand that you are dealt in life." You cannot ask for a redeal; you must play the hand that you have. The important thing is, however, that there are several ways to play the hand and that each person has a choice as to how to play it. Too much of psychotherapy is aimed at trying to deal clients a new hand. If one is abused as a child, that is the hand that must be played; if one is the child of an alcoholic, that is the hand to be played. Counselors cannot change that, but we can help our clients play their hand in the way that will be most beneficial or satisfying to them. The same is true with terminal illness. It's the hand the person has been dealt, and in only a very few cases will there be a redeal. Most persons must play the hand they have, but how they play it is their choice.

A counselor's first goal in facilitating a person's journey through this final stage of life must be to try to understand how the person perceives the hand that has been dealt and what choices he or she sees. It is not the counselor's role to tell the person what the choices are, but to create an atmosphere of freedom for the person to examine his or her own perceptions of what those choices might be. To increase our effectiveness, counselors must approach work with the terminally ill from a broad spectrum orientation. Our overall purpose should be to facilitate movement toward wholeness while realizing that help focused toward the development of a worldly self, whether physical, emotional, or mental, is going to have limited importance to the person who is in the process of accepting the inevitable death of that self. As counselors, our approach must be developmental and broad enough to encompass those levels of development that are within the personal and those that are beyond.

APPROACHES TO COUNSELING

The various theories or approaches to counseling can be viewed as oriented to one or another of the levels on the spectrum of consciousness (see chapter 4). Wilber (1986) made the case that the four forces of psychology, and various theories within those forces, have focused their attention on the development of the self at different levels of the spectrum and that each remains ignorant of the characteristics of development at other levels. Psychoanalytic theory has traditionally perceived mental health problems to be a function of faulty self-development in the early years of the child's life, thereby focusing its work at the lower levels of the spectrum. Cognitive approaches have drawn their boundaries around the level of the mental self, and humanistic and existential approaches have developed concepts of psychopathology that relate to the highest level of the first half of the spectrum, that in which the development of the self is seen as the highest order of human achievement. Success in counseling is, to a great extent, a matter of matching the level of the individual's development with the approach that is most oriented toward that level.

With this picture in mind, it is now possible to understand how the advocates of a given theory can believe in the correctness of their approach and reject those that are focused on different levels of the spectrum. A theory may very well be accurate for the level of consciousness at which it was developed while being quite inaccurate for other levels. Theorists are asking questions that pertain only to the development of the individual at one level. Approaches that answer questions that come from different levels of development are simply responding to irrelevant questions and consequently coming up with faulty answers. For a person whose developmental needs occur at the level of a particular theory, the approach of that theory may be the best available. For a person whose life is being lived at another level, however, the approach will likely miss the mark altogether. Therefore, any useful approach to psychology must in fact be a megatheory that involves all levels along the spectrum of consciousness.

Following a spectrum approach to psychology allows counselors to use all modes of knowing rather than just the empirical one (posited as the predominant mode of knowing in Western culture). In fact, the empirical way of thinking, being oriented to sensory input, is associated with the lower levels of the spectrum of consciousness and is primarily pertinent to persons who are living their lives at these lower levels. In particular, behavioral and psychobiological approaches are appropriate to the lowest levels on the spectrum because they are focused on maintenance and restructuring activities that are most needed by persons who have not yet developed an adequate sense of a separate physical or emotional self. Restricting ourselves to either a behavioral or psychobiological mode of thinking would cause us to deal with all persons at this lower level, in spite of the fact that some may be operating at a higher level of consciousness. Conversely, dealing with all persons from a humanistic orientation could cause us to be of little help to the many people whose development has not moved beyond a lower level.

Once more we can refer to Mike as an example. His movement from a high prepersonal stage of development to the beginnings of self-perception as a physical–psychological person is within the primary purpose I have delineated. This movement took place within the context of a therapeutic climate that is part of counseling at all levels of the spectrum. (This will be discussed in detail in chapter 10.) Yet even though the purpose and facilitating climate were the same as they would be for any person facing a life crisis, Mike's level on the spectrum of consciousness dictated that procedures be different than they would be for someone at another level.

Self-reflective thinking was certainly beyond the realm of Mike's level of consciousness. If I had expected that he could look into himself and understand abstract values that defined his self-concept or that he could comprehend the meaning that various personal relationships had with respect to his satisfaction with life, we would not have been working in the same realm of consciousness. What Mike could understand and deal with were the relationships between what he did, his very concrete overt behaviors, and what happened following those behaviors. He was virtually unable to connect what he did with how he felt in any causal way. He was living his life at a very low, concrete operational level of development.

As described in chapter 7, Mike attempted to respond to his impending death in terms of the meaning it might have for others. This was a beginning in opening up his consciousness to a new and higher way of seeing the world and his relationship with it. To accomplish the first small steps in this direction, Mike needed to work his way through this transition in a very step-by-step concrete way. To have asked Mike what he thought his death would mean to his wife, for example, would have been to ask him to think in an abstract way that was beyond his level, but helping him explore how she might behave after he died was concrete enough for him to handle. He could remember how she had behaved in situations that had similar characteristics and transfer those perceptions to his own death, and then he could infer that she would behave the same way. It is questionable that he was able to determine how she might feel as a result of the loss, other than to attribute to her the feelings that he might have in the same situation.

Another aspect of Mike's level of consciousness at the time he started openly facing his death was that he did not see himself in terms of belonging; that is, he did not define himself through values that came from having membership in specific groups or other human entities. He did belong and have membership, but that was not the focus of his self-definition. When he defined himself, he returned to physical, behavioral descriptions—I am a large, male, assembly line worker who is a good fisherman, and so forth. As he struggled to begin seeing his death from the perspective of others, it was reasonable to expect that he would also begin to have more of a sense of being a part of self–other relationships, the beginning of awareness of his membership role. This awareness would come, however, from a working through of the pattern of behavioral responses and their consequences and not through an abstract understanding of those relationships. So our work together was focused on exploring his self and his self–other relationships in a concrete, behaviorally oriented way. The purpose of transformation, the climate conducive to exploration, and the process of exploration itself were a necessary and integral part of counseling with Mike just as they are with all clients, but the level of process was specific to his level on the spectrum of consciousness.

My view of the purpose of counseling, regardless of the setting in which it occurs and under what title (e.g., marriage counseling, substance abuse counseling, hospice counseling), is that it should be to help individuals transcend their current level of development and move on to the next level. In one circumstance this may involve analyzing unconscious material and in another it may involve clarifying values, but in either circumstance the purpose is to provide the basis for moving on through the spectrum that defines the direction of life. In this way, what may appear to be therapeutic in nature is actually the facilitation of movement, and it is in this sense that all counseling is growth oriented, not curative oriented.

This single purpose is viewed by some to be so global as to be unmanageable without further differentiation, however. As these further differentiations are made, the one primary purpose gets divided into subgoals, each of which may be legitimate for persons who are living their lives at the same level as the theory's orientation, but which is inappropriate for those whose level of consciousness is different. The mistake counselors must guard against is believing that any of these subgoals is the endpoint, that it constitutes *the* single megapurpose of counseling.

Some therapists, as an example, might state that differences in ego structure dictate differences in goals. They would point out that a person who has not achieved a level of self-differentiation cannot handle standard uncovering techniques and that therefore the counselor's goal must be to build structure. The point is, however, that the goal should be to help such a person move to a higher level of development through the process of differentiating a self-structure, and for this level of consciousness, structuring techniques that are behaviorally oriented may be most appropriate. It might seem trifling to say that building structures is not a goal, but if we do state the purpose in this manner (e.g., "the goal of counseling is to build structure"), we reduce the process of growth and therapy into pieces, and we lose sight of the overall movement of life. Once we have done that, the next step is to make the use of structuring techniques the goal of counseling and to work with each client from that perspective only.

If as counselors we remain aware of the overall purpose defined by the underlying progression of the people with whom we work, we should talk of the various theories not as equal to and competitive with each other but as representing a hierarchy paralleling that of human development. From this point of view, successful counseling necessitates the use of different approaches for different persons depending on their level of development, and each theory's success should be evaluated at the level for which it is appropriate.

TRANSPERSONAL COUNSELING WITH DYING PERSONS

With this brief description of the relationship between theoretical orientations and the spectrum of human development, we can now turn attention to the transpersonal aspect of a model for working with terminally ill persons. All persons who come to the final stage of life do so having developed their own selves up to a specific level on the spectrum of consciousness. However, during a terminal illness many people realize for the first time that the personal self is no longer important or at least that it is losing its potency. The crisis of dying seems to have greater power to move a person beyond the realms of the outward arc than do other crises in a person's life.

As a means of facilitating the process of transformation through the stages of the developmental spectrum, counseling involves helping people achieve awareness and acceptance at their current level and actualize the potential they have to transcend that level and progress to the next. When counseling is viewed in this way, it is termed *transpersonal*—not because all persons with whom we work are at a level of development beyond the personal realm but because we perceive the teleological pull toward the transpersonal and because, at whatever level we work, our vision and direction are transpersonal.

Much of modern psychological theory is behavioristic in its framework, subscribing to some form of an "existence precedes essence" concept that denies the idea that a deep structure characterizes all of humanity. Behavioral and cognitive approaches and most humanistic psychologies all deny any preexistent nature, claiming that what we are is that which becomes defined solely through our interaction with the environment. These represent most of the approaches that have been prevalent over the past 25 years, when the growth of counseling has been so prolific.

In very recent years, however, there has been increasing interest in psychologies that account for deep structures, or what H. Smith (1982) referred to as the *sacred unconscious*. He traced the decline and rebirth of metaphysics, and in the process showed that human development, regardless of race, culture, time, or place, follows a basic direction. In clinical experience, a counselor's observations lead almost inevitably to the conclusion that something more fundamental than sexual concerns, striving for social power, or the desire for material possessions dominates the lives of our clients—it is a universal striving for an understanding of the inherent meaning of life. As counselors we are led to accept the concept of a perennial psychology that defines the deep structure of humanity. The absence of such an understanding has been an extremely limiting factor in our understanding of human development and has limited the growth of counseling.

A transpersonal approach to counseling accepts and tries to account for levels of existence or consciousness that transcend the personal. This approach, then, necessarily posits a deep structure to consciousness and assumes that there is an essence that precedes and follows the worldly birth and death of the individual. The personal is differentiated from the transpersonal in terms of the separation of the self from the cosmos versus the transcendence of this duality, and there is some sort of process occurring within each person that goes beyond that person. Whereas the third force of psychology (i.e., the humanistic or phenomenological psychologies) are concerned with maximum development of the self, transpersonal psychologies (the fourth force) are focused on transcendence of the self.

Within the spectrum of consciousness, higher order structures encompass and include lower structures. In this way, the person becomes more complex and integrated as he or she moves to a higher level. The contents of the stages, however, are specific and are not integrated or included at succeeding levels. This is why on the one hand the person becomes increasingly more complex and on the other hand must let go of important self-defining values that are pertinent only to certain stages. For example, the need to belong and a law-and-order orientation to morality are stage specific, and these are values that must be given up or left behind for the person to move to the next level. Thinking processes, such as object constancy and propositional thinking are part of the deep structure that, once brought into consciousness, remain part of the individual at succeeding stages. The self is defined to a significant degree by the stage-specific contents, however, and this results in the need to continually give up the self to make room for developing a new one.

A transpersonal approach to counseling is like a deep structure in that it does not necessitate giving up the ways of the earlier levels of the spectrum.

One does not give up knowledge of behavioral, cognitive, or perceptual approaches to working with persons in order to be transpersonal. A transpersonal perspective means that one's work is now understood from a higher level yet includes knowledge gained at the lower levels, thereby making the work more encompassing. (On the basis of this conception, humanistic psychologies should encompass those focused on the lower stages, that is, the cognitive, behavioral, and psychoanalytic psychologies. In fact, they do, although in many instances this is neither admitted nor recognized. Nevertheless, analysis of humanistic theories shows considerable incorporation of cognitive, behavioral, and psychoanalytic concepts.)

This concept of a spectrum of psychological theories corresponding to that of consciousness is helpful in developing an encompassing model for working with terminally ill persons. When transpersonal psychology is viewed from the perspective of individual contents and concepts, the tendency is to make it other, opposed to, or in competition with the other forces of psychology. This would not significantly improve our understanding of psychology or the people we work with; it would simply cause us to create more boundaries. When understood from a spectrum perspective, transpersonal psychology becomes appropriate for all the persons we work with in a hospice-type setting.

It is well accepted that in counseling and psychotherapy, as in most of the helping professions, we are culture bound. We are limited by our assumptions about reality, which are linked to our scientific heritage, and this inhibits us from venturing into the realm of the spiritual. Yet the latter is simply the *nonmaterial*, that which exists beyond the realm of the senses. If our approach is to encompass all the modes of knowing, it necessarily will include the spiritual.

Psychology is the study of the mind, though advocates of the empirical (in this case behavioristic) have redefined it as the study of behavior, reducing the activities of the mind to that which can be overtly observed. Accepting the broader and more correct definition, however, still limits the study of the mind to the worldly or nontranspersonal realms. To be complete, psychology must include the transpersonal or spiritual. To describe such approaches to helping, we can use the terms *transpersonal* and *psychospiritual.* Each term implies a viewpoint that encompasses all levels of the spectrum of consciousness both in our understanding of the people with whom we work and in the development of the ways we work with them.

SUMMARY

This chapter outlines the underlying philosophy of a transpersonal, facilitative model for working with dying persons. It is an approach designed to help the person move toward greater wholeness, achieving higher levels on the spectrum of consciousness, which defines the direction of human life. The time of dying is seen as the ultimate of life's crises, and as such, is viewed as an opportunity for growth rather than intervention.

The process by which this growth comes about involves most importantly an increased awareness of the nature and meaning of loss to the person's sense of self. Relief from the suffering and anxiety associated with death comes through exploring its meaning and facing it in an open, nondefensive manner. The counselor's purpose is to create a climate in which this process can unfold.

Chapter 9

The Process of Facilitative Counseling

I turn now to an exploration of the way in which counselors can facilitate the terminally ill person's transformation to a higher level of development. I do this first by examining the overall process of movement, then by looking at the nature of the counseling relationship and how that facilitates movement, and finally by discussing ways of communicating with the dying person, using the counseling relationship as the vehicle. This chapter examines how one brings into greater awareness those aspects of the self that are critical to transformation.

Facilitating a person's movement through a crisis involves a sequence of phenomenological unfolding that is characterized by (a) awareness of the meaning of one's life and the crisis of dying, (b) an acceptance of that meaning and an assimilation and integration of the new awareness into relationship to the self, (c) a transformation from the level at which that awareness has occurred, moving to the next higher stage in the direction of wholeness, and (d) actualization of the self at the new stage. It also involves creating an atmosphere in which the client feels safe enough to begin the process of exploration that leads to increased knowing of the self.

ANXIETY MANAGEMENT

The first stage of a loss is often one in which the person denies the experience full access into awareness, and therefore it is one during which the counselor very likely will be blocked out. There is a common understanding, even among persons who have never been involved in formal counseling, that if they enter into a relationship with the counselor, they are expected to talk about themselves. Yet that is exactly what the person is stubbornly avoiding by denying the existence of a crisis. To talk about oneself is paramount to acknowledging the threat to the self, thereby allowing the anxiety to come closer to the surface. It is better just to stay away from the counselor altogether. Over 300 years ago, Pascal (cited by May, 1950) noted this phenomenon, commenting that people engage in diversions to avoid the awareness of being alone and to avoid thinking about themselves because if they paused for self-contemplation, they would become miserable and anxious.

When this is the situation, facilitation can best take the form of leaving clients alone to work through the denial in their own way. We may need to allow time for the person to assimilate the meaning of the loss and let the anxiety produced by the threatening experience come into appropriate bounds of its own accord. We certainly cannot force clients to stop denying, and we cannot force them to talk about themselves. It is a time for caring and understanding and allowing them to proceed in their own time.

As a person begins to work through the denial, the anxiety comes closer to the surface, manifesting itself through common physiological and psychological symptoms. Facilitation at this point involves helping bring the anxiety into bounds that are appropriate for allowing the process of exploration to occur. Levels of anxiety that are too high are simply overwhelming and will cause a blocking of the process. This is similar to individuals who have such great anxiety over having to take a test that they can't even think clearly about the questions and therefore have no chance of giving appropriate answers. To expect that dying persons, overwhelmed with anxiety, can explore the meaning that dying has for them is just as unrealistic. Therefore, we must first help them free themselves from the debilitating aspects of fear that may accompany the threat of loss. In doing so, we must not seek ways to block the anxiety but instead must encourage and facilitate the client in feeling the anxiety, knowing its source, and working through the need to be afraid.

Although at this stage people are not ready to work on becoming more aware of their experience of loss, they may accept the help of a counselor if it comes under the term of stress management, or perhaps, in the case of terminally ill persons, pain management. If the anxiety and pain are so great as to cause considerable discomfort, yet their meaning is too threatening to be allowed into awareness, the person may be willing to try relaxation or imagery procedures. This is seen as acceptable because the person is willing to acknowledge that there is pain or stress, although there is no recognition that there is anxiety stemming from a threat to the self. The person will usually make it quite clear that some active process, such as the use of imagery, is what is wanted and that there is no desire to just talk.

In other cases, persons may want to talk, not for the purpose of exploring the meaning of the loss, but just to express the anxiety—the anger, fear, frustration, or depression. They may find an accepting relationship to be comforting in this process of venting their negative feelings. It is important to let them have their pain, their grief, or their anger. We do not want to take it away or help them hide it but to facilitate them in the process of exhausting it. The more one expresses negative emotions in an environment of understanding, the less need there is to have the emotions. From an outside point of view, a counselor or family member can see the uselessness of the anger or fear, but we cannot transfer that perspective to the persons who are experiencing it. We can only allow them to come to their own experiential understanding of its limited worth. When they do, however, and the uselessness of the emotion becomes clear to them, they will let it go of their own accord. That process will not and cannot occur if we block the expression of the emotions.

Before we can facilitate the process of exploration and increasing awareness, then, we must help the person bring the anxiety and accompanying negative emotions into balance, and we can do this through relationship and with the use of imagery procedures. The nature of the counseling relationship is discussed in detail in the next chapter, and the use of imagery is the subject of chapter 12.

AWARENESS

A person moves through a fairly natural sequence of stages in the process of transcending to a higher level of consciousness. This is the loss paradigm that characterizes all psychological crises. The meaning of the loss must come to the surface in such a way as to begin to break apart the boundaries that have been rigidly maintained during the period of denial. Having reduced the anxiety to a level where there is enough comfort to want to explore the meaning of the loss, the client must then be willing to become aware of the present self and to acknowledge the values and beliefs by which that self is currently defined. The client must bring into awareness all those aspects of the self that are being lost as a result of the crisis.

Self-awareness and transformation begin at the moment we consciously become dissatisfied with our lives. When the suffering becomes great enough, there is a push to begin the process of awakening to deeper, truer realities. At every level of the spectrum of consciousness, we gain an understanding of our nature that continually approaches more closely the true essence of our existence. Moving from the eye of the flesh to the eye of reason, and then on to the eye of contemplation, our knowledge becomes more complete and less illusory. The pain, anxiety, and depression of a crisis break apart the complacency created by our normal distortions of reality and who we are, and this frees us to become more in tune with our true nature.

The road to transformation is not an easy one. It involves first of all a willingness to let into consciousness the dissastisfaction that we are feeling. We must move beyond the need to maintain our selves as they are and allow the boundaries of those selves to loosen enough to provide room for the work of exploration to begin. The desire to explore must come from within the individual, but the counselor can help bring this desire into the open by creating an atmosphere of safety.

There are few approaches to helping that do not acknowledge the importance of knowing oneself and therefore the importance of the role of increased self-awareness in successful counseling. There are those who approach awareness from a cognitive basis and those who see the affective experiential aspect of awareness as more critical. Still, it is almost universally accepted that knowing oneself more fully is part of growth and therapy.

Within the loss paradigm, awareness comes primarily during the bargaining stage. In fact, that is what bargaining is all about. The anxiety and depression are present in some form and at some level of consciousness throughout the crisis, whereas denial, bargaining, and acceptance follow in a sequential order. Therefore, following a person's emergence from denial and the bringing of the emotional manifestations of anxiety into manageable bounds, the process of bargaining begins. This involves becoming aware of the meaning of the threat, the way it affects the self-concept, and the nature of the loss of values and beliefs. Awareness may come in bits and pieces over a long period, or it may come flooding into the person's consciousness almost at once. The person's first inclination as this awareness comes into consciousness is to look for ways to avert the loss of the self, that is, to begin the process of bargaining. Given appropriate circumstances, however, the person will continue on to the point of knowing, cognitively and existentially, that maintenance will not be satisfactory and that there must be movement beyond the present self.

When we approach counseling from a transformative view, we perceive our work to be successful only when persons have accepted the nature of the loss and realize that movement to a higher level of self-understanding is positive within the inherent direction of their lives. Although they may be able to come to an accommodation within themselves by which they restructure their lives to maintain the precrisis self, the lack of acceptance of what the crisis means in terms of the opportunity for movement to a higher level represents unsuccessful progress through the loss paradigm. It should be defined as an arrest even though the person may be satisfied and the anxiety and depression may subside. Maslow (1968) said that if you set out to be less that you can become, you will be dissastified with your life. To not use the crisis as a means of becoming more of what you can be will lead to ultimate unhappiness.

DEEP-STRUCTURE UNCONSCIOUS

Awareness of the meaning of loss and its relationship to the self does not come easily. Some people are consciously aware of certain aspects of such meaning while other aspects remain hidden in the unconscious. For many, however, virtually all of the meaning is at an unconscious level. Therefore, we need to look at the nature of the unconscious mind and how we can facilitate persons in bringing into awareness those aspects that relate to their loss.

Two aspects of unconscious processing are particularly relevant to increasing awareness: The first relates to knowledge that is inherent within us from birth, the basic structures that need to be brought into awareness for the first time. The second relates to knowledge that was conscious at one point but was so threatening and anxiety producing that it was repressed into the unconscious as a protection to the self. The first of these is the *deep-structure unconscious,* and the second is the *repressed unconscious.*

The deep structures that give direction to our lives are a part of us at the time we are born. They come into being in their own time as is appropriate to our level of development. This occurs through our interaction with significant persons in the environment, and at times a counselor is part of the process by which the emergence of these structures is facilitated. An example of this type of deep-structure emergence is the emergence of a mental self. A concept of a mental self and all that it entails is a part of the structure of the individual from birth. It is not learned, but simply emerges or is remembered when it is appropriate. It comes out of the unconscious into the conscious awareness of the person.

In the absence of an appropriate growing environment, however, these structures do not emerge from the unconscious. They may simply not be encouraged to emerge because the climate created by significant persons in the environment is not adequately positive, or they may be perceived as inconsistent with a person's sense of reality and therefore threatening and are thus kept in the unconscious. They are not repressed, that is, pushed out of consciousness, but simply are not allowed to develop, thereby inhibiting the growth of the individual. The person gets stuck at a specific level of development.

A crisis provides an impetus to exploring aspects of the unconscious that have been blocked from conscious awareness. Because the self of which the person is aware is now threatened, one of the choices is to look at other possibilities. Under these circumstances, a nonthreatening environment provides the security to explore the self in relation to previously blocked experiences. Because an inappropriate environment during development originally blocked awareness of these experiences, replacing that environment with one that is now perceived to be free from negative conditions will facilitate the exploration that did not take place earlier. In this sense, the counselor is simply removing what was a roadblock in the process of development.

One example of such a blocking of the deep-structure unconscious has to do with the relation of mind and body. As humans develop, we form a concept of being a physical self, then a physical and emotional self, and finally a physical, emotional, and mental self. At this point we pass from the prepersonal to the personal. We must then develop through the egoic stages and come to an awareness of the *centauric self,* which is a comprehension of the self as being an integrated mind and body (Wilber, 1980). Having arrived at this awareness, we conceive ourselves to be an integrated whole of all that we knew in lesser pieces in the lower stages. We now understand the integrated nature of the body and mind aspects of the self, and we understand that they work together as a unit. We experience for the first time the knowledge that the mind affects the physical working of the body and that the physical body affects the mind.

On the way to this understanding, however, we must go through the process of dying to the current self and restructuring it at a higher level, and this is always threatening. We may abort the development process before arriving at the centauric level. If we do, the integration aspects of the whole self will remain outside of our conscious awareness, and we will have no conceptualization of the mind having an effect on the workings of the body and vice versa. We will continue to see ourselves as having a body—out there—that operates on principles of its own that we don't fully understand and over which we have little control. The notion that we can control our pain or the physical symptoms of anxiety through the use of our minds is an alien concept and likely to be dismissed out of hand.

As counselors, we cannot talk someone into believing that the mind can affect the body. A person living at a lower level on the spectrum of consciousness does not understand the conceptualization of the higher levels, and individuals currently living their lives at a level below that of the integration of mind and body simply will not understand what we are talking about. We must facilitate their movement into the level of the centaur. This is not corrective treatment, for there is nothing to correct. It is simply helping them to free the natural movement, the bringing into awareness of the inherent deep structure that has so far been arrested in their lives.

The use of imagery in the process of controlling the negative effects of pain and anxiety has a dual role—that of control itself and that of facilitating awareness of the integrated relationship of body and mind. Persons operating below the level of the centaur may accept the counselor's use of imagery to help in symptom control, but they do so on the basis that it is something that the counselor is doing to them. In the same way that drugs can affect the body from a point external to the individuals themselves, people believe that perhaps guided imagery can, too. However, as we show them that they are doing the work, that we are only facilitating them in the utilization of their own resources, they begin to experience the relationship between their own mind and body. This is the beginning for many of allowing this deep structure to come into awareness.

THE PERSONAL UNCONSCIOUS

The second realm of the unconscious is generally referred to as the personal or repressed unconscious because experiences that are too threatening to be left in the conscious mind are repressed into the unconscious. Unlike the deep structures of the unconscious, these are experiences that are first in the awareness of the individual before being pushed underground. This realm of the unconscious is personal in the sense that it is unique to the individual, its contents having been learned from personal experience, whereas the deep-structure unconscious is the same for all humans.

Rogers (1951) stated that any experience that is inconsistent with the self-concept of the individual is likely to be distorted to fit the self-structure; that is, the original experience as perceived by the individual will be repressed in favor of an altered perception that is more acceptable. Movement through life, then, is based in part on distorted perceptions of experience, providing an inadequate foundation for growth. During the bargaining stage of the loss process, the counselor can facilitate the person in bringing these experiences into awareness and understanding them in an atmosphere in which it is not necessary to distort.

A full discussion of the repressed unconscious is not necessary here, but I will examine one aspect that is particularly pertinent to movement through the loss paradigm. That is the process by which self-defining values are developed and the relationship of those values to the repressed unconscious. Rogers (1951) noted that the values that we attach to perceptions of ourselves at any level of the spectrum come from an interaction with other persons in the environment and that these values are formed in one of two ways. The first of these is through a process of direct evaluation, unencumbered by conditions placed on us from outside. We simply evaluate the experiences pertaining to the self-perception and make a decision for ourselves as to whether that perception has positive or negative value. The perceptions and their values are then incorporated into the self-concept. If the value comes into conflict with experience at a later time, we are free to change those perceptions that have negative value. For example, if a man perceives himself to be a religious person, and this perception is based on nonconditional evaluation, then at a later point in life when the perception of himself as religious may become negatively valued by him, he is free to change his behaviors and relationships in such a way as to alter this perception of himself. He can simply quit going to church, stop believing in God, or what ever else he deems appropriate.

In much of one's interaction with others in the environment, however, conditions are placed on the satisfaction of needs, and those conditions often relate to the acceptance of values. For example, during the preschool years, according to Erikson (1963), children's primary task is to develop a sense of initiative. To do this, they must try out new and different roles. At the same level of the spectrum, children also have a need for security. If a child's parents communicate, intentionally or inadvertently, that psychological security is dependent on accepting the roles they have determined to be appropriate for the child, then the child will forgo the exploration of roles and will develop a definition of self according the role values insisted on by the parents. When we take over a value from others and accept it for our own because of the conditions placed on us, the value is introjected. This is the second process of valuing the self described by Rogers (1951).

These introjected values create a particular problem in the process of in-creasing one's awareness of self because they are not easily accessible to the conscious mind. Such values were taken over and accepted so that the need to be accepted could be satisfied, whether that was in the form of security, love, belonging, or esteem. The condition placed on the person was that if you have this value, that is, define yourself in this way, you will be accepted. The threat of not being accepted, of course, gives rise to anxiety, and to manage that anxiety, the person simply takes over the self-value without evaluative consider-ation. The experience of exploration, of entertaining the idea that another value might be preferable, is relegated to the personal unconscious so that the anxiety over acceptance can be kept within acceptable bounds.

When, at a later time in life, the person wants to consider an alternative value, a different way of looking at the self, the anxiety arising from not being accepted rears its ugly head again, and in many cases this causes the explora-tion to be aborted. To rewrite my previous example, instead of being religious on the basis of an open evaluation, suppose that a man goes to church to be accepted by his parents and perceives himself to be religious on the basis of introjecting from his parents the value that "being religious is good." If he begins to have experiences that cause him to perceive that being religious is now a negative value, he does not have the same freedom to change as he would if the value had been directly evaluated. As soon as he begins to alter behaviors and feelings to fit a more positive value, the experience that caused him to introject the value in the first place, now hidden in the unconscious, causes anxiety, or what he might describe as feelings of guilt. What he really is experiencing is the assumed loss of acceptance by his parents. He is now caught in a conflict of having to choose between the negative value and feelings of anxiety and guilt.

The climate in which conditions for acceptance were placed on this man, where it was communicated to him that his need for security and belonging were contingent on accepting this value, is the cause of his blind incorporation of the value in relation to his self. Therefore, the opposite climate should free him to explore his values within a more appropriate level of anxiety. If the man felt originally that a certain value had to be accepted for him to be loved, then removing that condition should provide a basis for a freer exploration. This is exactly the premise on which a facilitative climate is based.

In chapter 7, I discussed the experience of Marty, a woman who was dying from lung cancer. She defined herself primarily through her memberships, by being a self that belonged to her family and her church. When we started work-ing together, Marty did not know she defined herself by these memberships; she simply described herself this way. This was her identity. Moreover, the thought of giving up these memberships and consequently her identity was very threat-ening. Because of the rigidity with which she held on to these perceptions, it seems reasonable to assume that they were based on introjections and that she was not free to explore their worth to her. Whenever she would consider not being a part of the church, for example, she would experience all over again the anxiety that accompanied the original development of the value.

Marty originally introjected the value of perceiving herself as being part of the church because she realized that accepting this value was a condition for love and acceptance by her parents. At a later point, when it became appropriate for her to give up defining herself through her memberships and she had the first experience of moving beyond that stage, it was inconsistent with her self as she perceived it, and it was therefore threatening and anxiety producing. She had the choice of reinforcing the boundaries around her current self by pushing the inconsistent experience of letting go of the need for membership into her unconscious or of facing the threat and anxiety and examining the meaning that this experience had for her and incorporating it in relation to a new self. Marty had chosen the first of these alternatives and had thereby cut off the possibility of further movement through the spectrum of consciousness.

During the period of terminal illness, Marty began to explore the meaning that the loss of her own self had for her. She slowly brought into awareness the realization that she was being forced to let go of the memberships because of her impending death and that reinforcing the boundaries around the self would not work as it had during earlier experience. She entered into this exploration during counseling, however, in a climate that was free of the conditions origi- nally placed on her and in which the need to deny her experience was lessened, if not removed.

This is the process of phenomenological unfolding, gradually bringing into awareness those perceptions of self and one's relationship to the world that are momentarily significant in the process of transformation. It is not a delving into the past of the individual to see what the occasion of the repression was or to understand the personal dynamics of developmental arrest. It is, instead, a mov- ing forward by uncovering more of the underlying potential of the person, some of which is deep structure and needs to be brought forth for the first time and some of which is repressed and needs the appropriate climate for it to reenter the conscious realm. In Marty's case, it was a matter of her allowing the expe- rience of transcending the need to belong to come into awareness anew. This was done in a climate that provided enough security for her to fully explore its meaning.

EXPLORATION AND AWARENESS

Self-awareness at increasingly deeper levels is necessary for positive growth. As we facilitate exploration toward this awareness, questions arise as to whether an analysis of the etiology of problems or current circumstances is appropriate or helpful. When one deals with issues surrounding dying, however, this is not a meaningful question. Living with a terminal illness, regardless of the course of the disease, is to deal with issues related to the death of the self, and counseling must deal with deep structures and process, not surface structures and contents.

It is not appropriate for counselors to ask themselves questions regarding where their clients are on the spectrum of consciousness. This focuses the counseling around a process of external evaluation. Rather, we must understand how individuals are *living* their lives and how that can be used to help them move up the spectrum. As stated in chapter 4, the metaphysic that views material phenomena as giving rise to consciousness is what drives much of psychotherapy, and in this orientation counselors seek out the causes of behaviors on the principle that the causes are what give rise to consciousness of the self. A woman whose behaviors stem from being abused by her father has a consciousness of herself as a rejected, not-belonging, and unloved being. From the material-into-consciousness metaphysic, the causes of the behavior must be rectified before the conscious awareness or identity of the self can be altered. The sensory, material phenomenon is the cause of the consciousness, and only by a change in that phenomenon can the self-perception change.

The transpersonal approach sees consciousness as occurring first, however, and giving rise to one's sense of the material. From this viewpoint, then, the counselor's interest is in the consciousness of the persons with whom he or she is working, in helping those persons to be more aware of their own consciousness, and in trying to understand empathically what that awareness is. External causes of behavior do not fit this understanding, so as counselors we simply try to help the person uncover those parts of the self that are hidden and bring them into awareness, where they can provide the person with a stronger basis for moving forward. The structure that is the necessary aspect of growth is within the individual, waiting to be remembered. The causes of the conscious awareness of who the self is are not relevant to the process of moving forward; only a free and open view of the deep structures that are an inherent part of the self is necessary.

Solving problems or resolving conflicts gives us something tangible to point to as the positive results of counseling. Both counselors and clients often need this. We cannot just focus our attention on greater knowledge of the self because that gives us no product. This need, however, focuses our attention on the contents of the current stage of development and on how we can rearrange that content to create a better living environment for the client. In accepting this orientation, we naturally focus our attention away from the client's possible need to let go of the contents of the current stage to move to the next stage. We must choose to do one or the other because we cannot do both.

The view that open awareness of the self is the key to positive growth has been most completely expounded in the West by Carl Rogers (1961), and that view is examined in detail in the next chapter. This understanding is also found in the traditions of the East, however, where the transpersonal has had its greatest emphasis over the centuries. In the Buddhist tradition, for example, the basis for growth to higher levels of consciousness is found not in examining the history of persons but in facilitating the expansion of their awareness of self and the world around them. Through the process of meditation, individuals are facilitated in the process of uncovering their selves, in becoming more aware of who they are by bringing more and more of the self into their conscious awareness. Engler (1986) reviewed some of the aspects of the uncovering process as it is outlined in Buddhist psychology, particularly the form called *insight meditation*.

There is first of all the necessity of keeping reactions, interpretations, analyses, and elaborations out of the process of being aware. The person should simply allow events, mental and physical, to come into awareness, note them, and allow them to move on. There is no room for trying to make something out of the awareness. It is just there and is to be noted.

A second aspect of gaining insight is to remove censorship from the process. The person is to let into awareness whatever thoughts and feelings come forth. Engler pointed out that this is equivalent to the process of free association in psychoanalysis, where the client is instructed to not impose censorship. This is also a key factor in phenomenological approaches, especially that presented by Rogers (1951, 1961). Little in the way of knowledge of one's self will be gained if the self is allowed to limit perception only to those aspects with which it feels comfortable.

A third characteristic of the insight meditation process is that of abstinence from the gratification of wishes, impulses, desires, and strivings. The awarenesses that come, the thoughts and feelings that appear to the person, are not to be the subject for working through any problems or conflicts but are simply to be registered as a part of the increasing understanding of the self as subject and object of the thoughts and feelings.

The final concern of insight meditation is with the person's ability to step back and observe what is happening. It is the equivalent of being self-reflective and seeing or noting; in essence, it is being aware of what is going on within the entity that one calls self. Counselors who are accustomed to the self-reflective mode are sometimes surprised when they work with clients who cannot accomplish this seemingly simple process of stepping back and observing their experience. A practicum counselor was working with a teenager and reflected the feeling that the teenager had just expressed, using virtually the identical words. The teenager asked, "How did you know that?" He was unaware that he not only had the feelings but also had expressed them. One could suppose that in the absence of the reflection by the counselor, the feeling would have remained hidden from the teenager's conscious awareness.

Phenomenological unfolding, then, begins with individuals becoming increasingly aware of their own experience—their feelings, thoughts, values, and the way that they define themselves. In a developmental crisis, knowledge of this definition will also include awareness of the extent to which these aspects of self continue to be viable and the extent to which they no longer hold their worth to the individual.

STAGES OF PROCESS

When we become aware of who we are, we become aware that who we are is nothing other than a series of relationships. Rogers (1951) stated that the self-concept is developed on the basis of evaluational interactions with other people. The contents of the various stages by which we define ourselves are developed in relationship to others—according to Maslow (1968), we are secure, we belong, we have esteem; according to Kohlberg (1981), we do what we should, we obey laws, we abide by social contracts. Post-Freudian developments of psychoanalysis have centered around object relations, which define the essence of the ego.

Facilitation of the exploration of self is to encourage people in finding the nature of their relationships and understanding that they *are* these relationships. When a person enters the bargaining stage during a life-threatening crisis, it is done with a certain level of self-rigidity, which has been developed within that person's current stage of consciousness. In the process of increasing awareness of that self, there will be a movement from the more rigid position to one of experiential fluidity. As this awareness comes forth, people move through stages on the way to wholeness, although these stages are not always clearly delineated. The stages can be used to describe movement through life in general; they can be used to describe the process of counseling; and they can be descriptive of the movement through the bargaining stage during the experiencing of the loss that occurs through one's own death.

In the early stages, there may be little perception of a need to change the self. Such change is not perceived to be related to solving the problem of dying. In fact, the problem is to keep from dying, which means to keep the self as it is without change. Descriptions of the self at this point will be in terms of a separate entity buffeted by external circumstances. The problem does not exist within the individual but is being created for the person by other people or other things. This is a common reaction even though, prior to the crisis, the person may have achieved a much more advanced perception of the self as a fluid process in relationship with others. The crisis tends to initially create a regression to earlier defense strategies, which means also a narrowing of awareness away from the relationship aspect of self toward a more separated perception of entity. The person will be able to move through this level of self-perception much more quickly if it results from a regression, however, than if it is a continuation of a low level of self-development.

Clients tend to see themselves as objects to be analyzed and worked with, just as would be done with any other external object. Yet as they allow their perceptions and values to come into awareness, they achieve a growing understanding that these perceptions and values exist in direct relation to other people and do not stand alone. Mike was not a good fisherman per se; he perceived himself to be a good fisherman because of the way others behaved toward him. Although his perception of himself came from being part of a relationship, he could only define himself in terms of the concrete, sensory aspects of the inter-action. As a result of his process of exploration, however, he took the first steps in realizing that "good fisherman" had meaning only in terms of relationships. He certainly did not come to a level where he knew that he was *only* a part of the relationships and that there was no Mike independent of those relationships, but he made the first step in this direction.

There is a strong similarity in the way that Buddhists and psychoanalysts describe the development of the self (Engler, 1986). Buddhists describe the self as a sense of personal continuity and sameness in the felt experience of existing as an ongoing being, with this sense coming from a synthesis of the inner life and the outer reality of personal relationships. The psychoanalytic point of view is that this same experience of personal continuity and selfhood comes from a gradual differentiation of internalized images of a self from the internalized images of outside objects. It is this differentiation that creates one's self-representation.

In discussing the meaning of boundaries, Wilber (1979) noted that there can be no thing in isolation from other things. A tree can only be a tree in relationship to other things that are not a tree. A self cannot be a self except in relationship to other selves. The process of differentiation can only occur if there are others from which to differentiate. Yet the differentiation process is also one of perceiving the entity we call self in relationship to these other beings. The values by which one defines the self are not perceived in a vacuum but only as a part of relationships.

The term *object relations* is descriptive of the orientation of the prepersonal level of awareness. Out of the undifferentiated fusion state of birth, children separate what is self from not self in an object fashion; that is, they see others as objects and themselves as a different object, and they begin to define the self in terms of the relationships between these objects. As they develop into the personal realms of the spectrum, however, they begin to see themselves as subject of the relationships in the sense that they control their self-concepts through the ways in which they subjectively perceive themselves. They have moved from the prepersonal notion of interrelated objects to one of interdependent personal relationships. They are now subjects participating in the relationships. It is this same movement from self-as-object to self-as-subject that Rogers (1961) saw as the result of successful counseling, in which movement is from a less developed relationship to a more developed relationship. The counseling process recapitu-lates the overall development process.

Developmental psychology teaches that healthy development involves es-tablishing a concept of object constancy, that is, understanding that significant others exist physically and emotionally separate from oneself. This is a part of the process of differentiation of the self. Yet within the context of transpersonal theory, the self is not different from those relationships but is an integral part of them. The differentiation is an illusion. We are all connected. If not, none of us exists. This is the enlightenment that can occur during the crisis of dying.

We are only relationships. There is no other aspect of self. It is not simply the self that changes but the relationships through which we get our sense of self. And it is the changing nature of relationships the defines the spectrum of consciousness. Higher and more complex structures demand new kinds of relationships. The relationship of dependency of the very young child is no longer adequate for developing the deep structure of competence that is appropriate for the preteen years. A relationship that is built on mutual satisfaction of esteem needs is not appropriate for seeking the meaning of existence. Different relationships are necessary to bring out this more complex deep structure.

Henry Stapp (cited by Wilber, 1979) stated that "an elementary particle is not an independently existing unanalyzable entity. It is, in essence, a set of relationships that reach outward to other things" (p. 37). The same is true of persons. What we have differentiated is not a separate being or self that stands alone, but is, in essence, a set of relationships that reach outward to other persons. When we become aware of who we are, we become aware that we are *only* relationships, and this is what will be destroyed by death. To die is to end our relationships. It is not the physical body that will no longer exist, but our relationships with other people and hence our self.

The point, then, becomes not one of separating opposites into a unique self but of unifying and harmonizing the opposites, both positive and negative, by discovering a ground that transcends and encompasses them (Wilber, 1979). When we become aware of the true nature of our experience of being a self, we can see that protecting the boundary around that self makes little sense. If we are only relationships, then we are only one, not two. We do not want to separate the parts of the relationship but to unify them. The Hindu *Bhagavad Gita* says that liberation is not freedom from the negative but freedom from the pairs altogether.

THE MEANING OF WHOLENESS

The process of individuation, according to Jung (1971), is one in which the unconscious parts of the self, those unconscious sides of the many dualities that characterize our personality, are brought into consciousness and integrated with their counterparts, bringing the self into a greater sense of wholeness. It is a process of moving from a prepersonal, unknowing state of undifferentiation to an actualized individual self (in which the separateness of one from other is complete), and then beyond to the point where all of the aspects of separateness are transcended and there is only oneness again. But now it is a transpersonal unity, one that the individual has become aware of in the fullest sense.

When we become more aware of ourselves in the process of working through a crisis, concomitant changes occur along the way. Four of these changes are discussed in this section as examples of the movement toward wholeness that comes as one lives through a loss. The changes are (a) a greater openness to one's experiences, (b) an increasing internalization of evaluation, (c) greater empathy, and (d) a willingness to live in the present moment.

Openness

Openness to experience comes from a lessening of the fear of one's own feelings. When a person facing the crisis of dying begins the process of exploration, there is often a lack of deep feeling. Part of the denial is to shut out of awareness the fear, anger, loneliness, and other emotions that are connected to the threat of loss. As has been presented, many of the values surrounding the self-concept come through the process of introjection, which causes the knowledge of the source of the values to be relegated to the unconscious. Unable to freely examine these values, and afraid of the feelings that accompany experiences related to them, we distort our experiences to keep the feelings hidden and out of awareness. We separate our body from our mind so that what the body feels can be denied access to the mind.

Just as the awareness of self moves from object to subject, feelings move from being things to be examined to the point where the person fully experiences them. The person sharing the journey with a dying person might first notice a lack of acknowledgment that there are any significant feelings working inside the person. "I seem to be doing okay" or "I'm taking things pretty well" are statements that may indicate that feelings are being shut out of awareness. The feelings are "out there," things remembered but not felt, something that belongs to the object self but that is not being experienced in the moment of exploration.

Through the process of exploration, however, we begin to realize the nature of the self and the values that define it, and with this realization the feelings associated with our experiences become less fearful. We are therefore able to open ourselves up and be more consciously aware of those experiences. We begin to understand that our selves are not defined by an object out there controlling our values but that they are simply part of the relationship. We are not worthy or unworthy, liked or unliked; we just *are* a part of the relationship. In a sense, we have seen the enemy, and it is us, or at least it is our perceptions.

Internalization of Evaluation

A second characteristic of increased awareness is movement from an external locus of evaluation to a source that is inside of one's own self. As we begin to understand the relationship nature of our selves, this is accompanied by a lessening of dependence on introjected values as the source of our self-definition. Early levels of the spectrum of consciousness are characterized by the external—the needs of Maslow that are dependent on an outside source, the moral stages of Kohlberg that are related to approval, law and order, and social contract, the basis of which is determined from the outside. These are transitional characteristics that depend on structures of the self that are not capable of the internal examination needed for a self-determination of values.

Awareness of the self opens up new and more complex structures from the unconscious, however, enabling the individual to begin moving from this necessary external basis of evaluation to one in which the self, its values, and its direction are determined from within. As we facilitate an individual's movement through the crisis, we enable the uncovering of more and more of this hidden structure. For example, as Marty continued to work deeper into her unconscious knowledge of self, she became more accepting of the reality of the control she was allowing others to place on her because she perceived of herself as an entity defined by others. Awareness of her self in relationship to these others began to open up to her a different understanding of who she was; she was not just an object that belonged to this group or that, but a person acting and reacting in relationship to others. She began to perceive that she had a say in how she perceived herself within these relationships. This is a necessary step in the movement from being a person (object) defined from the outside to the ultimate level of knowing that one is not a separate self at all. In between, we must come to a place where we know ourselves to be the subject of our awareness, not the object of someone else's knowledge. From this point, we can bring into being the deep structures that transcend the personal.

Empathy

In the process of moving toward a more subjective orientation to self-perception, we also begin to move away from seeing others as objects and begin to see that they also have their own subjective views of the world. Just as we understand our own selves to be defined by an increasingly open evaluation of experience, this experience tells us more and more that others also have their own perceptions of their experiencing in the world. In developing a sense of emotional constancy, children first understand that significantly important people in their environment have emotional lives that are separate from their own and that remain constant regardless of their own emotions. They can only guess what another's emotional life is, however, by observing that person's objective behaviors and drawing inferences based on their own world view. This is how one perceives a world of objects.

Knowledge of the interrelatedness of persons, the understanding that one is, at the core, only relationship, brings one to a point where it is the relationship that is the subject of understanding, not the objects that make up the relationship. Feelings and perceptions no longer get projected onto the other from the person's own framework but are now understood to be the result of the other person's own experiencing in the world. And the only way that experiencing can be understood is from the subjective view of the person doing the experiencing. This marks the beginning of empathic understanding. Progress, then, is from (a) assuming the experiences and feelings of the other person to be the same as one's own, to (b) understanding that the other's emotions are separate from one's own but interpreting them from one's own world view, to (c) realizing that the other person's emotional life is different *and* subjective and can only be known from that person's frame of reference, to (d) knowing oneself as relationship, which means, by definition, knowing the emotional life of the other as an integral part of the relationship.

Living in the Present

A fourth aspect of movement toward wholeness is a greater focus on the present moment, a moving past the duality of now and not now. The behavioristic orientation, which is focused on the lower levels of the spectrum of consciousness, sees human behavior as resulting from the environmental contingencies related to that behavior. One tends to behave in ways that have previously led to positive reinforcement, both immediate and delayed. This view necessarily focuses us on a time sequence in the sense that we always have our eye on the past (what has been rewarding) and the future (what will we get from this behavior).

Existentialism, on the other hand, attempts to focus our concern on direction and not destination. Even though we still see a destination, we only live authentically if we keep our attention in the moment that is now occurring. Our anxieties are all about the future, fears that we will not achieve that which we feel is critical to our self-concept. The anxieties all come from the past; we remember what was, but no longer is, as if it continued to be. Only as we transcend this duality of present and not present can we find the serenity that is afforded by freedom from this anxiety.

When we view our relationships from an external locus, we are concerned more with how the other object of that relationship reacts to us than we are with the meaning of the relationship itself. We don't live the relationship, we act it out. We play roles, wear facades, and do as we ought to do. We worry about how we are perceived as object and how that will affect our future self. Once we become aware of the illusory nature of the boundaries of relationships, however, we are also able to see the illusory nature of the boundaries of time, and we begin to know the immediate moment without any understanding of the future or past. Through the efforts of bringing the self out of the unconscious and more into awareness, there is an increased acceptance that "this is the way I feel now." This is the experience that I *am* having, not one that I had at another time that can now be remembered and discussed. We move more toward being an experiencing individual rather than an observed one. We begin to truly live in the now, which means to be aware that the now is all there is.

THE MEANING OF ACCEPTANCE AND ACTUALIZATION

Awareness is the first step toward transformation. When we become more aware of our experience, our feelings, our self, the meaning of our life, and the meaning that death holds for us, we must then come to an acceptance of this new knowledge. In this context, acceptance means that the awareness must be incorporated into relationship with the self. Knowledge without acceptance will not further our movement toward wholeness.

In discussing the self-system, Wilber (1983) noted that one of its characteristics is metabolism, by which he meant the taking in of experiences and using them in the process of growth, much in the same way that the physical body takes in nourishment and uses it for growth. As we have seen, self develops out of relationship with others, but this only occurs if the experiences of the relationship are metabolized, that is, if they are assimilated into a self-structure. This means that at each new level of consciousness, the experiences that make up the self must be integrated into a relationship with the structure that remains after the person has discarded the self-defining values of the previous stage that are no longer pertinent. Only when this has been accomplished can we say that the person has accepted the new awareness of self.

The acceptance described by Kubler-Ross (1969) as a part of the loss paradigm is reached only at the end of one's life, just prior to the dying itself. It seems to be a realization of the illusory aspect of life and the connectedness that is the essence of unity consciousness. Yet when we apply the paradigm to losses other than the one that occurs at death, the meaning of acceptance must be understood in a different light. When one goes through the grieving of self that accompanies any transformation within the spectrum, acceptance refers to a higher but not complete realization of the illusory nature of life and a move toward a greater but not complete understanding of the connectedness of all people and things. In other words, the loss paradigm refers not only to that which occurs at death, but that which occurs at all levels of the spectrum, and involves the same but lesser degrees of understanding of the nature of life, the self, and the connectedness that is unity consciousness. Each transformation on the spectrum of consciousness is a microcosm of the loss that occurs at death.

The person must go through the process of unfolding at each level of development. Because the self is only relationships, then at each level the relationships must be evaluated anew. This is the essence of metabolism—that each level calls for different and more advanced ways of taking in the food, the relationships that nourish the self. To take in the food is to become aware. Yet once the body takes in the food, it must digest it for it to be usable, and this is acceptance. Once we become aware of the new nature of relationships and self, we must digest this food, incorporate it into relationship with our lives so that we can grow, that is, move to a new level on the spectrum of consciousness. If we do not digest the food, growth will not occur. Awareness will be lost and we will remain at the same level.

Self-actualization is a process that goes on in bits and pieces, each piece adding to the other until we can say that individuals are self-actualizing, meaning they are living more in the realm of self-actualization than they are living in the realm of self-esteem. From this perspective, we can say that at each level of the spectrum of consciousness, they have actualized the potential that is inherent within the deep structures of that level, so that every time they successfully negotiate a level or sublevel, they move a little more into the realm of being a self-actualizing person.

SUMMARY

The process of movement involves an unfolding at each level of consciousness. When we have integrated the deep and surface structures of a level into relationship with the self, we begin to become dissatisfied; we realize that we are not all that we can be. The teleological pull begins to exert itself. It is this dissatisfaction that leads to the search for the meanings of the self within the structures and surface contents of the current level. As new awareness comes into consciousness, and we come to accept and incorporate this awareness into relationship with the self, energy becomes available for movement to the next level. Hence, awareness and acceptance provide the basis and the motivating force for transformation to the next level. At the new level, we repeat the process of actualizing the potential of the structures of that level, integrating them with those that were actualized at the earlier stages. Once the process of actualizing is complete, we become aware of the dissatisfaction of our life at that level, and the process begins all over again.

From the perspective of the spectrum of consciousness, this process is specific to the outward arc, to that half of the spectrum that is focused on the development of the self. Beyond the level of the self, however, is the transpersonal. As we bring into being the deep structures and actualize the potential of being a separate self at increasingly higher stages, we begin to feel dissatisfied not just with the self of the present level, but with the self as self.

At the highest of the levels of the outward arc, there is an increasing awareness that the self is only relationship, that it is not a separate being. As awareness of the nature of relationships and particularly of the self as relationship begins to come forth, the boundaries between self and other become more fluid, and we come increasingly to an understanding that we are nothing other than the relationships that we live. As a part of this understanding, we also come to a greater sense of the interconnectedness of ourselves and the other parts of the relationship. Just as death cannot stand alone without life to give it meaning, so the self that is defined through relationships is necessarily and essentially connected to the other selves that are part of those relationships. This dawning of the transcendent nature of the self is characterized by what Wilber (1979) called the *transpersonal bands,* which are a sort of bridge between the personal and the transpersonal.

The point is that who one is is determined through relationships and that growth is accomplished by understanding one's relationships at continually higher and more complex levels, up to the point that the individual selves that constitute the relationship transcend into a unity. If this is the essence of growth, then it should also be the essence of facilitation, and that is exactly the point that Rogers made. Counseling is living a relationship in such a way that each person can experience increasingly higher levels of the connectedness that transcends our differentiated separate selves.

Chapter 10

The Nature of Relationship

Having looked at some background on the developmental aspects of humanity and their relationship to death and dying, it is now time to discuss in greater depth the process of facilitation. For those looking for a description of how to counsel a dying person, however, these chapters may be disappointing. As indicated earlier, sharing the journey is not a matter of techniques or formulas but a process of living with dying persons in such a manner as to enable them to find their own way toward greater unity. How that may occur with one person is unique to that person and cannot be generalized as a prescription for others. Each time we begin the journey, we must start with a new outlook.

Two distinguishing aspects of a facilitative approach should be discussed as they relate to other counseling orientations. The first is the concept that change, particularly transformative change, does not result from what we know in a cognitive sense. The struggle to use our reasoning powers to solve the problems of dying hinders us from experiencing the pain and dissatisfaction with our lives and therefore keeps us focused within our current level of consciousness, cutting off the possibility of transformation. We create illusions about our separate selves through the process of reasoning, and we maintain these illusions when we try to work through a crisis using our cognitive knowledge.

Psychotherapy seems to be based on theoretical formulations about our clients. As counselors, we are especially concerned with making correct diagnoses and interpretations. We are the experts in exploring the unconscious of another person (Pande, 1968). Even though cognitive theories do not subscribe to the concept of unconscious dynamics as being critical to health and pathology, this interpretive approach to counseling is as true of cognitive orientations as it is of psychodynamic therapy. When, as psychotherapists, our world view tells us that reasoned knowing is the highest order of understanding, we raise it to a level of the utmost importance. The result is that we tend to feel good about ourselves as interpreters of human behavior, but we fail to achieve the desired results of successful counseling.

All of this is not to say that we do not need to know anything to be good counselors. An understanding of the way in which people develop, what their needs are, and the ways that they fall off the path of psychological health are all necessary to the process of counseling. This is all background that helps us in being empathic and helps us to recognize the need to create a facilitative environment. It gives us the basis for determining our purpose. Wilber (1983) pointed out that we use the rational mind to operate on knowledge that is gained both from the world of the senses and the world of the mind. The difference is where we get the data (or to which realm we restrict the data) about which we think and reason. In like manner, we can think about the world of the transcendent, even though in doing so we only create a map. We do not know the world of the transcendent by thinking, but only through the eye of contemplation. In the same sense, we cannot know about our client's inner experience through our own thinking processes; we can know it only through an empathic understanding of the client. We can, however, and in fact must, use our rational thinking mind to develop a map of this nonrational realm as a means of guiding our efforts toward empathic understanding. It is our thinking that tells us the importance of knowing the inner experience of our client and the likely consequences that communicating this understanding will have on the client's growth, but the understanding itself is beyond the realm of thinking.

What we understand as facilitators should therefore precede our entering into a relationship with another person and not become our method of treatment. It will only lead us away from our goal if it becomes the basis for interpretation and objective analysis. Our facilitation comes from being able (knowing how) to help the person experience a renewed sense of unity, and cognitive knowledge of that experience is not adequate for our purpose.

I have discussed at some length the development of a person and the process of experiencing a loss. This has all been presented as a cognitive basis for understanding how to facilitate a person's movement through the crisis of dying but not as the basis for making interpretations about the client's situation. The question has been asked, "How do you determine where a client is on the spectrum?" Yet this is to misunderstand the nature of the spectrum of consciousness and its meaning for counseling. Knowledge of the spectrum of consciousness is a framework within which one understands the basic direction of a client's life and from which one develops a purpose focused on facilitating the process of transformation. Moreover, it provides us with an understanding that each client must be helped at the level where that client is currently living. It does not imply evaluation of developmental levels, however. Rather, it guides the counselor to explore experiences with clients wherever they are on the spectrum as a part of the process of freeing them to move to a higher level. This necessitates an empathic understanding of clients, not an external evaluation of where they are on the spectrum.

Techniques of intervention, treatment procedures, and expert analyses have nothing to do with a person's becoming more aware of the meanings of a crisis that lie hidden in the unconscious. What we do understand from this background knowledge is the reason for creating an environment in which the need to defend the self is lessened and freedom to explore is promoted. On the one hand, there are professionals who attempt to force meaningful exploration, and on the other hand, there are those who attempt to facilitate the person's own natural flow of experiencing. In the latter approach, the focus is on entering into a meaningful relationship with the client, not as a technique, but as a way of sharing the experience of the crisis in a way that enables the client to feel a sense of connectedness and compassion that is, in and of itself, therapeutic.

Descartes' dictum, "I think, therefore I am," does not satisfy human needs with regard to personal development. We are not human simply because we think, and more important, what we are does not depend solely on our thinking. It is our ability to reason, and therefore to rationalize, intellectualize, and project that enables us to develop a persona, to reason out an illusory self that we think is the one we want. Distortion of one's experience, even though it may be motivated by emotion, is a process of rational (or irrational) thinking. In other words, we do not defend ourselves through our sensing mode nor through the eye of contemplation but by using logical thought to develop patterns of thinking that we find acceptable to the self. Yet in this process of creating an acceptable self, we cut off other aspects of our total being. We create a division between who we think we are and who we really are, between persona and shadow, thinking and feeling, mind and body. By separating out (denying) the nonthinking side of our being, we create the dualities that cause us to live segmented lives.

If, in the process of helping a person to uncover the integrated self, we use the same method by which the distortion came into being (i.e., focusing on the rational, thinking aspect of the client's experience), we create a climate that is highly conducive to continuation of the same distortion. Counseling becomes an argument, with counselors presenting one side and the clients countering with their own reasoned distortion as a means of continuing their defense against attack on the self. Having developed a self-image that might include being sexually inadequate, for example, the client needs to maintain that aspect of self. There was a need that created the perception, and we must assume that the need continues to operate at some level of consciousness. Attempting to talk the client's need away is akin to trying to take a gun from a mugger who believes he needs the gun to protect himself. The mugger will simply work harder to keep the gun; the client will simply work harder to maintain the distorted perception. We should concern ourselves, instead, with removing the client's need for defending that position.

The second aspect that differentiates among counseling viewpoints is related to the focus of the content of the helping process. Because our purpose is to help persons who are dying become increasingly aware of their own subjective meaning of crisis and loss, the content of the counseling is the internal experiencing of the person. This is not something that can be determined from the outside and applied from an external position. It can only be known through a knowledge of the inner world of the persons with whom we are working, and we must therefore listen to them to understand the needs, feelings, and meanings that make up their world. There is no other way to know them. (The term *experience* is used here to mean personal apprehension of the world through all of the modes of knowing—sensory, mental, and contemplative. It is not restricted to the empirical experience of science, which can be understood from a point external to the experiencer.)

As shown in chapter 4, objective, empirical analysis excludes certain kinds of knowledge—purpose, extrinsic value, quality (of life), and existential meaning (H. Smith, 1982). Yet it is this knowledge that makes up the content of the counseling that we can offer to a person who is dying, and these qualities of self can only be known from that person's frame of reference. When we talk of the values that define the self and the meaning that the loss of those values will have for the individual, there is no way to know them other than through the internal realm of subjective meaning of the person who holds them. To speculate on the basis of our own knowledge would be to place the meaning into an alien framework. It is akin to placing a round peg into a square hole, forcing it to fit the only viewpoint we have.

It is a difficult proposition for those of us who have lived in a world of experts, where analytical thinking and knowledge is supreme, to let go of our own conceptualizations and accept those of the nonexpert (the client) as being more valid. Many counselors believe that their education and experience place them in a better position than the client's to make decisions about what the client thinks and believes and what courses of action would be best for the client to take. Their belief is that the client's neurotic distortions and defensiveness prevents the client from seeing the truth or reality of the situation clearly or accurately and that the client needs an objective expert to clarify and interpret the situation.

The question, then, becomes one of what reality is important and what determines the best direction for the client to take. We cannot know the nature of a client's reality; we can only know what it seems like to us from our own framework. Judgments can be made about consensual reality, but not that which applies on an individual basis. So our orientation must be to facilitate our clients in coming to a more open awareness of their own inner reality, rather than trying to make external observations fit our own conception of reality. Erickson (Erickson & Rossi, 1983) believed that the individuals he worked with had within them the resources necessary to solve their own difficulties, and his purpose was to help them utilize those resources. He did not need to interpret their problems and give them solutions; instead, he enabled them to get in touch with their own inner experience and find their own best solutions.

One point of dispute in the field of counseling relates to whether a person who has had experiences similar to the client's is in a better position to be of help. Does having been there make one more understanding and better able to help? This concept perhaps first arose through the work of Alcoholics Anonymous, in which recovering alcoholics offer to help those who are struggling with the same problem. Since Alcoholics Anonymous was created, many other support groups and counseling programs have been developed in which the counselor or facilitator has been through the same problems that are the source of the clients' distress. A person recovering from breast cancer works with women who have the same disease; adults who were abused as children work with abused children; and those who have lost a spouse through death become counselors to others experiencing the same loss. The concept here is that only if we have had the same kind of experience can we truly understand what the client is going through. Such a perspective ignores our ability to be empathic, however, and relegates counseling to the world of the concrete.

Suzuki (1970) said that we must begin our task with the mind of the beginner, free of preconceptions and habits of the expert, ready to accept and open to all possibilities. Only in this way can we come to know the inner experience of the client. If we feel that we have to have been there to understand, then that belief will automatically lead us to interpret the clients' expressions of their experience within our own framework. The content of the counseling will no longer be the inner experience of the client but an abstracted cognitive model of human behavior.

CHARACTERISTICS OF RELATIONSHIP

Keeping in mind the differences between an approach that attempts to facilitate the client's own inner growth and one that works to provide externally determined solutions on an expert basis, let us now begin to look at how the process of facilitation comes about. The process is primarily (perhaps even solely) a matter of helping individuals become more aware of the personal meaning of loss, of freeing them to bring into consciousness more of the hidden experience of self that will enable them to struggle toward movement to a higher level of consciousness. It is a matter of creating a relationship that is conducive to this free and open exploration. Put another way, it is creating a relationship in which the client can achieve a more satisfying self.

Creating a climate in which caring about and understanding the experience of another person are the primary ingredients constitutes theoretical simplicity, so much so that it lacks character. It is not the kind of thing that requires several years of graduate school to master and often is done more effectively by untrained persons. Anyone—neighbors, club members, friends, colleagues—can have a relationship. To say, then, that an attitude of caring is a critical factor in counseling success is to make the process less formal and rigorous. It denies the empirical cause and effect relationship that is essential to a scientific approach.

To be professional, we believe that we need to be able to do more than just care. In an attempt to make our counseling and psychotherapy scientific, we develop healing rituals that must be learned through the rigor of graduate training programs. This is much like the hierarchy of a church that develops rituals and practices only the church elders can undertake, thereby separating the elders from the masses and making them necessary to the process of being religious. Counselors develop techniques and assessments that only they can perform and then create a belief that these are the necessary ingredients for helping one solve problems. We put considerable effort into determining just the right physical environment for creating a certain ambiance in which the counselor and client can work—not too formal with too many barriers and appropriately stylized to create a "sense of warmth and caring." We go through a process of analysis and diagnosis so as to appear knowledgeable and authoritative, and we perform our techniques to create an aura of professionalism. In many cases, the ritual of mind healing is calculated to give the impression of spontaneity and intimacy, but the calculation itself belies any real sense of meaningful relationship.

In a facilitative approach, the focus is on the relationship that we create with a client and its use as an environment that is conducive to unhindered exploration and acceptance of the self. The creation of that environment is the goal in itself and not a means to some other end. In much of psychotherapy, we use our need for cognitive understanding and interpretation as a rationale for establishing and maintaining what we call a therapeutic relationship, without recognizing the importance the relationship has even in the absence of our cognitive processing. The knowledge gained from the reasoned insight is not the source of growth but simply a reason for being involved in a warm, loving relationship (Pande, 1968). As counselors, we must come to the place where we can accept the relationship itself as the goal and the source of growth and not as simply an adjunct to the techniques of analysis.

Relationship is spontaneous and charged with one's whole being. When working with a client, what we say must not be calculated, but free and natural, coming from a deep understanding of one's own experience within the relationship. "The admired live word is the gut word, concrete and vibrant with feeling. The dead word is the explanatory word, dry and lifeless, issuing from the head. The first unifies, the second separates. Now, the important thing is not to wobble but to respond at once" (Kapleau, 1989, p. 17). When we make reasoned responses to our client, we wobble, losing the spontaneous and natural meaning of our relationship.

UNCONDITIONAL POSITIVE REGARD

A discussion of relationship, as it pertains to counseling and therapy, must begin with Carl Rogers. More than any other theorist, Rogers has defined the conditions of the therapeutic relationship, and he was responsible for instigating the large amount of research that has been conducted around this concept. Three aspects of a therapeutic relationship are presented in this section: (a) what constitutes the appropriate relationship, (b) the theoretical assumptions underlying the concept of therapeutic relationship, and (c) how relationship leads to success in counseling.

Rogers first described the climate that he perceived to be the essence of facilitation early in his career and elaborated on it many times (Rogers, 1951, 1957, 1961). A facilitative climate is characterized by an unconditional positive regard for the client, one that says "I believe you to be a totally worthy person regardless of what you are now, or what you may become in the future." It is characterized by an empathic understanding that enables the counselor to see the world from the client's perceptual frame of reference. In addition to having these genuine feelings of positive regard and understanding, counselors must be able to communicate them to their clients, and they must be perceived by the clients as being genuine persons. It was Rogers' belief that the relationship we create is the most significant aspect in determining whether our clients are able to use counseling in a positive, life-enhancing manner. Relationship alone, based on these conditions, is sufficient to enable clients to explore the self that they are and that they choose to become, without intervention on the part of the counselor. In such a relationship, people will move through the process of awareness, acceptance, and actualization, transforming themselves from one stage of consciousness to the next.

To have unconditional positive regard means that the counselor perceives clients to be persons worthy of genuine love and care regardless of what they are or what they may become. It means total acceptance of persons as persons, in all of their human facets, with no conditions placed on that acceptance. Clients are prized as persons without evaluation and are recognized as having their own valid experiences. The person experiencing unconditional positive regard for another cares about what happens to that person in a way that can be described as emotionally involved but not emotionally attached. This means that the counselor will feel joy and pain in relationship to the client and will have an emotional response to what clients express and to what happens to them, but it also means that the joy and pain that we feel as counselors does not define our own person. We can live in the immediate moment with the client while respecting the client's right to be a separate individual. There is an ability to have deep concern for another without losing one's own individuality in the process.

It is a relationship based on an open and honest caring, which distinguishes it from one characterized by over-involvement, rescuing behaviors or codependency.

Although Rogers considered unconditional positive regard to be a single condition of climate, Barrett-Lennard (1962) was able to show that two distinct aspects are involved: the positive regard itself and the unconditionality of regard. Most counselors would agree that it is important, if not necessary, to have positive regard for one's clients, although most question whether it is wise to hold such positive feelings without condition. The latter aspect, it is felt, leads to condoning negative behaviors and growth patterns on the part of the persons with whom we are working. A lack of trust in clients' ability to make adequate choices for themselves causes counselors to fear giving the freedom to choose. To say to a client that "regardless of what your choice is, whether I agree with it or not, whether it makes me appear successful in the counseling or not, I will still consider you to be a person of worth" is a posture that is difficult to achieve. Unconditionality of regard puts tremendous pressure on the counselor who perceives success to be dependent on bringing the client to the "right" choices.

Unconditional positive regard is a way of being that is integral to the self of the counselor. It is a genuine belief that clients are worthwhile individuals and have the capacity to make decisions and assume direction for their own lives. This is not a way of behaving to achieve results but an attitude that is part of the counselor's person. One must have a belief in the ability of clients to take charge of their lives and must genuinely feel that they are persons worthy of care and love. Only a person who is trusted will become trustworthy, and in like manner, only a person who is perceived to be worthwhile will behave in a worthy manner.

If an appropriate relationship is critical to facilitation of a client's movement through the spectrum of consciousness, then what is the basis on which unconditional positive regard, as an aspect of that relationship, is hypothesized to further these goals, particularly when working with one who is dying? What is the rationale on which we base our assumption that having a genuine attitude of caring for the clients, and communicating that attitude, will help them to move forward?

We assume that when people enter into a counseling relationship, they are dissatisfied with their lives. People are constricted in access to their full potential by the ways that they have structured their own selves and their understanding of the world. Distortion and denial protect against threat to one's identity, but they also limit one's capacity to move forward. The stage of bargaining that occurs as a person moves through a crisis is the period when there is a willingness to begin the process of exploring those distortions and delusions. There is a force that motivates the person to move forward, created by the anxiety of the crisis, and at the same time an inability to let go of the restrictions that hinder that forward movement. This is the dual aspect of the basic need to maintain the self on the one hand and to enhance it on the other, to keep the self as it is and yet to make it better.

As already seen, growth necessitates giving up the transition characteristics by which one defines the self at one stage to develop a new self-concept defined by higher order transition characteristics. For example, the belonging, conforming, conventional self of the early personal levels of the spectrum of consciousness must be let go to allow the development of a self-reflective and individualistic self. For this to happen, persons must become continually more aware of who they are, what meaning the current self has, and the potential for becoming a higher self. Communicating an acceptance of persons regardless of how they define their current selves or, more important, how they suggest they may define themselves in new terms is critical in encouraging them to explore their selves and the meaning these have for them. By communicating acceptance regardless of what the self is or may become, we remove the need to defend the self in order to have security, belonging, or esteem. We communicate that, regardless of which direction the person chooses, needs will be satisfied, at least within the relationship with the counselor.

As stated in the previous chapter, self is nothing other than relationships. In the prepersonal stages of development, we go through a process of differentiation in relation to others, coming first to an acceptance that we are physically other than those in relationship with us, then gaining an experiential understanding that we are also emotionally and mentally separate. At these early stages, however, there must be an environment of freedom to explore the meaning of separateness and assimilate that into relationship with the dawning concept of self. If the environment impinges on us in such a way as to communicate that we are not acceptable if we do not mirror the same emotions or if we do not follow the same values and attitudes as others in the environment, then our ability to explore our own separate self is hindered. As children begin to develop the ability to become autonomous beings and to try on new roles of personhood, they are faced with the threat of loss of acceptance if that autonomy and those roles do not coincide with the ones that others in the environment consider acceptable. If conditions are placed on the direction and amount of children's autonomy and initiative in trying new roles and making choices for themselves, feelings of alienation will develop, causing a constricting of self-development. In such a context, children come to understand the meaning of conditional acceptance: "I will be considered worthwhile and a member of the group *if, and only if,* I choose the direction of self development that others want." In such a context, the relationship one has is based on subservience, and the self that becomes defined from the relationship is restricted by roles and rules.

Within a counseling context, we have the opportunity to reverse this process of conditioning. Bargaining is the phase in which the terminally ill person begins to deal with the distortions and delusions surrounding the self and moves toward a readiness to work through these distortions to achieve an understanding of the irreversibility of the loss. This can be regarded as the first movement away from denial and distortion of experience. There is an emotional release that equates with the expression of anxiety, although the anxiety may not be perceived by the client as being "my" feelings. The anxiety may be manifested as anger, frustration, or depression—all stemming from circumstances in the outside world that are playing havoc with the client's life and over which the client perceives little or no control. These feelings of anxiety are painful and make exploration of the self tenuous. It takes little at this point to drive the individual back into the shell of denial and distortion. The slightest indication that current feelings as they are being expressed are not appropriate or acceptable will close the door to continued exploration.

As these first tentative steps away from the need to defend the self are attempted, individuals will be aware of the degree to which they are considered worthwhile even if the current self is not maintained. If conditions are implicitly placed on their communicating to the counselor a certain kind of self, if the feelings that come into awareness are labeled as bad or inappropriate, if indications of a desire to move forward are met with injunctions about what that movement should look like, the person will fall back to a defensive posture. By creating a climate in which clients need either to accept our point of view or defend their own alternative ones, we will foreclose the open exploration of choices that are available in the movement toward a new self.

In an appropriate environment, however, one that is not based on conditions, the client can move increasingly from distortion to awareness and from delusion to insight. When conditions of acceptance are removed, the perception of the person changes to "I will be considered worthwhile and accepted by this person no matter what I discuss, no matter what feelings I experience, no matter how I define myself." Relationship within the counseling context is based on openness, respect, and trust in individuals to choose that which is right for them. Within this relationship at least, clients can discover a freedom to explore all aspects of their experience without the need to deny or distort.

EMPATHY

As discussed earlier, empathy involves understanding the world of experience of another person as if one were at the center of that person's world. It means perceiving the world from the other person's internal frame of reference, with all the same feelings, cognitions, and understandings that the other person has. It is seeing the world as if you were experiencing it from the same vantage point as the other person. This is distinguished from feelings of sympathy, in which one accepts an understanding of another person on the basis of agreement with one's own feelings—an "I know how you feel" understanding because you have been through similar experiences or believe that you would have the same feeling if you were to go through a similar experience.

We must enter the relationship with the terminally ill person free of preconceptions. Gautama Buddha has been quoted as saying that we should not accept what we hear from others, nor should we accept a statement just because it is found in our books; neither should we accept things because they are tradition or in accord with our beliefs, nor because they are taught to us by teachers (Pratt, 1928). The test of every approach is to be found in one's own experience and phenomenal understanding, and it is from this vantage point that we must approach our clients.

There is a tendency when working with terminally ill patients to do what we have done in other counseling situations or to follow a preset model. We must empty our minds of preconceptions, allowing our approaches to grow out of an empathic understanding of the person living with terminal illness rather than borrowing from other settings and other persons with other needs. Gilligan (1987) noted that Milton Erickson "repeatedly stressed that therapeutic communication should be based on neither theoretical generalizations nor on statistical probabilities, but on actual patterns distinguishing the clients' present self expression (e.g., beliefs, behaviors, motivations, symptoms). This requires therapists to begin each therapy in a state of experiential ignorance" (p. 14). It has even been noted that patients are people who have had too much programming (Erickson, Rossi, & Rossi, 1976). The implication certainly has to be that therapists should refrain from adding to this programming, but in fact that is often exactly what we do. Erickson et al. went on to say that psychological disease, or a lack of mental health, can be a consequence of the counselor's using conceptual systems that are too detailed and rigid. The worst approach we can take is to attempt to facilitate growth by applying another system with the same characteristics.

The ability to generalize is one of the most important characteristics of being human. It enables us to be intelligent in our behavior, eliminating much of the trial and error that would be necessary in the absence of such a characteristic. The ability to differentiate is even more critical, for it allows us not only to see the sameness in situations but also to be aware of different aspects that call for different responses. Being empathic in one's understanding is the ability to differentiate how another person is perceiving the world rather than operating on generalizations. It is empathy that enables a person to work with another in a free and open manner. If we are able to enter into each relationship as a beginner, not needing to have a set of predetermined rules and procedures, then we can listen to the other freely and openly, understanding their experience as it is to them. Empathy is, as Moustakas (1961) said, the ability to notice the longing for response and to make that response with compassion and understanding.

If we describe a client as untrusting, or narcissistic, or the child of an alcoholic, we are attempting to portray that person as an object. We are likely, then, to ignore the effect the observer, the counselor-in-relationship, will have on the observed. Ignoring such an effect, we close our eyes to the client-in-relationship and tend to "observe" preconceived patterns of characteristics and behaviors. In discussing the lack of usefulness of theoretical presuppositions in one's quest for enlightenment, the Buddha told a story of a man who was struck by a poison arrow. He refused to let anyone remove the arrow until he knew who had shot the arrow into him—was the person a Brahman, to what family did he belong, was he tall, short, or of medium height, what village did he come from, and so forth. In the process of seeking the answers, he died (Eliade, 1982). The point is, of course, that such knowledge does not contribute to one's journey, and the same can be said of facilitating a person's movement through the spectrum of consciousness. Knowing that a person is a schizophrenic, or a borderline personality, or grew up in a ghetto does not describe that person's concept of self or present experience.

A counseling relationship with a person who is dying is a relationship of interconnectedness. The counselor cannot be separated (a professional) from the client (a treatment object). Quantum theory, in determining that distance is necessary for making unaffected observations, has abolished the notion of fundamentally separated objects (Capra, 1975). Effect is a function of closeness, and the concept of the participator replaces that of the observer. A teacher cannot observe a class as an unaffected or independent object because what that class is is affected by the teacher. If the class is unruly, or more accurately, behaves in an unruly fashion, they do so in part as a function of the teacher. In like manner, if clients are defensive in a counseling relationship, they behave that way in part because of the counselor. We cannot separate the clients' behavior from our own effect on them. Persons are never unaffected by other persons with whom they are in relationship, no matter how insignificant the relationship might be. Separate selves, therapist and client, are a hindrance to transformation. We must work together as a unit(y). Only as counselors struggle with their own transformation within the relationship can they facilitate their clients' movement toward their own transformation. In this sense, the relationship is one in which both members, living in the now, redefine themselves, and in so doing come to a greater experiential awareness of the unity that characterizes such a relationship.

Living in the now leads to a sense of unity, and empathy is crucial to living in the now. It is true empathy that causes one to transcend the separate self and to be able to communicate that transcendence. We can know (i.e., have empathy for) another person at three levels: We can know the meaning of the words of the other person without having any real sense of the inner experience; we can sense that inner experience but only as being a part of the other person and having no effect on our own self; and we can have the deepest sense of empathy, in which we only know our selves as a part of relationship, but by knowing our own selves, we also know the self of the other person, which we experience not as other but as unity.

At this third level, the relationship has power even if it is not experienced by the other—*Thou* is more than *It* knows (Buber, 1970). A person does not have to be consciously aware of the process of transformation for the relationship to have an impact. An understanding of the movement from one level of consciousness to the next is not a prerequisite to the movement itself. As one person (i.e., the counselor) enters into the relationship in a unitive manner, the other person, without cognitive acknowledgment, experiences the depth of the relationship and consequently its meaning. In this way, through sharing the journey with a dying person, we can have a positive effect during this final stage of growth that does not depend on cognitive interpretations or behavioral manipulations.

May (1958) noted that psychotherapists, when assailed by doubts about what they are doing, become preoccupied with technique. Perhaps the most anxiety-reducing strategy is to abstract oneself from the humanness of the client by adopting a technical emphasis. We are a nation of practitioners, but May asked the question, "Where shall we get what we practice?" The answer lies in an empathic understanding of our clients, in living with them in a relationship that is free of preconceptions.

Morton Kelsey (1986) described his own experience in counseling thus: "I had been listened to without judgment by someone showing genuine caring about me and my family, having a vision of what wholeness meant and an understanding of the necessity of having me find my own particular meaning as a part of a meaningful universe" (p. 8). How different this is from treating the client from a preconceived notion about the techniques that are effective in changing the behaviors we have determined to be unproductive. As Palmer (1988) said, "It is important to stress the ways that people are different from each other, because so much of the suffering that we experience in our relationships with other people is caused by the fact that we are blind to their point of view" (p. 6). The person living with a terminal illness deserves the dignity of being perceived as a unique individual.

EFFECTS OF RELATIONSHIP

The self is the heart of growth and transformation; it is defined through relationships. It therefore stands to reason that relationship should be the focus of counseling. Through personal relationships we touch the ultimate meaning of our existence at a depth that is impossible in any other way (Robinson, 1963). If one accepts the Christian concept that God is love, this points to an understanding that through personal relationships we encounter the deepest truth about the structure of reality. Relationship is not something into which we enter as a means to an end, it is the end itself. It is the essence of our existence and meaning, and thus it is through a counseling relationship that both client and counselor come to a greater understanding of self in terms of existential meaning.

Buber (1970) talked about *I–It* relationships, in which the *I* is the subject and the *It* is the object, in which there is a self and an other. Relationships perceived in such a manner shut us off from knowing the unity out of which our lives emerge. As shown earlier, the prepersonal stages of development involve the differentiating of the *I* from the other, of coming to an understanding of the *I–It* nature of the world. This process is based on an open experiencing of the world but pertains only to the development of the self. Whereas *experiencing* others *as* others is part of growth in the personal realm, *relating* to others (i.e., entering into an intimate relationship, which Buber called *I–Thou* and which is beyond the normal bounds of experiencing) is the route to development beyond the personal. It is the route to understanding the deepest meaning that life holds.

Relationship operates differently at different levels of the spectrum of consciousness. At one level, relationship aids in the development of a sense of belonging, at the next, a sense of self-esteem (unconditional positive regard), but at the higher levels of the personal realm, relationship works in two specific ways. First, by diminishing the need to defend, it enables introspection, allowing the person to understand the self more completely and to bring into balance or wholeness the various aspects of the individual, personal self. At the highest level, it is the bridge to the transpersonal and ultimately to unity consciousness. The transcendent nature of this unity cannot be known simply by searching the depths of the individual soul. Because God is love, God is only encountered in deep encounters among men and women (Buber, 1965). Once we move past the humanistic level of development, we can enter into a love relationship with others that transcends the love of separate-person relationships, thereby beginning the movement toward the transpersonal.

Rogers' conceptualization of relationship provides the basis for the sharing, community, and connectedness that are the antidotes for pain, anxiety, and depression that we find among persons who are terminally ill. Even though his approach is most often classified as humanistic, the process of sharing and relationship that characterized his counseling is a means of entering into the transpersonal. It allows one to move from the sense of intimate connection of worldly self–other relationships to the experience of the transpersonal connections that characterize the inward arc of the spectrum of consciousness. The natural movement of a person's life is from prepersonal fusion to a state of a highly differentiated self, from which the person begins the process of transcending that self toward unity consciousness. Behavioral and psychodynamic psychology are most appropriate to the early processes of self-differentiation, and humanistic approaches, such as Rogers', are focused on the highest levels of the development of the self after it has been adequately differentiated. However, a natural part of self-development at its most advanced levels also involves greater comprehension of the concepts of globality, empathy, and social conscience, all of which are bridges to an increasing sense of connectedness. It is in this way that relationship, as defined and applied to counseling by Rogers, creates the beginnings of a bringing into awareness the connectedness that frees the individual to explore these higher levels of self-development, thereby providing a basis for transformation into the transpersonal bands.

Relationship provides the means of moving through the spectrum of consciousness, and it leads to the spiritual levels of being. Relationship constitutes the essence of the psychospiritual facilitation that we can offer persons who face the crisis of dying. It serves as a freeing agent for the dying person, as a self-defining process, and ultimately as a means of transcending the self as the person moves toward greater unity.

RELATIONSHIP AS FREEING AGENT

Ultimately, the capacity to respond to a life concern lies within those who have that concern. They must have the power to respond. Counselors can do nothing more than provide the appropriate conditions for this to happen; we cannot force the person to respond. Searching is the process through which this capacity is brought to bear. Psychotherapy is needed when the clients' access to their own capacity to search is impaired, and they are constricted in the realization of their full potential by the ways they have structured their own identity and the nature of the world. Our job is to free up our clients' searching process. Through a facilitative relationship, we help them regain a power already present in them.

The searching process is begun when the client can describe the concern in a way that begins to expand awareness of the concern. The key elements in such a description are genuine presence, fullness of description, and an expectancy of discovery. The focus must be on the individual as the source of healing and growth, not on externals. Within the person there must be a sense of autonomy and initiative, and if these are not present, we must facilitate, through relationship, an increasing sense of ability to take on responsibility for one's personal healing. There is a focus on a sense of personal power that must be felt within the client.

The hypothesis that the therapeutic conditions of relationship are necessary and sufficient to provide for maximum growth is predicated on a philosophical principle that within each human there is the capacity and tendency toward positive growth. This is perhaps the concept in the Rogerian system that draws the most disagreement, being disputed on the basis that it seems to attribute to human beings inherent characteristics of goodness without a corresponding accounting for the evil side. It is argued that Rogers' position does not adequately provide for all of the negative, violent, and evil deeds that are part of humanity. Yet positive growth is not defined by Rogers as good in any evaluatively moral sense but rather as defining an inherent direction to one's growth. The growth of a tree provides a good example. Within the seed from which the tree springs there is contained a knowledge of what constitutes positive growth for a tree— up, out, and full of leaves. Given the appropriate climate (sun, water, adequate space, etc.), the tree will grow in that inherent direction of its own accord. One does not need to go out each day and push it toward the sky or pull out its branches. We just need to provide it with the proper environment. Humans are like that. Within the seed from which each of us comes there is an unconscious knowledge of the positive direction of our development. Given the appropriate environment, which is described by the conditions of relationship, each of us will naturally grow in that direction. It is not a question of good or bad, it is simply the natural (positive) direction of human development.

This concept of positive direction is philosophical in the sense that it is empirically neither provable nor unprovable; it cannot be known through the eye of the flesh. One can only speculate on it through the eye of reason or know it through the eye of contemplation. The position is therefore discounted by those whose system is based on the eye of flesh, primarily the behaviorists and psychoanalysts, although a number of humanists other than Rogers dispute its accuracy. It is not a concept that is by any means unique to Rogers, however. Huxley (1970) pointed out that throughout the ages, philosophical systems have claimed that humanity's single greatest drive is to rediscover the infinite and eternal wholeness that is lost at birth. It is this that is perceived by so many traditions to be the basic inherent positive direction that is both the tendency and the capacity of humans. Wilber (1980) talked of this as being the ground unconscious—"all the deep structures existing as potentials ready to emerge, via remembrance, at some future point" in the person's life (p. 83).

When working with persons who are dying, we cannot know what is best for those people, what is the appropriate direction for them to take at this stage of life. Is communication with family the positive direction? For many, yes. Perhaps we could even say that such a direction falls within the confines of consensual reality. But is it the right direction for the specific person we are working with? How can we know, other than by fitting that person into our own framework? A round peg in a square hole? If it is the correct path, how do we know? And if we know, why can't the person we are working with know the same thing?

The answer is very simply that the person *can* know. As discussed earlier, by removing the need to defend the self, we allow individuals to freely explore their inner drives, values, sources of joy, and so forth and to come to an awareness of the direction that is most beneficial and satisfying for them. When people do not need to hold to any particular orientation, they can see things as clearly as the counselor. The latter is no longer an expert in the sense of being able to determine what path would be best, for the path is now obvious to the client. By removing the need to defend (i.e., by removing the conditions placed on valuing and behaving), the counselor creates an environment that allows the inherent positive direction to take hold. We do not need to pull the person up any more than we need to pull the tree up; this will happen of its own accord.

We cannot work with clients without having some kind of relationship, and the kind of relationship we have will be instrumental in determining the self that develops within the client, regardless of what else we try to accomplish through the relationship. If the counselor holds and communicates a belief that the clients cannot solve their own problems and need an expert to direct the process, the clients will incorporate into their relationship to self a perception of needing to be directed by others. The ability to follow the natural direction of life will only be fulfilled through a relationship in which the counselor holds and communicates a belief that the clients can best solve their own problems, and in so doing, will continue to be persons worthy of being cared about regardless of the nature and direction of those solutions.

When the counselor establishes such a facilitating relationship with persons who are dying, questions of the quality of remaining life, dying a good death, and how to relate to family and friends are questions that are left to the individuals themselves. By freeing them to look openly within themselves, we allow them to bring out the natural positive direction to their lives and, in this case, to the dying stage of life. What is best is known only to them, and our purpose is only to allow that to open up.

RELATIONSHIP AS SELF-DEFINING PROCESS

Beyond the level of choosing direction, we move to the level of defining the self. Choosing direction can be conceived as moving the furniture around within one's present stage of development, whereas defining the self comes at the point of moving to a higher level of consciousness because of perceived dissatisfaction with the current one. The counseling relationship is experienced first as a self–other relationship, a freeing process that enables exploration of the deeper meaning of one's life. As time goes on, however, the relationship can become one in which individuals experience themselves as a part of a unit relationship, part of the *I–Thou*. At this point, therapy begins to move from an exploring of feelings and experiences to living in relationship with immediate experience. In this latter mode, the awareness of connectedness begins to come through.

Carse (1980) discussed the role that relationship plays in defining our selves: "To be a person we must exist in what for the moment we shall refer to as a web of connectedness with other persons" (p. 4). The web consists of dependency, along with freedom to enter into relationship or not, and it is the web of connectedness that defines our continuity, our personhood. Death has the immediate effect of revealing that interconnectedness of life. Often we do not know how closely our self-understanding is developed in relation to another person until that person has been taken by death or until we ourselves face death. Death can therefore be understood, in part, as irreversible damage to the web of connectedness between persons, to the continuity and definition of our very personhood.

So long as one looks at a relationship from a historical orientation, it will maintain a self–other quality—a relationship between two others that has continuing impact on the client based not on the moment of experiencing but on past dynamics that the client continues to use to define the self. When we learn to live each relationship in the now, to arise each day and begin a relationship as if it had no history, then we can define the self anew each day and through each relationship. Abuse from the past, disagreements from the past, low esteem from the past can all remain in the past. The self can be defined through the now relationship.

Imagine, for example, a woman in her late 30s who was sexually abused by her stepfather when she was a teen. In part because of this relationship, the client has developed feelings of self-disgust and low esteem. Furthermore, she is angry with her stepfather and consequently with much of the rest of the world. Her relationship with this man continues to be one colored by anger and self-degradation, and each time they meet she enters the relationship with a self that is defined in this way. If she could, however, meet the man who abused her without the memories from the past, if for example she could be given a short case of amnesia, how might she find the man? Caring, understanding, pleasant? How could she relate to the man? Could she be kind, could she listen to him without the need to be critical? Could there be a relationship that was to some degree positive in the sense that there was mutual caring and understanding? Quite possibly so, once the memories of the past were erased. If the stepfather could be experienced devoid of the history of abuse, that is, if he could be known only by what he brings to the present moment, he might be found as a person able to create a positive environment. People do change, and what the stepfather feels and believes might be quite different now from what it was 20 years ago. By the same thinking, could the stepdaughter allow herself to experience the positive feelings emanating from the stepfather without need to evaluate those feelings in terms of former experience and self-definitions? What is needed for this to occur is for her to come to a point of being able to live in the now.

Perhaps even more important, can this woman enter into relationships with others without assuming the label of "abused"? At the point that she enters counseling, the answer is most assuredly "No." She will bring with her an identity that includes her abusedness, part of which will likely be conscious and much of which she will be denying to awareness. The ability to set aside such past memories will seem an imponderable task—unrealistic and ultimately outside the realm of the achievable.

Yet this is what we as counselors must seek to do on our own part. We must ask ourselves whether we can enter into a relationship free to redefine ourselves through that relationship rather than having to live out an established identity. Can we allow ourselves to grow through the counseling relationship as much as we expect our client to grow? Can we let go of our own historical role and identity? Can we set aside the biases of the past, even though these may be transferred from other relationships rather than built on in a relationship with the clients themselves? In each session we must be able to be open to the clients without letting the knowledge we have gained from them intrude in a prejudicial and foreclosing manner. In short, we must live the relationship in the now, experiencing the client as an evolving person, not as an other that brings this or that characteristic, these feelings, or this problem. And we must be open to the redefinition of our own self that such an openness would demand. To be able to let go of the past and to accept a person only in the present moment is the essence of forgiveness.

One can make a comparison between being live and being on videotape in our relationships. It is a distinction between awareness of oneself in the moment and making choices from that basis and simply responding as in the past without present awareness. In the first instance, therapy becomes designed to help the person become more aware, more alive. But can each of us achieve such a status?

The starting point in bringing about meaningful change is a concern for one's life. Life changing means growth promoting. It means being able to be involved with one's life in a dynamic way. This consists of living the pain, the hope, the commitment, and the inwardness of one's life. But it does not mean continually reliving it. To live means to let go of the past because there is only the present. It means redefining the self through each new relationship.

Rogers tried to focus counseling and growth toward experiencing, awareness, sensing, and actualizing (self-responsibility). The reason for the decline in acceptance of Rogers' perspective is probably more a lack of "scientific aura" than anything else. Rogers' approach is too intuitive rather than rational, too subjective rather than objective, too phenomenal rather than behavioristic. It is also fraught with too much insecurity. To let go of the past and one's self to live in the present is an anxiety-producing proposition.

SUMMARY

If we start out as counselors thinking that therapy is designed to treat an illness, we will work with our client in one way. If we believe it is to correct certain developmental arrests or deficits, we will work in a different way. And if we understand therapy to be a process of facilitating a client's quest for greater wholeness, we will operate in an even different way. The way the counselor works when understanding the purpose of counseling to be one of facilitation is characterized by efforts to create a relationship that is growth producing. In this chapter, I have examined unconditional positive regard and empathic understanding as integral parts of the counseling relationship.

Bringing into awareness feelings and experiences that are presently hidden to consciousness is a necessary part of understanding the self on the way to letting go of that self in the interest of developing a new one at a higher level of consciousness. Exploration of one's experiences requires an atmosphere of freedom to look at the negative and anxiety-producing aspects of self that have either been denied awareness or have been repressed into the unconscious because they were perceived as a threat to one's sense of worth and belonging. When counselors are able to develop a relationship in which clients feel accepted and worthwhile regardless of what feelings and experiences they may have and express and in which they are understood from their own phenomenal frame of reference, the clients are able to try on different aspects of self; to explore openly feelings, values, and beliefs; and to explore the meaning of their existence. Through this process, they can evaluate and choose for themselves the direction that will be most beneficial to their own growth.

Caring for and prizing a person as a worthy human is a way of being, not a way of behaving. It must be consistent with the inner experience of the counselor. We must enter into relationship with our client with the mind of the beginner, able to shed any need to play the role of expert and professional therapist. It is necessary that we perceive the other persons as subjects struggling with their own meaning and identity rather than as objects to be analyzed, evaluated, and judged. If we are able to create such a climate, clients will be able to grow in the direction that is inherently a part of each of us. For the person who is terminally ill, to grow in this way until death defines quality of life and quality of dying.

Having looked at unconditional positive regard and empathic understanding as essential elements of the counseling relationship, I now move to the third element—communication of that positive regard and empathic understanding.

Chapter 11

Communication

When working with terminally ill patients from a facilitative approach, it is necessary for the counselor to bring to the counseling relationship feelings of unconditional positive regard and empathic understanding for the client. However, having such feelings and attitudes toward the person with whom one is working is not, in and of itself, enough to bring about changes toward positive growth; it is necessary to communicate these feelings to the client in such a way that they become an integral part of the client's experience of the relationship. The process of communication is the subject of this and the following chapter, in which I discuss communicating feelings of worth, caring, and understanding through verbal interaction (this chapter) and through guided imagery (chapter 12).

There is a danger when discussing how to communicate one's experience of the relationship that the process of communication itself will be perceived as a technique to be performed whether or not the conditions are a part of the counselor's own experience. The methods of response may become a substitute for the feelings and attitudes themselves, and the entire process will then degenerate into technique for technique's sake. This is exactly the situation that Rogers saw occur when he proposed nondirective techniques or responses as a way of communicating the therapeutic climate. His advocacy for creating a warm and accepting climate was distorted into the belief that counselors simply had to learn to use the techniques designed to communicate understanding and caring without regard to actual feelings and perceptions. *Why* nondirective techniques were used was lost in the process of focusing on *how* they were used.

Let us consider the first principle of communication, then, to be that whatever works to communicate the counselor's feelings of empathy and unconditional positive regard is appropriate. The suggestion of specific techniques serves only as a guide. Counselors, in evaluating their own responses to the client, must simply ask, "What was I experiencing? Did I communicate that experiencing? Was my response the best way to communicate it?" It is inappropriate to ask, for example, "Did I make a good restatement?" Evaluation of the quality of the response will take attention away from the relationship.

CONSCIOUS VERBAL COMMUNICATION

The discussion regarding the process of responding verbally to a client will be brief for two reasons: The subject has been thoroughly reviewed in a number of other books, and my intention here is not to teach techniques but to emphasize the importance of communicating positive feelings and empathy to the client. Therefore, I provide only suggestions and examples, not a definitive lesson on responding to a client. In the last analysis, each moment in a counseling experience must be judged within its own context in terms of whether the counselor was experiencing positive feelings for the client, whether what the client was feeling was understood, and whether the counselor's feelings and understanding were communicated. It is quite possible that making a restatement can, in a particular context, communicate a lack of warmth or that a clarification can communicate a lack of understanding.

As a general rule, responses that communicate acceptance are appropriate. By acceptance, I mean simply a communication of understanding what the client is feeling and expressing; that is, the counselor accepts that what is being expressed is the client's experience. Simple responses such as "I see," "I understand," or a short repeating of the client's words can express the counselor's willingness to listen and to attempt to grasp the meaning of what the person is saying. When clients are quite involved with expressing their experience and feelings, it may not be appropriate for the counselor to interrupt with his or her own responses, and making short acceptance responses can communicate that the counselor is listening, trying to understand, and that it is appropriate for the person to continue talking about the feelings.

Clarification responses are often appropriate in communicating a willingness to know what the other person is experiencing. They tell the person that the counselor wants to know what their feelings are and needs some help. The counselor is not completely sure what the person is saying and needs some clarification to more fully understand the client's experience. Such responses have the positive value of showing a willingness and desire to understand, but they have a negative aspect in that they also communicate that the counselor doesn't yet fully know what the person is expressing. If a woman says, "I don't know if I can get through this without some help," and the counselor is not sure what that means, he or she can request clarification by saying, "I'm not sure I know what you are saying. Do you mean you may want some medicine to put you to sleep?" Such a response shows that the counselor wants to understand what the woman is feeling but needs some clarification to do so. On the other hand, if the counselor knows from what the woman has previously said that the help she thinks she may need is sleep-producing pain medication, then it is more effective to directly communicate that: "You're not sure you can get through this without having enough medication to put you to sleep so that you do not have to endure the pain and agony." By making such a response when the person's experience is understood, the counselor communicates not just a desire to understand what the client is feeling but that he or she in fact does understand. In this way, there is a communication of seeming oneness in terms of working with the client's experience. The result is not an objective analysis made by an outsider but two people working together in an intimate relationship to understand and accept the client's inner experiencing.

Restating what the person has expressed and reflecting the feelings as they are brought forth are responses designed to communicate both understanding and caring. Such responses do not make for good normal conversation because they are focused solely on what one person is saying, but in the context of a relationship in which one's empathic understanding of the other person is of primary concern, they are extremely effective. So long as they are used at the appropriate time, that is, when individuals are exploring their own feelings in a meaningful way, they have the power to communicate "I am listening to you, I hear you, and what you are feeling and exploring is the most important thing right now." Such responses enhance the flow of exploration, encouraging increasingly deeper probing by the client. They communicate a willingness to let the client control the direction of the flow, thereby moving away from the concept of an expert who analyzes and interprets. Moreover, such responses communicate that the clients' own experiences are the most critical aspect in working through whatever crises they are dealing with.

Asking questions continues to be a controversial realm of communication in counseling. When the desired approach is perceived to be nondirective, there is a natural inclination to stay away from asking questions, as this causes the counselor to dictate the direction of the exploration. In some ways, however, this may be a false concern in that the direction the counselor may dictate could very well be one of increased understanding. To ask, "Have you thought about the option of . . ." or "What do you think might happen if you . . ." are questions that may increase the counselor's understanding of the person's experience and, in fact, may communicate that the counselor genuinely wants to understand, so much so that these questions are being asked about what the person is experiencing. The problem is not so much whether or not the counselor asks questions, but where the questions come from. So long as they come from the flow of exploration that is occurring within the person, they are likely to further the communication of understanding and caring. If, on the other hand, they come from a nonempathic, counselor-centered framework, they are likely to appear to have little to do with what the client is experiencing and may seem more like the questions of a treatment expert than those of someone attempting to understand the inner world of another person. This is an area in which it is easy to get trapped by the techniques themselves and to ignore the purpose that one has in working with the client. To avoid asking questions for the sake of not asking questions is as stultifying as forcing oneself to make a restatement of everything the client says. Neither case is natural, and in doing so the counselor would become a simple technician, responding in preconceived ways rather than living and responding in the moment of the counseling relationship.

People come into periods of crisis and terminal illness at different levels on the spectrum of consciousness. The person's current level will determine the effect of different kinds of responses in terms of communicating understanding and positive regard. To ask individuals to tell you how they are feeling about something, for example, to say, "Can you tell me how finding out you have cancer makes you feel?" is to assume that they have the capacity to look inside and know what they are feeling. It is to assume that these persons can relate visceral feelings to external events or that they can label the feelings. Such abilities come only as a person moves higher on the spectrum, developing the ability to be self-reflective, to know the self as subject rather than simply object. To a person who has not developed abilities to this level, asking "What do you feel about . . ." is to communicate a *lack* of understanding, not empathy. The counselor is essentially saying, "I don't know you well enough to realize that I am asking you to do something that is beyond your understanding."

One of the things that will occur when there is a high level of empathy is that the counselor will have an accurate sense of the way in which the person is processing the exploration that is occurring. When one responds, "You seem to be pretty angry about not being told what your treatment options are," it is necessary to also understand what this communication means to the client and how it will be processed internally. Does it trigger further inner exploration, or does it simply get filed as a labeled behavior? Does the person relate what you have said about being angry to what is felt inside or does he or she externalize it into a non-self objective experience? It is too easy for the counselor, not understanding the inner experience of the client, to assume that the reflection of the feelings is processed by the client in the same manner as the counselor would process it. That will only occur, however, if the client understands things at the same level of consciousness as does the counselor. True empathy means, in this case, that the counselor knows how the other person experiences and understands the reflection of feelings.

This relates to the question of making interpretations in the counseling relationship. It is generally considered, with good reason, that to interpret what the client is feeling or experiencing is to perceive the person from an external, evaluative orientation. The word *interpretation* itself means to make a judgment from an external position. Yet there is another side to the concept of interpretation. In the original psychotherapeutic sense, to make an interpretation was to understand what the clients were experiencing when the clients themselves did not consciously know and to communicate that knowing to the clients. If such knowing comes from an externally determined framework of understanding, one based on the "expert" knowing of the counselor, then the interpretation comes from a nonempathic source. However, if the knowing comes because the counselor is tuned into the feelings and experience of the client, and the counselor's interpretation is simply a realization of the client's experience that comes ahead of the client's own realization, then the interpretation can legitimately be classified as empathic. The question is whether the interpretation can be made in such a way as to communicate empathy rather than an external judgment.

In making such determination, counselors must be carefully focused on their own experiences. It is easy to believe that one's interpretation is based on an understanding of the client's inner experience when it is not. This is why the first condition of communication is to *be* empathic, to genuinely have an understanding that comes from focusing on and listening to the client's own internal world. Empathy is a way of being, and when it is a genuine part of the counselor, responses that are classified as interpretations will naturally be based on understanding the client as a unique person and not on preconceptions about people in general. Counselors must develop an ability to listen and hear what clients are experiencing and then trust themselves to respond spontaneously in an empathic manner. As Kapleau (1989) said, to wobble is to lose the effect of genuine understanding.

When interpretations come from an empathic orientation, they will be offered as tentative suggestions: "It seems to me that your pain is serving to help you not have to talk to your family" as opposed to "By having pain you keep yourself from having to talk to your family." The first statement communicates that the counselor perceives a feeling that is there but has not yet been recognized or expressed and is offering the perception as something to be considered by the client. The second communicates "Now I know what is going on within you, and I am going to tell you." The implication is that the counselor has figured out the client. The question then becomes not one of whether the interpretation is correct or incorrect, good or bad, but whether it comes from an empathic understanding of the experience of the client that lies hidden just beneath the surface and whether it can be communicated as based on an empathic understanding.

It is important to focus on the idea that the subject of an interpretation is the client's experiencing something that is hidden just under the surface of awareness. A person's natural inclination is to move to higher levels of self-awareness. As the freedom to explore the self becomes felt and the need to defend lessens, the natural direction will be toward increased self-exploration, increased perception of the self as subject, and increased awareness of feelings. The person will move toward a more internal locus of evaluation and toward self-reflective thinking. These are aspects of consciousness that will be strange to the person, however, and may be resisted even though there is a natural tendency in that direction. As the counselor understands these feelings to be ready to surface, interpretations made as empathic suggestions can both encourage more open exploration of the feelings and communicate that the counselor understands the hidden experiencing of the person even though it has not yet been expressed. The key is to understand the client well enough to know what the feelings are, to know that they are ready to surface and that the client is in a position to be able to work with and come to an acceptance of the feelings, and to know that the client has enough trust in the counselor to hear the suggestion in a nondefensive way. In this sense, the question is not whether a counselor should interpret a client's experience but what the counselor's awareness of the client is, how accurate it is, and what it demands in terms of a response.

What response is most appropriate at any given time can only be determined within the context of the moment in which the response is made. Counseling is relationship, and a great part of empathy is knowing the relationship. The ability of specific responses to further the communication of positive regard, the unconditionality of that regard, and empathic understanding is not within the responses themselves but within the meaning that the relationship has for both counselor and client. The ability to become more aware of one's inner experience and feelings depends on being able to let go of the need to defend the self and maintain a facade. It depends on there being a sense of deep trust that the other person can accept what one is experiencing and is able to know the meaning that the experiencing has in terms of one's self-identity. The freedom to explore the self within such a context is the reason for creating the facilitative climate I have been discussing. Knowing the relationship that has developed between counselor and client and working within that relationship is an integral part of the process of therapy. Responses cannot be appropriately made nor can they be evaluated with regard to their effectiveness outside the context of the relationship. To ask the question, "Are you afraid of dying?" cannot be evaluated as a response abstracted from the relationship in which it is presented. Whether it is appropriate depends not just on whether it is an issue in the present experience of the client but also on whether that client has a level of trust in the counselor that provides for an acceptance of such probing. Can the client trust the counselor to respond with acceptance and understanding to whatever the answer might be?

Counselors can comprehend and use the abilities related to the structures of levels on the spectrum of consciousness that are lower than the level at which they are living, but not those of a higher level. As one moves up the spectrum, the higher order structures incorporate the lower, but those that have not yet emerged from the deep-structure unconscious remain hidden and incomprehensible. Just as the people we work with are at different levels on the spectrum, so counselors are at different levels. Even though certification programs require advanced course work, which in turn requires a certain level of cognitive ability, it is still possible for persons whose consciousness is at the level of concrete operations to become counselors. Such people will have a difficult time creating a climate based on empathy because their ability to abstract themselves from their own perceptual framework in the interest of entering the other person's world will be limited. High levels of empathy require high levels of abstract thought so that we can see the world *as if* we were the other person. Levels of empathy that are even higher come from an ability to intuit the experiences and feelings of another person that lie hidden below the surface. Therefore, we must continually work to raise our own level of consciousness in the interest of becoming more empathic. Making what seem to be appropriate responses will not be satisfactory if the counselor continues to see the person as a separate object to be heard and the responses are simply at the level of overt hearing. Individuals must know, in a spiritual or transpersonal sense, the relationship that is present between them and others and respond spontaneously from within that knowledge. Within such a level of understanding and caring, the counselor will respond naturally at the level of the spectrum that is appropriate for the client. No analysis of where the client is on the spectrum will be necessary.

THE COUNSELOR–CLIENT RELATIONSHIP

In chapter 7, I briefly discussed the situation of Rob, a man who was dying of leukemia. We can see through this example how the relationship between counselor and client affects movement and the way in which the relationship grows. When I first met Rob I didn't know what he might be looking for in the way of help, and he very likely did not know what kind of help I might provide. He probably could not accurately verbalize what he himself was looking for, yet there was a desire on his part to establish a relationship and that desire was reciprocated by me. In this sense, we started as beginners, working our way toward greater wholeness moment by moment.

My goal in working with Rob was to understand him and be available as the situation called for. I did not have any ideas about what he needed to be able to more effectively deal with his illness or about what direction the relationship should take. I let Rob determine what we would talk about, that is, what aspects of himself he was willing for me to know, and given this choice, he first began to talk about the disease, the likelihood that he would die, and how he wanted to form a small group with other patients so they could help each other cope with what was happening to them. He talked about what he wanted his funeral to be like, who should take what part in it, and what it meant to him to be able to make such plans. For several weeks, our communication centered around these topics because they seemed to be of most immediate concern to Rob.

As his early reaction to the leukemia and the treatments subsided, Rob began to focus away from his feelings about death and dying, and he began to share with me information about his background and the effect that he perceived it to have had on who he was. Because Rob was highly verbal, self-reflective, and able to see himself as an active participant in his own life, he was able to take the lead in assuming the direction of our sessions. He was able to sense what was most important to him at the moment and to express it, exploring the deeper meaning below the conscious level of awareness. In this situation, I was able to communicate caring, feelings of worth, and a willingness to listen and understand through the primary use of clarification, restatement, and reflection of feeling. The use of these responses, however, was dictated by the level at which Rob was experiencing and expressing his life to me and not by any formula abstracted from the situation itself.

For nearly 4 months our counseling proceeded in this manner. No problems were solved because neither of us saw that as our goal. Rob's thinking was not corrected or altered in a direction that was more in keeping with "reality." Our time was spent simply building a relationship, one in which I increasingly understood Rob's perception of himself, the meaning that life had for him, where that meaning came from, and the direction in which he saw himself moving. In turn, he increasingly accepted me as a person who genuinely cared about what was happening to him and who was trying to understand his inner feelings. It was a relationship that we entered into for the sake of relationship alone, not one that was a vehicle for solving problems or correcting inadequacies. The relationship that I had with Rob and the process of communication that it entailed was characterized by four aspects that are pertinent to working with terminally ill persons.

The first of these relates to the nature of relationship that Rogers originally referred to as nondirective and later as client-centered. Even though these terms have come into poor repute and are generally not used, they have significant meaning that must not be overlooked. As Rob and I worked together building a positive relationship, he was given the freedom to bring out those aspects of himself that were of most concern at the time and especially those aspects that he was ready and willing to let surface and to let me hear. This is a substantial part of our clients' experience—not just what they are feeling but also what they are ready to let surface into awareness. What they perceive to be necessary for them to bring into consciousness, their struggle to allow it into awareness, and what they are willing to share with another person is as much a part of their experience as the content involved, and understanding this is as important to the counselor as is understanding the content. This aspect of the person's experience can only be known if clients are allowed the freedom to choose their own direction. If the counselor makes the determination as to what should be discussed, then this understanding will never be available. As Rob chose his own direction, it became clear that his first consideration was dying and what his death meant to him. It also became clear that his sense of identity was of concern, and particularly the question of whether or not he would be able to maintain the concept of himself as a self-directing person independent of his mother. My understanding of the importance of these issues to Rob and his level of readiness to let me know them became extremely important when he became severely depressed.

The second consideration in our relationship was the effect of the relationship itself without regard to content or its end product. A person's self develops through relationships with others, and in fact the self *is* those relationships as they are perceived and interpreted by the individual. A counseling relationship then is not just a vehicle for understanding but also is, in and of itself, a part of the world by which people define their selves. How clients perceive themselves in relationship with the counselor is a factor in how they conceptualize the self. The counselor cannot simply see the person as an object to be studied and evaluated because who the person is to some extent will be defined by the relationship with the counselor. Relationship is not a contact between two separate entities but a single event involving the two people as an integral whole.

The extent of the counseling relationship's effect will depend on how intense and intimate the relationship is, how important it is perceived to be by the client, and how it relates to other significant relationships in the client's life. To Rob, our relationship was extremely important because he had been stripped of many of the significant relationships that were important to his self-identity at the onset of his illness. Having had to leave the town where he was working, his job, and many of his friends, he was unable to continue to perceive himself, at least for the time being, as a part of these relationships. In such a void, it is understandable that a person would place more significance on the relationship with the counselor. This is not atypical of persons who are dying, because often and for several reasons, significant relationships in their lives are disrupted by the process of dying.

The relationship Rob and I created was one in which Rob perceived himself to be a worthwhile person, capable of making his own choices. It was one in which I communicated trust in his ability to find meaning through his own inner exploration without needing to depend on an outside source for definition. In such a climate, he was able to continue to use his own abilities and resources to explore and increase awareness of himself, and this was assimilated into his sense of self. When we began our relationship, Rob was in the early stages of experiencing himself as a self-directing, well esteemed, and, to some extent, self-actualizing individual. However, after he found out he had leukemia he began to question himself and his ability to live consistently within such a concept. He saw the possibility of not being able to be the subject of his life but instead reverting to the point where he was an object controlled by his need for security and belonging—a need that had led him to discontinue his growth at an earlier stage of his development. Having struggled through that crisis with great effort, he now perceived the danger of regression. The ability to see himself, instead, as able to direct his own exploration, evaluate his own experience, and to find acceptance in the process of doing so enabled him to maintain his hold on the self that he had discovered prior to his illness. In this sense, our relationship not only aided in Rob's process of exploration but was growth producing in and of itself.

A third aspect of the relationship that a counselor creates with clients is the importance of knowing how the clients perceive the counselor, knowing the degree of trust that they have in the counselor and their willingness to allow the counselor into their world of experience. In Rob's case, this aspect became important when he was depressed and did not want to communicate with anyone. At that point, there was nothing for me to rely on other than this experiential knowledge of our relationship. To be empathic and to be perceived as such, the way that I responded had to be based on an accurate sense of how Rob experienced me and our relationship together. This is a critical factor in working with persons who are severely depressed, particularly in response to a major loss. If one waits until the depression is already present to work with such persons, not only will it be very difficult to establish a relationship because of the lack of communication, but it will also be virtually impossible to understand and therefore to communicate understanding of what the person is experiencing, other than by guessing. With Rob, although I had little forewarning of the impending depression and, at the time, he did not want to tell me why he was depressed, I was able to understand his depression because I was aware of what he had been experiencing and what he had been feeling up to that point. This was not an educated guess based on knowledge of the stages that one goes through during a crisis but was actual awareness of what was occurring in Rob because I had come to know him empathically. Even more important, because I had developed an understanding of Rob's experiencing, his feelings about what was happening to him, and the meaning that it had for him, I was able to talk about these things without his having to tell me anything at the time. And because I was aware of the depth of our relationship, I was able to know the level of exploration and communication that was acceptable to him even when he would not respond. In other words, empathic understanding allowed me to continue to work with Rob at a meaningful and facilitative level at a time when he was noncommunicative.

This raises the fourth issue, that of how such communication occurs and what the consequences are. It is possible to make an educated guess as to what is depressing a person who is terminally ill, and this often may prove helpful. However, in such a case, any response to the person must remain in the realm of generalities and not refer to specific feelings and experiences, which can only be known from empathic understanding. This relates to the question of interpretation. Did I interpret, from my own frame of reference, what Rob was experiencing during his period of depression or did I know on an empathic basis? Was I making judgments from an external position and imposing them on Rob, justifying them on the basis that they *could* have been what he was experiencing? It is difficult, if not impossible, to actually know the degree to which one or the other was occurring, perhaps other than by examining the consequences and drawing inferences. In the actual circumstance, however, I made every effort to remember Rob's earlier expressions and to respond as if they had been made anew. Restatements and reflections were posed in an explorative manner rather than in an authoritative way. Such statements as "It's difficult right now to imagine going on, being able to get back to where you were before" and "Having to come back and live with your mother seems like a step backward and that's really hard to accept" were simply restatements of what Rob had himself expressed in earlier sessions. Given an understanding that he was feeling the loss of his independent self, it was possible to respond to the exact feelings that he had expressed earlier regarding that loss. In this sense, there was not so much an interpretation as a sensing of a continuing struggle to deal with these concerns.

Realizing that Rob was struggling with the issues of independence and the meaning that his life now had for him, I could recapitulate the exploration that occurred in prior sessions: "You have talked about not fearing death, yet not being ready to accept it, and it seems like right now you are struggling with those questions. Maybe they are even closer to the surface now than they have been before." Again, these were not statements that came from an external evaluation but statements that actually had been a part of the counseling process in previous sessions. They were based on knowledge that these were the questions that Rob was struggling with and of the direction that his struggle was taking. These statements are quite different from a response such as "It must be very difficult to have to accept not being able to go back with your friends." The last statement implies an external judging—"it must be"—which communicates something different from a response that actually reflected what Rob had shared. Compare that response with "You have talked about how difficult it is going to be not to be able to go back with your friends." This statement communicates that I had heard and accepted this as Rob's experience rather than that I was guessing on the basis of some external evaluative criterion.

The process of focusing developed by Gendlin and his colleagues (Gendlin, 1978) is aimed at helping a person bring experiential feelings into congruence with cognitive understanding. It involves, in part, getting a tentative handle on what one is feeling and then resonating that with the continuing experience until there is a felt congruence between what is going on in the mind and what is going on in the body. One doesn't simply know what the deep inner experience is but must continually work to get an accurate sense of it. It is a process of approximating the feeling as closely as possible, measuring that against the total experience, and correcting the labeling of the feeling on the basis of that measuring. This continues until there is a felt sense that what the person has called the feeling is, in fact, an accurate description of the actual experience. This is similar to the communication process that occurred with Rob during his depression. On the basis of my understanding of his inner experience, I would attempt to label what I sensed he was experiencing, for example, "You may be wondering if all the progress you have made in developing an independent life is going down the drain now." Rob would then resonate this with his inner feelings and respond accordingly: "I'm not sure it's all down the drain, but I sure don't feel very hopeful right now." My goal, then, would be to try to correct the labeling: "It seems to be more a fear that there is not much reason for hope than it is that you are certain things will never be the same." In this way, we worked together to bring into awareness exactly what Rob was feeling and what the specific source of the depression was.

The depression that occurs as a part of the loss process comes when there is a beginning realization that the old self is gone and that it can no longer be recaptured. Rob had struggled with the possibilities of returning to his job and friends, but the leukemia progressed in such a way that he became increasingly pessimistic that that would happen. The realization that his old self was gone came on him rather suddenly, precipitating the depression. In the struggle to maintain the old self, however, Rob had also naturally explored the possibility that he might not return to his job and friends, and there were times when he tentatively examined what that would mean. During the period of depression, then, we could reexplore those tentative ideas, but now they carried a sense of greater urgency. Again, knowing Rob's inner experience, I could respond, "You've talked before of the possibility of not being able to return to work and what that might mean, and I wonder if this is something that is on your mind now." I could not know if this was, in fact, on his mind, but I was aware that it was a continuing part of his struggle and would be very close to the surface. Such a response was able to communicate both an understanding that this was something that he was experiencing and could also encourage him to explore it further at a time when it was more crucial to his forward movement.

Working through the depression brought on by loss means grieving the loss of the self—letting go of what was and moving toward what can be. The person in crisis must have the freedom to do this, but when counselors understand the specific nature of the struggle, they can facilitate this process by responding to the experiencing that is going on inside the silent client. In the absence of this knowing, the counselor can only sit and wait for the processing to occur at its own inner pace. With Rob, the period of depression was simply a continuation of our work together, with me taking more of the lead because sadness, apathy, and withdrawal had lessened Rob's ability to communicate. These sessions were a natural and continuing part of the exploration we had been doing for several months, although now the focus took a different direction—that of looking past the predisease self. My goal during this time was the same, to understand and to communicate my understanding and positive regard to Rob. The way that I did this was not significantly different than it had been prior to the depression, and in this way, movement through the loss process was natural and continuous. The periods of anger and frustration, bargaining, and depression are not discrete happenings but are simply different phases of an overall movement.

Rob came through the depression with a different outlook. He had accepted that he would not go back to work and to the friends with whom he had been so close. More important, he was able to give up the need for the esteem that these relationships afforded him. It was not the friendships and the job that Rob gave up, but his need for the continuing sense of positive self-esteem that these friendships supported. He was able to move to a higher level of self-determination, in which he was more concerned about actualizing the potential he had as a human being. In the time he had left, he undertook several projects that were more altruistic and less ego-centered. He had satisfied himself to an extent that was adequate for him to feel that he was an esteemed and worthwhile person and that he did not need to continue to seek confirmation of this. This provided a sense of quality to Rob's life, enabling him to use the potential that was inherent within him. No such sense of quality and satisfaction could have been gained other than by this movement to a higher level of consciousness.

SUMMARY

Growth, and therefore quality of life, is facilitated through a relationship that is based on genuine caring for and understanding of the inner experience of the other person. Communication of these aspects of relationship is necessary to the process of facilitation. Although there are certain responses a counselor can make that will generally further such communication, and other responses that can detract from the therapeutic relationship, the appropriate way for the counselor to respond can only be determined on the basis of the client's experience within the moment. Therefore, as counselors we must focus on our goal of creating the relationship and not on making specific kinds of responses. We must continually ask, "Am I responding in a way that will communicate my understanding and caring?" If the answer to that question is positive—I do understand and care—then we will be facilitating our clients' growth.

Chapter 12

The Use of Imagery

The use of guided imagery as an adjunct to counseling has become increasingly common. Used properly, it has the capacity to significantly increase a person's awareness of feelings and experiences and to facilitate the person's growth. The term itself, however, implies a focus completely different from the client-centered orientation that is part of a facilitative approach. To guide imagery implies that the counselor knows the direction that the imagery should take and, like an expert, will guide the client to a successful solution. As discussed in relation to the use of interpretation, however, imagery has the power to facilitate exploration, awareness, and acceptance in a way that is different from, and in many cases more effective than, the strictly verbal communication that has traditionally been the essence of counseling.

Guided imagery, or visualization, is the process of helping a person explore the self and bring about changes through the structure of imagination. It is simply a different mode for apprehending and processing data. The ability to form internal images comes into being at an early level of development, preceding the use of language. It appears during the phantasmic structural level on the spectrum of consciousness, just before the introduction of language at the representative mind level, and the ability to use that language to do operational thinking at the rule/role mind level (Wilber, 1983). This does not mean that the use of imagery within a counseling context should be restricted to persons who have not developed higher levels of thought, however. Lower structures are maintained and incorporated into higher levels of consciousness, so that once the ability to use images has been developed at the early stages, it remains as a structure to be used where appropriate at the higher levels. Concrete objects, abstract concepts, and the transcendent nature of the self are equally available to the process of imagination.

When a person is directed to imagine the destruction of cancer cells in the site of a tumor, and that imagining involves white blood cells taking the form of little men who eat the bad cells, this is a use of imagery at a very concrete level of operation. On the other hand, if a person imagines the spiritual connection among all persons filling the body/mind/spirit with love and forgiveness, thereby creating an inner healing energy, this is imagery at an abstract and holistic level. Each image may be effective in fighting cancer, but they operate at different levels of the spectrum. One can create internal images of a person-God who looks after His separate children, and one can create an image of a unity in which there is no separation between self and other, person and God. If the latter image is based not on cognitive belief in a transcendent realm of being but on a contemplative knowing of the higher realm, then it represents the use of imagery at a high level on the spectrum of consciousness. Imagery is simply one way of working with data, with the level of its use being determined by its contents and processes.

Working within the mode of imagery can provide a direct and holistic apprehension, without the intervention of linear thinking. One explores the self by means of mental images rather than cognitive concepts. Operational thinking can be used to evaluate, alter, understand, and otherwise work with the awareness that comes from imagery, but the imagery itself is different from the operational thinking. The important point here is that the distortions we develop to protect or defend our self-concept come from the realm of operational thinking. Rationalization, intellectualization, projection, introjection and other defensive maneuvers come through the power of the reasoning mind. Even the process of denial requires an intellectual assessment that the experience would be better left out of consciousness. By whatever name we call it—facade, mask, persona, role—the self that we allow the outside world to see and, in fact, the one we accept as our own concept of self is developed through the rational powers of the mind. The child whose level of development is presymbolic and prior to language, whose highest level of data apprehension is through images, is not yet capable of developing such a facade.

Because imagery does not involve the cognitive reasoning of symbolic language, its use as a means of exploring the self has the power to bypass the strategies of defense that are part of verbal interaction. One can allow the images of self to come into awareness out of the realm of the unconscious, without the mediating censorship of cognitive evaluation. In that sense, the use of imagery does not involve defensiveness, whereas conscious verbal exploration does. When counseling is centered in the latter realm, the counselor and client must continually work to overcome the distortions, whereas with imagery, perceptions of the self come into awareness spontaneously and holistically, leaving little room for distortion.

When awareness comes through imaging, it is much like that which comes through dreaming in that it is real at the moment it is occurring but may or may not be remembered in the conscious mind after the imaging period is over. Distortion can be applied after the fact of imaging; that is, the conscious thinking mind can deny the images access to consciousness or can distort them as they are allowed into the conscious mind, but the initial awareness that comes during the process of imagery is undistorted. The question then can be raised as to the benefit of imagery if the awareness that is gained can be distorted before it becomes a part of the consciousness of the individual. There are two parts to the answer. First, knowledge that comes through the process of imagery is not always distorted or denied access to the conscious mind. In many cases, what is brought forth during the imaging is allowed to remain as a part of conscious awareness and becomes available for the person to use as a means of increasing knowledge of the self. The second part of the answer is perhaps more important, however. Imagery is not limited to increasing awareness but also has the capacity to help a person in the process of acceptance and actualization. Through the process of imaging, the person may very well be able to alter perceptions and feelings in such a way as to lead to movement toward greater health, without having to consciously process the self-data through the power of the rational thinking mind. Awareness, acceptance, and change can all come about at the unconscious level.

Take as an example an individual with a terminal illness who is struggling with the fear of death. Counselors have at least three choices for helping such a person work with this fear. We can ask the person to directly discuss what meaning death has, trying to help in the process of overcoming the resistances that are present and that inhibit the ability to adequately explore the issue. There may be an unwillingness by the person to discuss what this means, or if there is a willingness, it may be distorted in such a way that the true meaning remains hidden. The person may not have the ability to cognitively understand whatever it is that death means; this may be a conceptualization that is beyond the person's level of consciousness. Therefore, even though such an approach seems most direct and straightforward, it well may be beyond the scope of the person with whom the counselor is working.

A second course of action is to transfer the meaning of death and dying into a symbolic representation, for example, by asking the person to think about his or her own funeral, moving through it step by step, and talking about the meaning that this has for the person. Often in such a case, the word *image* or *imagination* is used in the directive, such as, "Imagine yourself at your own funeral." This is simply a way of transferring the meaning of death from the abstract conceptualization of the first case to the secondary and more concrete process of using a tangible symbol to represent what was first presented in the abstract. The counselor is still dealing with cognitive operations, but at a different level. The counselor is still working in the realm of the rational mind where the person has the ability to distort the meaning. The drawing up of an image does not, in and of itself, constitute a transfer from the cognitive realm to that of direct perception. The difference is not simply in the process by which the content is brought forth but, more important, is in the process by which the content is assimilated.

The use of guided imagery should take the processing of the person's inner contents out of the realm of the rational mind and into the realm of the holistic, intuitive mind. This is the third means of dealing with the idea of death. If a person is guided, for example, to imagine his or her funeral as a symbol of being dead and to bring forth such a vision without analyzing or evaluating, he or she can directly apprehend the experience of being dead. This is a whole-person experience rather than an intellectual exercise, and acceptance of the meaning that comes through the imagery comes as direct experiential insight. Through the imagery the person grasps an undistorted knowledge of the meaning that death has for him or her, and this experience can be incorporated into relationship to the self without resistance. When the imagery process ends, the person may or may not be able to recall the total imagery and feelings associated with it: The person may recall it but not want to share it with the counselor, or the person may bring it forth into the counseling session to be dealt with there on a verbal basis. Whichever option the individual chooses, however, the effects of the imagery will be significant.

What has just been described is not empirical knowledge of the process but is inferred from the experience of many. *What* happens during imagery remains in the realm of hypothesis, but there is considerable evidence regarding the changes that occur in people after they have gone through a guided imagery experience. Achterberg (1985) said that imagery is the energy that directs the movement of our mind, body, and spirit. It has the power to change beliefs, values, and personal mythologies. Often after people go through the experience of guided imagery, they find it difficult to remember or describe the visualizations, or at least all of them, but there is a noticeable change in their feelings and behaviors. A person may experience less worry as a result of guided imagery, an experience that can be substantiated with biofeedback. Or, in the case of imagery used to help a person stop smoking, the person may quit even without remembering many of the visual symbols that occurred during the guided imagery. The changes that occur can be substantiated and often logically inferred to be the result of the imagery process, even though the way the changes occur is not fully known.

Bloomfield (1983) noted that Western hypnotists tend to focus on the techniques of trance induction and behavior change, whereas those in Eastern societies tend more toward a belief in the development of inner powers—a kind of energy that enables them to communicate with and affect the minds of others.

With the continuing development of imagery practices, however, practitioners in the West have also become more concerned with processes of internal change. Suggestions (direct or indirect), metaphors, imagery of rituals, and other procedures are all designed to change beliefs, personal paradigms and mythologies, and perceptual orientations in ways that benefit the person in the growth of consciousness. Symbols and images are vehicles for conceptions, which may be rational–linguistic, imaginal–intuitive, or feeling–evaluative. The counselor's goal is to make these symbols imaginal–intuitive, allowing the person to directly assimilate new awarenesses into relationship to the self.

Certain principles regarding the use of imagery need to be mentioned. For guided imagery to fit into a facilitative approach, it must promote self-direction, it must be individualized, and it must further the creation of a positive relationship, that is, it must communicate empathy and unconditional positive regard.

SELF-DIRECTION

I mentioned earlier that the term *guided* carries a connotation that the person who is guiding the imagery is directing the process in an authoritative, treatment-oriented way. In fact, many persons, particularly those who are faced with a life-threatening illness, accept the use of the procedure because they have a belief, or hope, that the expert is going to do something to them that will help. This is typical of the developmental stage in which persons perceive themselves to be externally controlled objects rather than subjects whose direction is based on an inner determination. This expectation is not, however, different from expectations that can arise when the mode of communication is conscious verbal interaction rather than guided imagery. The same persons will still expect the counselor to do something to them to bring about change.

The term *autogenics* was used by Johannes Schultz in referring to guided imagery but has not appeared to any significant extent in the literature in recent years (Pelletier, 1977). The process to which the term refers has its own characteristics and is somewhat different than current practices, but the process is not so different that the use of *autogenics* as an alternative term for *guided imagery* cannot be justified. There is certainly some merit to using the word *autogenics* to describe the general process of imaging or visualization because it literally means that the self is the source, that is, that the person doing the autogenics or imaging is the source and effect of the images. The counselor, or whoever is doing the guiding of the imagery, is simply facilitating the other's own process of healing. If the client can come to understand that he or she is actively directing the process and is the source of whatever change results, then there will also be an increased sense of inner control, which in and of itself will be a partial basis for growth.

Like most of counseling, or growth in general, the use of imagery is something that is often not effective as a one-time thing. In training to run a marathon, a person, over a period of time, gets the body accustomed to reacting in ways appropriate for long-distance running. In a similar fashion, imagery is a process of training the body, mind, and spirit to perceive and respond in ways that are appropriate to an on-going pattern of increased awareness of the total self. Though the counselor may guide the imagery during the counseling session, the client must be responsible for the process at other times if there is to be a pattern of continual, day-to-day imaging. As this pattern continues, the client will become more aware of being his or her own source of growth rather than simply being the object of the counselor's expert direction. The client will become continually more accepting of the idea that there is something that he or she can do independently to bring about positive changes. Such an awareness is consistent with movement from a perception of the self as object with an external locus of control to one of self as subject with an increasing internal locus of control. This awareness, in and of itself, constitutes movement up the spectrum of consciousness. As this awareness becomes incorporated into the self, the client's perception of self will change accordingly. Regardless of the specific changes resulting from the content of the imagery and the way that content is assimilated, the perception of increasing control of one's own life will be a positive outcome. In this sense, the term *autogenics* may be more descriptive than *guided imagery* or *visualization.*

In counseling, whether or not we are using the process of imagery, our goal is to facilitate movement up the spectrum of consciousness, which involves helping clients increase their ability to become more introspective and self-directing. It is not the content that the person learns about the self that constitutes growth, but the process of becoming more aware and whole. We have within ourselves, in the ground unconscious, all of the power and resources necessary to this growth. It is a matter of bringing them forth into the conscious. It is in this process that imagery is especially helpful. Erickson (Erickson & Rossi, 1983) referred to the hypnotherapeutic process he uses as *utilization* because it is designed to enable or facilitate people in utilizing their own inner resources, even when those are unknown to the counselor. According to Erickson, results in psychotherapy derive only from the client's activity. The counselor merely stimulates or facilitates this activity, often without even knowing what that activity may be. The counselor's purpose in using hypnosis (imagery) is to communicate ideas and understandings to get clients to utilize competencies that exist within them at both the psychological and physiological levels (Erickson & Rossi, 1983).

INDIVIDUALIZATION

If we can view imagery, or autogenics, in this fashion, then we can use it to further both the process of healing the sickness that the person is dealing with and to increase the growth that will come from a greater sense of inner control. This also implies, however, that the use of autogenics must be individualized to the person involved for such an orientation to prevail. Although we can draw on

the knowledge of the common structures of the psyche to create effective visualizations, the complete process involves filling out the structures with content
and meaning from the surface level of consciousness, and this, of course, can
only come from an understanding of the contents and meanings that are specific
to the person with whom we are working.

There are many tapes available for use with guided imagery, but obviously
these have not been made with any sense of individualization. Because of this,
their effectiveness is limited. Use of these tapes is akin to counseling with a
stock list of verbal responses and expecting the client to react to them without
any continuity or adjustments for the client's own particular needs. As a simple
example, in a tape made for common use, the person directing the visualization
might direct the imagers to allow themselves to be in a comfortable sanctuary
where they can be relaxed and at peace. If the procedure is built on a personal
knowing of the client, however, the counselor can know exactly where that
sanctuary might be, what its characteristics are, and in what way it is relaxing
and peaceful for the client. Then the counselor can make the guiding of the
imagery much more attuned to the specific inner framework of the client. This
will match up with the client's own cognitive and emotional sensing and will
create a feeling of empathy, as well as making the visualization more real to the
client.

Understanding a client from an empathic orientation involves, at the deeper
levels, a knowing (not a guessing or interpreting) of the current inner experience of the person. Grinder and Bandler (1981) talked of matching when doing
visualization (hypnosis) with another person. Such aspects as talking at a pace
appropriate to the level of concentration of the person, matching up with the
sensory mode that the person is using (i.e., talking about seeing things rather
than hearing things if that is the present internal frame of reference of the
visualizer), and making sure that what we say does not contradict what the person
is feeling (e.g., not saying "You are feeling relaxed" if, in fact, the person is quite
tense at the moment). At an outward sensory level, this is an understanding of
what the client is experiencing. We simply need to take our understanding to as
deep a level as is possible, and this can only be done through individualizing the
process. The model then becomes this: The counselor works with the client,
empathically understanding where that client is, and then uses the imagery in
whatever way that understanding calls for. This could be pain relief, anxiety
relief, physical healing, spiritual healing, acceptance of self, or something else.
To be most effective, the imagery should be done in the moment on the basis of
the counselor's awareness of the client's present experience.

COMMUNICATION OF EMPATHY
AND UNCONDITIONAL POSITIVE REGARD

Imagery can be technique *or* it can be a process of communicating relationship
that goes beyond normal, verbal, separate-self communication. It must first of all

be individualized and spontaneous, coming from an understanding of the other person, but to be truly facilitative, it must also transcend the separateness of the guider and the guided. Imagery will strengthen the experiencing of relationship if the counselor goes beyond talking to the "other" person and uses the imagery to enter into a direct, experiential relationship of connectedness with the client.

The inward journey into what we call the unconscious is not a spiral descent into an isolated cell but a discovery of the variety of ways in which the individual self is connected to the whole, and consequently it is the discovery of the way in which a person can abandon the ignorant and doomed attempts to preserve the self-contradictory existence of the individualized ego (Carse, 1980). Imagery is a means of facilitating that inward journey for the client, and it frees the person to transcend surface-structure alienation, allowing the experience of deep-structure connection to unfold. The dualities, boundaries, and illusions that one develops to maintain and enhance the self are abandoned within a relationship that transcends the *I–It* relationship. When one experiences connection *without* condition, the need for such boundaries fades.

Suspension of rational thinking during guided imagery also leads to the suspension of analysis of other persons and the relationship that the imager experiences with them at the surface level. This opens up the possibility of an increased sense of *I–Thou* connectedness, which is the essence of the facilitative healing power. It is not the guided imagery (or the hypnotic trance, the shamanic state of consciousness, the meditative state) that heals. Imagery is only the vehicle. Healing comes through an experience of the deep-structure connectedness, which removes the barriers and defenses to healing. At the surface-structure level, unconditional positive regard removes the need for maintaining nonhealing defenses. Connectedness (an experience of unity) removes those barriers at the deep-structure level.

Delores was a person who had grown up with very little sense of self-trust and no sense of autonomy. She entered the crisis of dying with what one might describe as very little coping power. At the beginning of our relationship, she was bothered by both a tremendous fear and a deep sadness at her impending loss of life. She appeared almost immobilized by an inability to make any decisions, to take any actions that might alleviate her condition, or to even explore what the possibilities might be. Our first two sessions were spent primarily with her expressing feelings of despair and hopelessness.

When I asked Delores what she was looking for in counseling, she stated that she did not know but that she just couldn't go on living this way. She talked about her faith in God, that it was being severely tested. She indicated that she was really questioning if there was a God, and the questioning itself was adding to her anxiety and despair. As we continued to talk, her lack of trust in herself to make decisions or take control of her life became clear, although where such feelings and beliefs originated did not come into the discussion. She stayed in the present, continually reviewing what was to her a hopeless and frightening situation.

During our third session together, I asked Delores if she would like to do some imagery. She had a vague idea of what imagery was (she sensed it was designed to relieve anxiety and perhaps her despair), and she said that she would be willing to do that. During the first period of imagery, we simply worked on developing a greater sense of calm and peacefulness in Delores, in reaffirming her present feelings of hopelessness, and doing some simple affirmations focused on her ability to determine for herself what might be the direction she wanted to go with her life. One of the important things in regard to the imagery at this point is that the last of these things, affirming her ability to control her life, was something that did not fit her current concept of self and would most likely have been denied or otherwise defended against if it had been presented in a traditional verbal counseling context.

In future sessions, we continued to use imagery to help Delores focus inward in ways that were not available otherwise. I worked from an understanding that she had little confidence in herself, felt that she could not control any significant aspects of her life, was totally at the mercy of her disease, and felt hopeless and depressed about the situation. During the imagery, these understandings were reaffirmed to continue a sense of understanding. We also explored the deep-structure connectedness that I assumed was there simply because it was a part of the ground unconscious. Delores was allowed to relate to persons or figures that she perceived to be important to her and to become aware of their caring and concern for her. No attempt was made to suggest solutions to Delores' hopelessness or lack of autonomy. The goal was to let her experience the sense of relationship and connectedness that was, at the time that counseling began, hidden from her awareness. It was this experiencing of connectedness that I assumed would have the power to enable Delores to work toward some greater feeling of trust and control. The imagery was simply a means of more efficiently helping her experience the relationship of unconditional caring and understanding. We were doing at the level of holistic, intuitive, direct experiencing what Rogers has advocated be done at the level of verbal, conscious counseling.

Delores' sense of hopelessness and despair gradually faded. It became much easier for her to talk about her disease and the course it would probably take. She began to talk about death in a more calm and peaceful way. Day to day events in her life did not change, and in most ways, she remained seemingly dependent and untrusting in herself when she would talk of decisions that had to be made, from those related to treatments to those focused on taking care of the house and her husband. Yet she did seem to have a much greater sense of trust in herself to die in a manner suitable to her. In the last major decision she had to make in her life, there did seem to be a significant difference in her level of self-trust.

SUMMARY

Guided imagery, or visualization, is not a panacea. At times it can even be counterproductive, as when a person is actively and positively exploring life and its meaning at a conscious, verbal level. On the other hand, it does give one access to the nondefensive level of consciousness where direct experiencing occurs.

During imagery, we cannot tell clients that we care and understand and expect them to accept this any more than we can do so at a conscious level in the traditional counseling relationship. What we can do in imagery is to facilitate the client's becoming aware of conditions that already exist but of which awareness is hidden because of a need to defend. In the traditional counseling mode, the counselor creates a positive relationship and lets the client experience it. In imagery, the counselor facilitates the client in bringing forth positive and growth-producing relationships that already exist but are denied to normal awareness. In many cases, these relationships are more potent than the relationship created by the counselor because they have, either inherently or experientially, more meaning than that created only in the counseling milieu.

If as counselors we can perceive guided imagery as a process of communication, occurring at a different level than that of the traditional counseling situation, and not relegate it to the level of technique, it can be a significant and powerful addition to our ability to facilitate our clients' growth.

Chapter 13

The Individuality of Death

Dying is an individual matter. Even though we can discuss common elements and find patterns that are similar from individual to individual, in the final analysis, we all will die in our own way. In this chapter, I share the experience of one person with whom I worked, a man who died in his own way. His story presents some of the common issues and directions discussed in this book but also demonstrates the individual nature of dealing with a terminal illness.

I have altered certain aspects of Art's story for the purpose of anonymity (including his name), but the crucial factors remain the same. I have not presented any verbatim conversations so as to focus not on the techniques I used but on the holistic aspect of Art's struggle. What occurred within Art's life is the important issue.

BEGINNING OF THE RELATIONSHIP

Art was a young man I worked with for nearly 2 years. When we first met, he had just been told he had a malignant brain tumor, which could not be fully removed and which would, in all likelihood, eventually cause his death. At the time that we first began our relationship, he seemed to be primarily concerned with needs of belonging and affiliation, of being a part of a family and having a place in the world of work that he could consider his own niche. In the 2 years that Art struggled with the crisis of dying, however, he was able to move to a level of existence where his primary concern was using his potential in an altruistic, self-transcending way. Perhaps as much as any person I have worked with, Art demonstrated the ability to use the time of dying to transcend the current level of consciousness and live at a higher level, at least for a short period.

I first talked with Art the morning after he had been told his diagnosis. He was in his hospital room, and the doctor had asked that I visit him. He was surprisingly (at least to me) bright and cheerful, and he was very willing to talk to me. He informed me almost immediately of his tumor and told me that the doctor had said that even though they would not be able to remove the tumor, radiation could perhaps allow him several years of normal life. These things were very difficult to predict, he had been told.

During the first session, Art talked little about the disease, the upcoming treatments, or the meaning that all of this had for him. His basic comment was that he was confident that he would have at least several years and that perhaps in that time they would find some new treatment that would lead to a cure for him. Rather than wanting to talk about his tumor and the future, he simply shared with me some of the things about himself that seemed particularly important to him at that time. I visited with him twice more while he was in the hospital. During those three sessions, it became clear that his marriage was on shaky ground; his wife was not sure she loved him and was thinking that maybe they should get divorced. He also told me that his relationship with his parents was poor, that he saw them very little because they did not approve of his marriage, and that they continually degraded him because he had not been as successful in his vocation as they had hoped.

Art told me that he had dropped out of college to get married and had not been able to fulfill his goal of becoming an architect. Instead, he had found a job as a draftsman, which he did not like. It continually reminded him of his unfulfilled goal, he found it too boring, and he did not relate well with his fellow workers. He very much would have liked to finish college and get a better job, but he perceived that to be out of the question because of his family's financial situation.

With regard to his marriage, Art agreed that perhaps a divorce was the thing for them, although he said he still loved his wife and would like to reach a reconciliation. That didn't seem likely, but he felt that further discussion about the divorce would be put off for at least a while because of the tumor, the impending treatments, and the unknown future.

At the end of these three sessions, we had not discussed the tumor or the treatments, nor had we talked about what was likely to happen to Art or what that meant to him. He was ready to leave the hospital at that time, as treatments would not begin for a couple of weeks. He said that he enjoyed talking to me during those first three days in the hospital, but he didn't feel he had a problem at that time and didn't see any reason to continue. He said that quite likely he would want to talk to me in the future but not at the present time.

Three aspects of this initial part of the relationship are significant. The first is that Art appeared to be in some denial, not of what his disease and diagnosis was, but of the likelihood that the tumor would lead to death. As is fairly common, Art was optimistic at that point that the best scenario would ensue and that it was not yet time to think about or discuss death. He perceived the tumor as a disruption to his life (perhaps even a welcome one), a circumstance that would cause him some pain and discomfort because of the treatments, but he did not perceive it as life-threatening. That aspect was blocked from his awareness.

At the same time, Art was willing to enter into a relationship with me. Certainly the convenience of his being in the hospital made it easier, yet he seemed to genuinely want to talk to me about himself and his family situation, even though he did not perceive that he needed counseling at that time. Because of this, we were able to establish the beginning of a relationship that would be important later.

The second aspect of this initial relationship concerns what Art was struggling with in life and where he was on the spectrum of consciousness. He entered the crisis of a life-threatening illness in the midst of another major crisis, the one centered around his marriage. In fact, the disease was a benefit to Art because it served to temporarily bring the marriage back to an earlier point. Whereas his wife (Nancy) did not feel she loved him and did not want to stay married, her initial reaction to the cancer was to feel guilty, which resulted in behaviors that communicated a restoring of earlier feelings of fondness, if not love. She responded to Art with much greater care, concern, and attention, which he interpreted as a return to more positive feelings on Nancy's part. As time went on, however, it became obvious to Art that Nancy's feelings were not genuine and were, in fact, based on a sense of guilt.

At the time that we began our relationship, Art perceived himself to be at a place in life where he could find little sense of belonging, of being a member of any significant group. He was alienated from his parents (he had no siblings), he was alienated from his immediate family (he had three children whom he perceived to be aligned with their mother), and he never felt he belonged on the job, primarily because it was only a job and not a profession, which could have given him a greater sense of belonging. It seemed that part of Art's problem in getting along with his coworkers was a feeling that if he liked his job, he would lose all reason to continue to want to pursue his career as an architect. As was revealed later in our relationship, Art had never felt any significant sense of belonging, either with his family or among his friends in school.

Art appeared to be living at a low level within the personal realm of the spectrum of consciousness. His concerns were with belonging and esteem, he was other-directed in his values, and his way of interacting with the world was concrete and behaviorally oriented. His approach to the world and his own life was one that could be characterized as problem-solving, one that called for very concrete solutions.

A final consideration regarding these first contacts with Art has to do with the process. As I have indicated, Art said he did not want to be in a counseling relationship, yet he was very willing to talk to me. We talked little about his illness or about death and dying. He seemed to want to share his current situation regarding family and work and to discuss the problems and concerns he had with these. My goal was simply to understand as best I could what his experience was and to communicate a desire to be available to him for whatever he might want to work on. It was a time when Art was denying the total reality of his illness, yet he was willing to enter into a relationship with me that would serve us later.

THE INTERIM PERIOD

Art and I saw each other only periodically during the first year after his diagnosis. The initial treatments were very positive, and his tumor remained well under control during that time. Various small problems necessitated his return to the hospital for short periods on three different occasions, and during those times we talked. Much of what I know of this period I learned after we became more involved during the second year of his illness.

The first year after Art found out he had a brain tumor was spent trying to reestablish good relations with his parents and working to save his marriage. Art told me that he spent a number of evenings with his mother and father, during which he would talk about his goals, his marriage, and his job. He said that they discussed these things in a very concrete manner, without any emotional involvement. He and his parents never talked about feelings, particularly those that related to their relationship with each other. Art believed that both of his parents were very nonfeeling persons and that they had learned over the years not to show emotions.

No matter how much effort Art made to communicate his side of the story, he felt that they could not forgive him for having married Nancy (the reasons were never clear, although Art believed it was because they felt that Nancy had forced the marriage and that the marriage had caused him not to achieve his goals). In addition, they could not get over their disappointment that Art had not completed college and had not become more successful in their eyes. These seemed to be unresolvable issues as far as Art could see.

With regard to his marriage, Art said that the first few weeks following his diagnosis were much better. Nancy showed considerably more caring than before, and there was no talk of divorce. As time went on, however, and the immediacy of the illness began to wane, old feelings and behaviors began to reappear. Art said the bickering increased and indications of a lack of love and caring on Nancy's part surfaced again. During the second 6 months of that first year, communication between Nancy and Art decreased significantly, and they spent less and less time together. Nancy and the children began to develop lives that did not include Art, and in turn, he became more of a single person. He said that divorce was not discussed during this time, and he suspected it was because Nancy was quite uncertain as to his prognosis and felt it was better to "weather the storm."

Just slightly over 1 year after the original finding of the brain tumor, the doctors found that it was growing again. They told Art that it would be difficult to control the growth over a long period and that he might only live 1 or 2 more years. At this point, Art said he would like to enter into a counseling relationship with me.

It is difficult to understand completely the dynamics of this period of Art's life because we had so little contact. It seems that the crisis brought about by the threat to his life caused a renewed effort to consolidate his self at the level of belonging. Art had never satisfied this need; he had never felt a sense of belonging because he was never accepted as a part of those groups that were crucial to his self-concept. His efforts were toward conforming to the expectations of others, and his values were those that were based on the approval of others. These are all transitional aspects of a low level within the personal realm of development.

During the first year following the discovery of his tumor, Art was no more successful in achieving a sense of belonging than he had been prior to that time. He was not able to reconcile the roles he was expected to play to be accepted by those with whom he was most concerned. He would have liked to attain a college degree, thereby approaching some sense of acceptance from his parents, but he was unable to do so. He would have liked to reestablish a positive marriage but was unable to do so because he could not satisfy the demands of his wife. (What those demands were is not important. It is enough to know that he did not have the ability to fulfill the role she demanded.) Art was faced with a no-win situation. He did not feel himself to be accepted, and he could not perform the behaviors necessary to do so. As he entered the second stage of his crisis of dying, he was no closer to a sense of belonging, but he was much closer to realizing that he would not achieve this with his parents, his wife, or his work.

THE MIDDLE PHASE

During the first session that we had after Art found out the tumor was growing again and that his illness was in fact terminal, we talked a little bit about what this meant to him. His feelings were fairly general and confused. He said that he knew he would die but was still hopeful that he could think in terms of at least 5 years, even though the doctor had indicated the likelihood was no more than about 2. His first reaction was that this changed his relationship with his wife, but he didn't quite know how. Even more important at that moment, he realized he quite possibly would not have to return to work, and for him, this was a real positive aspect of the crisis. (He had only been able to work on and off during the first year because of the need for treatments and some minor health problems that necessitated his being away from work for 1 or 2 weeks at a time. His supervisor had told him that if he was not able to return on a more regular basis, they would have to terminate his services.)

Art received more treatments at this time, and the growth of the tumor was again slowed so that he was able to continue a semblance of a normal life. He received disability insurance and never worked again as a draftsman. Art had no problems with pain, although there were negative side effects of the treatments (his energy level was low and he had some problems with nausea), but these periods constituted only about 3 or 4 days out of every 3 weeks. The rest of the time he was able to do much of what he wanted.

Gradually over the course of the next 6 months, Art distanced himself from his parents and his wife. As we talked about this in the counseling sessions, it seemed that these relationships simply lost their importance. The need to be a part of these relationships lessened, and Art showed a sense of comfort in letting go of them.

He visited with his parents only twice during that period. He considered the visits only as keeping in contact, and unlike before, he did not attempt to revitalize the relationship. He told me that he realized that his parents would never be happy with him because he had severely disappointed them and not just with regard to his marriage and vocational choice. He now realized that he had never been able to live up to their expectations, and he was through trying. He seemed to come to a place where it no longer bothered him that he was not accepted, it was just the way it was.

As indicated earlier, his relationship with Nancy had deteriorated during the first year of his illness. They had begun to live separate lives, talking little and doing virtually nothing together. After the recurrence, he moved into a small apartment. He saw the children once or twice a week but had very little contact with Nancy. He did not express anger or other negative feelings toward her as we talked in the counseling sessions. He seemed to be able to let go of the relationship without any lasting negative feelings.

At the same time, several changes began to occur in Art. He made the decision to return to school and finish the degree he had started over 15 years earlier. His wife protested that they didn't have the money for that and that it would be too demanding on him, but he chose to do so anyway. This was the first major decision he made that was not based on a need for acceptance and belonging. It was something he did because he wanted to and because he felt it would be good for him.

As he began the process, however, and we discussed the satisfaction he was getting from the courses, he determined that obtaining the degree was still a matter of needing to satisfy some external standard; not feeling the need to conform to others' standards, he discontinued two required classes he did not enjoy. Instead, he enrolled in two other classes, one in art and one in literature, that he wanted to take for his own sake.

During our counseling sessions, Art gradually moved away from talking about his parents, his wife, and his work. He no longer saw these as problems to be solved. His focus turned more to what he was doing now, exploring his sense of satisfaction with the direction his life was taking, and looking forward to new ways to fulfill his need to learn and understand more of the world around him. At times he would talk about dying, various aspects of his memorial service (he wanted to be cremated), and his hopes that he would not have pain or other negative consequences of the tumor. But this was still a future event, not something that Art was experiencing at that time. It represented the preliminaries of an exploration of what death meant to him more than the search itself. His concern was far more with living these months in a way that would let him fulfill some of the potential he had as a human being and which he had not been able to realize up to that point because of his continual focus on his relationships with his parents and his wife.

The first stage in moving to a higher level of consciousness for Art was letting go of the need to belong and to play the roles that he perceived would lead to satisfaction of that need. Precisely how Art was able to do this is impossible to know, but some considerations can be discussed. The first is that Art found the sense of affiliation and belonging that he had been unable to achieve up to that point. He had made some close friends among the other patients that he would see periodically when he was in the hospital, as well as among the nurses and staff. This occurred at a time when patients spent longer and more frequents stays in the hospital, and there was a sense of cohesiveness among many of them. This was a group that held significance for Art because of their common crises; to develop a sense of belonging with this group became very important for him.

Our relationship also provided a place where Art could find that same sense. My purpose was to create a climate of total acceptance and understanding, and in such a circumstance, there is a feeling of union or belonging between counselor and client (both persons feel it), which can satisfy such a need. The relationship was not one of dependency or transference but simply involved two persons being together for the purpose of mutual growth.

A second consideration as to why Art was able to let go of the negative emotional attachment to the relationships with his parents and his wife centers around the double-bind aspect of his need to find acceptance but his inability to live out the roles that such acceptance necessitated. After making a concerted effort to reestablish relationships that would serve his purpose and being rejected without hope for ever successfully achieving acceptance, Art finally determined to break the no-win situation, and the only way to do it was to let go of the relationships. Having made this intentional decision, he withdrew both physically and emotionally from his parents and his wife.

A third aspect to be considered is the development of a greater understanding of himself in relationship to others. For Art, as for others, movement up the spectrum of consciousness involved not only development of higher level needs and a higher sense of self but also bringing into being higher level cognitive structures. Art needed to develop an internal locus of evaluation, a greater ability to be introspective, and a sense of empathic understanding of others, all of which necessitate moving from a concrete level of thinking to a formal operations level.

As we began to work together on a weekly basis, we were able to begin exploring more deeply Art's unconscious experiencing. In addition to communicating feelings of warmth and caring and an ability to understand Art from his point of view, my purpose was to facilitate his ability to look inside at his own feelings, his values, his needs, and to help him understand and accept who he was. As he became better able to do this, several things happened. He was able to understand his parents and his wife more completely, realizing what their needs, feelings, and attitudes were. As he let go of his need to stay focused on his own needs, he could see their perspectives more clearly. As he did this, his feelings toward them softened. He no longer perceived himself in a competitive situation but in a situation where what he wanted was not what they wanted, and he decided that it would be best for him to seek satisfaction of his needs someplace else.

In addition to developing a greater empathy for others, he also began to move away from an external locus of evaluation. We spent a great deal of time exploring what he wanted and what would make him satisfied with his life. He began to understand that what would satisfy him was not playing the roles that others had in mind for him but living in greater harmony with his own inner needs. Art began to make some significant movement toward inner direction and satisfaction.

This movement might seem somewhat dramatic, occurring in such a short period of time. Yet we must remember that Art was in crisis, the most serious of his life. Who he was, or was striving to be, at the time of his diagnosis was torn away from him, and he had the choice of continually struggling with the futility of getting it back or of letting go of the former self and moving on to a new one. In such a climate, Art was able to fully delve into his life and come to understandings that were impossible when he was focused so intently on maintaining his former self. In a relationship that posed no threat to his self, his present one or his future one, he could use all of his energy to come to an understanding and acceptance of who he was and who he wanted to become. This is the positive side of a crisis.

THE DYING PHASE

About 1 year and 8 months after Art was first diagnosed as having a brain tumor, the doctor told him that treatments were no longer effective, and there was little more that could be done other than to see that he had no pain and was comfortable. Immediately after finding this out, Art asked if he could see me. He shed some tears during that session, but then he said he had known this was coming, and he was okay with it.

Art was very much alone during the last 3 months of his life. Having resolved the need to belong and having let go of his relationships with his wife, parents, and job, he had not sought any new relationships because they were not important to him at this time. He seemed satisfied to be able to work with me regularly and to know that the hospital staff was concerned about him. He was not lonely, simply alone.

Art spent a considerable amount of time during that final stage walking and sitting alone in the woods. He would go for walks each day, some lasting for as long as 4 hours. He said he would sit and just think, and then during our sessions he would share with me some of those thoughts. A great deal of the thoughts were about his life and impending death.

Death had become a welcome event for Art, not because he was tired of life, but because he saw it as a positive movement to the next level of existence. He had no remorse for the life he had led but seemed amused when he contemplated all of the ups and downs. He talked at length in the last few weeks of his relationship with his parents and the marriage to Nancy, but now it was from a point where he was only concerned with what the future held for them. There was no sense of anger, sorrow, pity, or other negative emotions, but simply an interest in these people that had shared his life.

In the last few weeks before entering this final phase, Art had become concerned with the world and what was to become of humanity. He studied environmental issues and the political situations in those countries that were in the news. He was not able to be actively involved in doing anything to resolve these issues, but he was genuinely concerned with them. He told me he wished that now that he was concerned with such things for the first time in his life, he could have more time to work to alleviate some of the problems. Then he almost immediately said that he knew that he never would have become interested if he hadn't been dying. A real paradox, as he expressed it.

During the last 3 or 4 months, Art also began studying Buddhism. He did not consider himself to be religious, never having belonged to an organized religion nor having attended church. Yet he found the concepts of Buddhism to be fascinating and chose to spend considerable time during our sessions discussing them. This was not an intellectual exercise, but one in which he was making an honest and deep effort to find meaning in his life through this Eastern philosophy.

Art was able to remain in his apartment until the end. Although he continued to become weaker and less able to attend to certain chores (such as cooking and shopping), his wife looked after these things for him so that he would not have to go to the hospital or nursing home. She offered to have him move back in with her, but he preferred to stay in the apartment. Their relationship during the last few weeks was amicable and was a pleasant encounter for Art. Three days before he died, he had a seizure and was taken to the hospital. He was unconscious until he died.

The key factor in Art's movement to a higher level of existence was his ability to let go of the self that he perceived himself to be at the time he was diagnosed as terminally ill. Having done this, he was able to openly explore other meanings and aspects of self, without the need to measure them against the needs for belonging, acceptance, and esteem.

During the counseling sessions, Art would share what he had learned from his readings, and he would then relate them to his own feelings and experiences. He became very interested in Buddhist beliefs in reincarnation and karma as they related to him. He had never seriously considered what happened after one dies, and these concepts started him on an exploration of the meaning of death. He said that during his walks in the woods, he would ponder what he had learned, and then he would go back to his apartment and read some more. What he learned about himself and his future is probably not so important as the fact that he entered into the exploration.

Art also tried to learn meditation on his own because his weakened condition prevented him from seeking instruction. Although he described his attempts as being crude, he did garner a sense of peacefulness from his practice. He described this as being instrumental in allowing him to forgive his wife and enjoy her company and help during the last few weeks, even though there was no love relationship left. He referred to her as a new-found friend.

SUMMARY

When Art first faced the crisis of a terminal illness, he had an identity that was confused because of never having felt he belonged and never having been a significant part of any relationship. He spent the first half of his illness struggling within that confused concept of self and reinforcing efforts to gain acceptance and a sense of belonging from his parents and wife. He finally came to understand that this would not be achieved because he could not fulfill the required roles, and he let go of his struggle.

During the final months of his life, Art was freed to explore new aspects of self and to move to a higher level of consciousness. Our relationship was characterized by a mutual feeling of caring, one in which my response was listening, understanding, and sharing the struggle that Art was making to find increased meaning and satisfaction in his life. For Art, the crisis of dying provided the final opportunity for growth.

Chapter 14

Sharing the Journey

Moustakas (1961) distinguished between the loneliness of anxiety and existential loneliness. The first is not a true loneliness but a feeling of isolation and separateness. We defend against it by seeking the company of others, by trying to belong, and by continually keeping busy, by seeking self-esteem. In this way, we avoid the crucial questions of life and death. On the other hand, existential loneliness comes from the reality of being human, of being aware, and of facing ultimate experiences of upheaval and change. It is a loneliness that comes naturally and inevitably from being born and from dying.

Separate selves, counselor and client, are a hindrance to transformation. They perpetuate the sense of loneliness and do not address its existential meaning. Therapy must be a sharing, each person equal and working together, for only as counselors struggle with their own transformation within the relationship can they facilitate the clients' moving toward a transformation. Progoff (1956) suggested that perhaps all psychological work since William James and Carl Jung has been implicitly seeking this psychological and spiritual union, having recognized that there is no lasting personal healing without an experience of meaning at the depth of one's being.

It is between persons that we find unity. Feuerbach even went so far as to profess that the unity of person-to-person relationships *is* God, although that proposition is not very well accepted (Robinson, 1963). The more common understanding is that human relationships are the way to finding unity consciousness but do not constitute it. One only knows ultimate unity through direct knowing, but the love relationship between person and person is that which frees one into the direct knowing (*A Course in Miracles*, 1975).

Empathy at its deepest levels occurs at the point of transition between the personal, nonunity self and the realm of direct experience. At the deepest empathic levels, one is totally in the present with the other person, knowing that person simply as a part of the now relationship. There is no question of past experiences, past meanings, or habitual roles. There is simply that which arises in the moment of the relationship. There is a precision, a complete matching, a unity of understanding and communication that are experienced and expressed without hesitancy, without analysis, or without evaluation (Truax, 1967).

The inner work, the esoteric comprehension that is integral to the highest levels of the personal and that represents the core of therapy in the high humanistic and transpersonal bands, occurs through a process of abstract knowing emanating from the eye of reason. From a cognitive development perspective, this is beyond the concrete level of thinking that characterizes many clients in therapy, many of the terminally ill persons with whom therapists work, and many therapists themselves. Yet there is evidence that such levels of self-awareness and acceptance are not dependent on cognitive ability alone. Near-death experiences, visualization, and some forms of hypnosis point to ways of knowing the self at levels that transcend the personal. The primary mode of many traditions for achieving such a level is meditation, which takes many forms but does not depend on conscious cognitive processing (Goleman, 1988). It is into this category that the immediate, now-present, *I–Thou* relationship falls. It is in this sense that relationship leads to transcendence.

The *I–Thou* relationship is not only immediate but also based on love (Buber, 1970). "The cosmos itself is composed of two movements: the movement of conflict, through which individuals emerge as distinct, and the movement of love, which leads back to unity" (Wood, 1969, p. 7). To define love as the ground of our being is to provide the bridge between the separate personal self and the separate other. Through love we come to know the unity within a relationship and ultimately the unity in all relationships—that which is beyond personal. What we know as God's love, then, is not the love of another separate personal being but the love that is the ground of our being as it extends beyond the separate personal self.

When we speak of love in this sense, we are, of course, speaking of a love that is greater than any ordinary sense of personal or possessive love. It begins with the essence of the unconditional positive regard that is a Rogerian condition of appropriate climate. It is a love that transcends any sense of attachment. It is the love that is said to be at the heart of all the major traditions. "Love is a mode of knowledge, and when the love is sufficiently disinterested and sufficiently intense, the knowledge becomes unitive knowledge and so takes on the quality of infallibility" (Huxley, 1970, p. 81). "There is no Truth higher than love. There is no method greater than ecstasy, or self-transcending love of the Radiant Life-Principle. There is no Destiny to which we may evolve that is more profound than the ultimate and spiritual sacrifice of the self, and mind, and body of Man" (Da Free John, 1980, p. 18).

The highest form of love, that by which one approaches unity consciousness, is an immediate spiritual intuition, by which knower, known, and knowledge are made one (Huxley, 1970). To transcend the personal, we must trust that to give ourselves to the uttermost in love is not to be confounded but to be accepted, that love is the ground of our being, to which we ultimately come home (Robinson, 1963). When we speak of a relationship built on empathic understanding and unconditional positive regard, then, we see that it not only frees one to explore the self more freely but that it creates the conditions necessary for one to take at least the first steps beyond the self. In this sense, it is the bridge to the transpersonal.

The most intimate motions within the depths of our selves are not completely our own. They belong also to our friends, to humanity, to the universe; they are the ground of *all* being, the aim of our lives (Tillich, 1948). This is another way to talk about archetypes or the collective unconscious. We are not separate entities, and the more we try to convince ourselves that we are, the more we alienate ourselves from the intimacy that Tillich was discussing. Only by accepting our commonality—our collectiveness—can we experience the unity that is beyond the separate.

Fritjof Capra, in his popular book *The Tao of Physics*, said that quantum theory in physics has abolished the notion of separated objects (Capra, 1975). Instead, we now understand the concept of a participator in the place of the observer, and we have come to perceive the universe as an interconnected web of relations whose parts can only be defined by their connection to the whole. Walsh and Vaughn (1980) noted that in a "truth is stranger than fiction" type of situation, evidence is beginning to suggest that each part of the universe is connected to every other part and, in fact, enfolded in every other part. All of this points to the conclusion that we, as humans, also are connected in an integral, nonseparable way, and our development must include an uncovering of that connectedness. To maintain a sense of the separate is to limit our growth.

Entering a counseling relationship free of preconceptions, then, follows this concept of interconnectedness. The observed cannot be separated, nor is it unaffected by the observer. In fact, no person is unaffected by another person with whom there is a relationship, no matter how insignificant that relationship might be. How one responds to a clerk in a store depends in part on how the clerk responds. Even though we can describe typical ways a person responds, in general, those are probabilities and fall under the uncertainty principle. How they are carried out depends on the actual interconnected parts of the relationship. Neither client nor counselor can ultimately be unconnected from the other, and each must have a significant impact on the other. This is true both in terms of the freedom to explore one's nature and meaning and in the process of continually defining the self at higher levels. Ultimately, the relationship has the power to facilitate the transcendence of the separateness altogether.

Knowledge of the transcendent can never be obtained by observation but only by full participation with one's whole being (Capra, 1980). We must learn how to *be* in relationship, not how to behave or play the role of therapist. When we interpret the relationship in terms of transference and countertransference or attempt to quantify empathy in a scientific manner, we destroy the meaning of participation and are left only with observation and external evaluation. We have only a self–other relationship, which can be used for a further end but serves no end in and of itself.

Different persons can each perceive differently the manifestations of a single phenomenon. Systems theory has been applied as a way of expressing the perceptions of the interactions of separate selves—interpersonal relationships as they are viewed from a point external to the members of the relationship. One can describe and understand the movement and interactions of the individual members in much the same way that one can analyze the dynamics of a basketball game. Certain of the separate selves are seen as responding in a team fashion (having common goals, plans, and responses) and in that sense are seen as a unit(y). There is an understanding among certain members of the same team, and often between members of different teams, regarding what their intentions are and what their responses will be. At the depth of these relationships, however, everyone maintains an understanding that each member is and remains a separate self—a self that can leave and become a member of another team or unit(y). When we seek to understand family units or counseling dyads from the same external perspective, we maintain a position of knowing that any sense of unity is dictated by the momentary circumstances and is therefore tenuous. There is no deep structure or lasting quality to the sense of unity that is perceived. When we work with dying persons, there remains an underlying knowledge that upon the death of one of us, our relationship will end, we will recapture our sense of separateness, and the unity will end.

On the other hand, we can perceive this same phenomenon from an internal orientation in which we view the team as an inseparable unit(y), that is, with each part having no existence other than the existence defined by the relationship. Such a perception is based on direct knowing rather than external impingements, meaning that the goals, plans, and responses are found within the relationship as relationship, not as brought in separately by the members of the team and molded to a single purpose through compromise and consensus. In this perception, one does not bring a self identity—a "this is who and what I am"—to the relationship but freely allows that self to be defined through the relationship. As one moves into each new relationship, there is the desire and ability to redefine the self rather than hold on to old definitions.

TRANSCENDENT OR SUPERNATURAL?

Relationship as discussed in this book does not have a supernatural implication. An integral part of the classic psychoanalytic thesis is that fantasies about spiritual forces are really projections of elements in our experience of personal relationships that we seek to avoid recognizing. Yet it is hard to see why the common projections made by the human race should have a numinous, transcendental character unless there is something numinous and transcendental in the experience of personal human relationships themselves (John Wren-Lewis, cited by Robinson, 1963).

To assert that "God (or god-consciousness, or unity consciousness) is love" is to believe that in love, or the deepest of human relationships, one comes into touch with the most fundamental reality in the universe (Robinson, 1963). The person who acknowledges the transcendence of god-consciousness is the one who *in* the conditioned relationships of life recognizes the unconditional and responds to it in unconditional personal relationships. To perceive the transcendent in this sense does not mean that we must establish a superworld of divine objects. It does mean that, within itself, the finite world points beyond itself. In other words, it is self-transcendent. I should also add that the self points beyond itself. The reinterpretation of transcendence in a way that preserves its reality while detaching it from the projection of supranaturalism allows us to understand it in a way that does not contradict current 20th-century knowledge but in fact is congruent with much that comes to us from modern physics itself.

To understand the transcendent is to be aware that ultimately there is no time and space; there is no temporal self with a past and a future, but only the now self. In his own training, Wilber (1991) came to an understanding that whatever has a beginning in time is not real. At the deepest levels of relationship, one experiences the timelessness of the relationship, that it has no beginning or end but that it just is, and in this sense the person experiences the transcendent. "Time is what keeps the light from reaching us. There is no greater obstacle to [unity consciousness] than time" (Eckhart, cited by Wilber, 1979, p. 62). Unity consciousness comes from the realization that one's true self has no boundaries, that it simply is a part of the larger cosmos. When the dying person comes to this realization, then each moment is lived for itself, without concern for past or future, and the fear of death loses its sting.

Genuine caring (love) and empathy occur at a spiritual level, not the level of the ego. Their source of energy is beyond the cognitive level of being. Through an *I–Thou* relationship the true *I* arises, conscious that it is different yet united to the whole in a higher sense. In this way unity consciousness is realized (Wood, 1969). It is through relationship that the unity is realized and that unity consciousness comes to birth, but it is in the totality of life and not in the isolated moment of ecstasy apart from things. One does not experience unity through any withdrawing from the world of experience but through the experiencing of life, especially the experiencing of meaningful relationships.

SIMPLICITY OF RELATIONSHIP

Sometimes the simple is the best, but because it appears simple, we convince ourselves that we need to make it more difficult. The good way must be clearly good, but not wholly clear, otherwise it would be too easy to reject (Kaufmann, cited by Buber, 1970). In recent years I have been struck by the simpleness of Eastern approaches to helping persons, compared with the complexity of most Western theory. (By this I do not mean that Eastern philosophy or psychologies are simple but that approaches to growth and development that are based on them are more straightforward than are many Western theories.) As I think about such a contrast, I return to the apparent simpleness of the Rogerian process of counseling and the extent to which awareness of that lies hidden from much of the counseling profession. To say that just being, simply creating a climate or relationship, is adequate to bring about whatever therapeutic change is called for is seemingly to oversimplify to the point of the ridiculous. It seems we have a need for complexity, intricacy, and rigor to make ourselves appear legitimate.

Much has been written about the authentic encounter and the role it plays in a helping relationship. But simply to relate to someone in a genuine, authentic way somehow seems unscientific or unknowing, so we make it more complex by defining, labeling, charting, and interpreting the many characteristics of the relationship to the point that it becomes anything but authentic. I had the opportunity a few years ago to spend an evening with a man I had been very close to during graduate school. He had been an avid follower of the Rogerian approach to counseling and had spent 14 years in private practice following completion of his degree. We had communicated only infrequently during that 14-year interval, and I had no sense of the direction his counseling had taken. During the course of our evening together, I asked if he was as Rogerian as he had been when we left graduate school. He laughed (I perceived with some embarrassment) and said, "No, I now approach clients from a more cognitive orientation." He said that when people are hurting and they pay money to have you help them over that hurt, they demand something more than the permissiveness of Rogerian counseling.

There have been attempts in the past to bring consciousness into a more central place in the knowledge system. Areas of endeavor such as phenomenology, introspectionism, and Gestalt therapy, as well as Rogerian counseling, have failed to gain acceptance as meeting basic methodological criteria; others, such as Tibetan Buddhist psychology, come from other cultures and are only now receiving serious consideration (Harman, 1988). Acquisition of knowledge, in the West, is primarily an intellectual undertaking; knowledge that comes through being an integral part of the experience, which implies an intense and close communion between the knower and the known, is relatively ignored (Pande, 1968). We posit a separation, if not a frank opposition, between individuals and their environment, and we focus our attention on a direct relationship to the world of external reality.

In trying to facilitate the final growth of persons who are terminally ill, the Rogerian simplicity works because the "problem" is so simple—separation anxiety inhibits transformation. Our help must be focused on connecting with the dying person, through unconditional positive regard and empathy, which will alleviate the anxiety and facilitate a transformation to a higher level of consciousness.

When we perceive ourselves to be professional counselors who are able to see the situation objectively, meaning without the distortion and defensiveness that the client brings to the moment, we become treatment specialists, not persons sharing the journey. If what hinders dying persons from seeing the picture (i.e., what is involved in moving toward transformation) is clearly only their distortion, why not simply remove the need to distort rather than try to get them to accept our position within their distorted framework? Once the need to be defensive is removed, the persons with whom we are working will themselves be in a position to see the matter as "objectively" as we do. This is exactly the point that Rogers made.

There is a tendency for us as counselors to be too analytical about what our clients' needs are, and in so doing, we begin to question our effectiveness. Yet when we focus ourselves on understanding the experience of those clients, and become aware of what they are struggling with, we realize we are successful to the extent that we have been a meaningful and authentic part of a relationship with them. Nothing else is needed. It is as simple as that.

SUMMARY

An intimate relationship, more than technique and procedure, is the key to facilitating one's movement through the spectrum. In such a relationship, we do not concern ourselves with external evaluations, problem-solving efforts, or counselor–client roles. Our goal is to create a climate in which there is no need to defend any particular concept of self, thereby removing the barriers to inner exploration.

For those who are dying, comfort and freedom from anxiety and pain are primary concerns. While medications and treating the physical body are appropriate means of helping with these concerns, we can also provide such comfort through an intimate person-to-person relationship. Pain and anxiety that result, at least in part, from a sense of alienation can best be approached by helping the client overcome the feeling of being separate and alone.

Freedom from anxiety and pain are not the only concerns of terminally ill persons, however. We also need to be aware of spiritual needs. Movement toward the transpersonal realms of development, involving the gradual giving up of the separate self, is a significant part of using the time of dying for one's final growth during this lifetime. A counseling relationship that is based not on roles and appropriate techniques but on establishing the most intimate union possible can help the dying person in this process. A sense of union between two people is a significant beginning to eliminating the barriers created by separate selves.

Working with the terminally ill is ultimately about fellowship and community, about sharing the journey. Wilber (1979) talked of the incredible voyage between the terminals of prepersonal unity and transpersonal unity. This voyage is the journey that we share when we work with persons who are dying. Our purpose is the maintenance and extension of human community in such a way as to promote growth. As Bonhoeffer (cited by Robinson, 1963, p. 76) said, "Transcendence consists not in tasks beyond our scope and power, but in the nearest *Thou* at hand."

References

A course in miracles. (1975). Tiburon, CA: Foundation for Inner Peace.

Achterberg, J. (1985). *Imagery in healing: Shamanism and modern medicine.* Boston: New Science Library.

Assogioli, R. (1965). *Psychosynthesis.* New York: Penguin Books.

Barrett-Lennard, G. T. (1962). Dimensions of therapist response as causal factors in therapeutic change. *Psychological Monographs, 76,* 1–36.

Becker, E. (1973). *The denial of death.* New York: The Free Press.

Bloomfield, F. (1983). *The book of Chinese beliefs.* London: Arrow Books Limited.

Borg, M. J. (1987). *Jesus: A new vision.* San Francisco: Harper.

Browning, D. S. (1976). *The moral context of pastoral care.* Philadelphia, PA: Westminister Press.

Browning, D. S. (1987). *Religious thought and the modern psychologies.* Philadelphia, PA: Fortress Press.

Buber, M. (1965). *Between man and man.* New York: Collier Books.

Buber, M. (1970). *I and thou.* New York: Scribners.

Butler, R. N. (1963). The life review: An interpretation of reminiscence in the aged. *Psychiatry, 26,* 65–76.

Byock, I. A. (1991). Physician involvement in assisted suicide decisions. *The American Journal of Hospice and Palliative Care, 8,* 6–7.

Campbell, J. (1988). *The power of myth.* New York: Doubleday.

Camus, A. (1955). *The myth of Sisyphus and other essays.* New York: Knopf.

Capra, F. (1975). *The Tao of physics.* New York: Bantam Books.

Capra, F. (1980). Modern physics and Eastern mysticism. In R. Walsh & F. Vaughn (Eds.), *Beyond ego* (pp. 62–70). Los Angeles: Tarcher.

Carse, J. P. (1980). *Death and existence.* New York: Wiley.

Cassel, C., & Meier, D. (1990). Morals and moralism in the debate over euthanasia and assisted suicide. *New England Journal of Medicine, 323,* 750–752.

Cohen, S. R. & Mount, B. M. (1992). Quality of life in terminal illness: Defining and measuring subjective well-being in the dying. *Journal of Palliative Care, 8*(3), 40–45.

Craven, J. & Wald, F. S. (1975). Hospice care for dying patients. *American Journal of Nursing, 75,* 1816–1822.

Da Free John. (1980). *Scientific proof of the existence of God will soon be announced by the White House.* Middletown, CA: Dawn Horse Press.

Eliade, M. (1982). *A history of religious ideas, Vol. 2.* Chicago: University of Chicago Press.

Engler, J. (1986). Therapeutic aims in psychotherapy and meditation. In K. Wilber, J. Engler, & D. Brown (Eds.), *Transformations of consciousness* (pp. 17–51). Boston: Shambhala.

Erickson, M. H., & Rossi, E. L. (1983). *Hypnotherapy.* New York: Irvington Publishers.

Erickson, M. H., Rossi, E. L., & Rossi, S. I. (1976). *Hypnotic realities.* New York: Irvington Publishers.

Erikson, E. (1963). *Childhood and society.* New York: Norton.

Erikson, E. (1968). *Identity: Youth and crisis.* New York: Norton.

Fawzy, F. I. (1994). The benefits of a short-term group intervention for cancer patients. *Advances, 10*(2), 17–19.

Fromm, E. (1941). *Escape from freedom.* New York: Farrar, Straus, & Giroux.

Gallup, G. (1983). *Adventures in immortality: A look beyond the threshold of death.* London: Souvenir.

Gendlin, E. T. (1978). *Focusing.* New York: Everest House.

Gilligan, S. G. (1987). *Therapeutic trances.* New York: Brunner Mazel.

Goleman, D. (1988). *The meditative mind.* Los Angeles, CA: Tarcher.

Grinder, J., & Bandler, R. (1981). *Trance-formations.* Moab, UT: Real People Press.

Grof, S. (1988). *The adventure of self-discovery.* Albany: State University of New York Press.

Grof, S., & Halifax, J. (1977). *The human encounter with death.* New York: Dutton.

Harman, W. (1988). *Global mind change.* Indianapolis: Knowledge Systems.

Huxley, A. (1970). *The perennial philosophy.* New York: Harper.

Johanson, G. A. (1991). Symptom character and prevalence during cancer patients' last days of life. *American Journal of Hospice and Palliative Care, 8*(2), 6–8.

Jung, C. G. (1961). *Analytic psychology: Its theory and practice.* New York: Vintage.

Jung, C. G. (1971). *The portable Jung* (J. Campbell, Ed.). New York: Penguin Books.

Kalish, R. A. (1987). The study of death: A psychosocial perspective. In H. Wass, F. M. Berardo, & R. A. Neimeyer (Eds.), *Dying: Facing the facts* (pp. 55–75). Washington, DC: Hemisphere.

Kapleau, P. (1989). *The wheel of life and death.* New York: Doubleday.

Kastenbaum, R. (1989). Death fears and anxiety. In R. Kastenbaum & B. Kastenbaum (Eds.), *The encyclopedia of death.* New York: Avon Books.

Kastenbaum, R. & Kastenbaum, B. (Eds.). (1989). *The encyclopedia of death.* New York: Avon Books.

Kelsey, M. (1973). *Healing and Christianity.* New York: Harper & Row.

Kelsey, M. (1986). *Christianity as psychology.* Minneapolis, MN: Augsburg.

Kohlberg, L. (1981). *Essays on moral development.* San Francisco: Harper & Row.

Kopp, S. (1977). *Back to one.* Palo Alto: Science & Behavior Books.

Kubler-Ross, E. (1969). *On death and dying.* New York: Macmillan.

Kutscher, A. H. (1980). Foreword. In J. P. Carse, *Death and existence.* New York: Wiley.

Lajoie, D. H., & Shapiro, S. I. (1992). Definitions of transpersonal psychology: The first twenty-three years. *Journal of Transpersonal Psychology, 24,* 79–98.

Levine, S. (1982). *Who dies?* New York: Anchor Books.

Levine, S. (1990). Expanding "my" pain into "the" pain. *Inquiring Mind, 6*(2), 1–6.

Lifton, R. J. (1979). *The broken connection.* New York: Simon & Schuster.

Lonetto, R., & Templer, D. I. (1986). *Death anxiety.* Washington, DC: Hemisphere.

Lovejoy, A. O. (1964). *The great chain of being.* Cambridge, MA: Harvard University Press.

MacDonald, D. (1991). Hospice development: Insights from four models. *American Journal of Hospice and Palliative Care, 8*(2), 37–44.

Maezumi, T. (1993). Life and death. *The Ten Directions, 16*(2), 9–12.

Maslow, A. (1968). *Toward a psychology of being.* New York: Van Nostrand Reinhold.

Maslow, A. (1971). *The farther reaches of human nature.* New York: Viking Press.

May, R.•(1950). *The meaning of anxiety.* New York: Simon & Schuster.

May, R. (1958). Contributions of existential psychotherapy. In R. May, E. Angel, & H. F. Ellenberger (Eds.), *Existence: A new dimension in psychiatry and psychology* (pp. 37–91). New York: Basic Books.

Moustakas, C. E. (1961). *Loneliness.* Englewood Cliffs, NJ: Prentice Hall.

Muzzin, L. J., Anderson, N. J., Figueredo, A. T., & Gudelis, S. O. (1994). The experience of cancer. *Social Science and Medicine, 39*(9), 1201–1208.

Neimeyer, R. A. (1988). Death anxiety. In H. Wass, F. M. Berardo, & R. A. Neimeyer (Eds.), *Dying: Facing the facts* (pp. 97–136). Washington, DC: Hemisphere.

Neimeyer, R. A. (Ed.). (1994). Preface. In *Death anxiety handbook: Research, instrumentation, and application.* Washington, DC: Taylor & Francis.

O'Connor, P. (1985). *Understanding Jung, understanding yourself.* New York: Paulist Press.

Palmer, H. (1988). *The Enneagram.* San Francisco: Harper & Row.

Pande, S. K. (1968). The mystique of "Western" psychotherapy: An Eastern interpretation. *The Journal of Nervous and Mental Disease, 146*(6), 425–432.

Pelletier, K. R. (1977). *Mind as healer, mind as slayer.* New York: Dell.

Plato. (1952). Phaedo. In R. Hutchins (Ed.), *The dialogues of Plato.* Chicago: Encyclopedia Britannica.

Pratt, J. B. (1928). *The pilgrimage of Buddhism.* New York: Macmillan.

Progoff, I. (1956). *The death and rebirth of psychology.* New York: Julian.

Rainey, L. C. (1988). The experience of dying. In H. Wass, F. M. Berardo, & R. A. Neimeyer (Eds.), *Dying: Facing the facts* (pp. 137–157). Washington, DC: Hemisphere.

Rando, T. A. (1984). *Grief, dying, and death.* Champaign, IL: Research Press.

Rhymes, J. (1990). Hospice care in America. *JAMA, 264*(3), 369–372.

Robinson, J. A. T. (1963). *Honest to God.* Philadelphia: Westminister Press.

Rogers, C. R. (1951). *Client-centered therapy.* Boston: Houghton-Mifflin.

Rogers, C. R. (1957). The necessary and sufficient conditions of therapeutic personality change. *Journal of Consulting Psychology, 21*, 95–103.

Rogers, C. R. (1961). *On becoming a person.* Boston: Houghton-Mifflin.

Rokeach, M. (1960). *The open and closed mind.* New York: Basic Books.

Sandner, D. (1979). *Navaho symbols of healing.* New York: Harcourt Brace Jovanovich.

Schulz, R. (1979). Death anxiety: Intuitive and empirical perspectives. In L. A. Bugen (Ed.), *Death and dying: Theory/research/practice* (pp. 66–87). Dubuque, IA: Wm. C. Brown.

Seale, C., & Addington-Hall, J. (1994). Euthanasia: Why people want to die earlier. *Social Science and Medicine, 39*(5), 647–654.

Sogyal Rinpoche (1992). *The Tibetan book of living and dying* (P. Gaffney & A. Harvey, Eds.). San Francisco: Harper.

Shneidman, E. S. (1973). *Deaths of man.* New York: New York Times Book Co.

Shneidman, E. S. (1980). Some aspects of psychotherapy with dying persons. In E. S. Shneidman (Ed.), *Death: Current perspectives* (pp. 202–213). Palo Alto, CA: Mayfield.

Smith, D. C. (1993). Exploring the religious–spiritual needs of the dying. *Counseling and Values. 37*(2), 71–77.

Smith, D. C., & Maher, M. F. (1993). Achieving a healthy death: The dying person's attitudinal contributions. *Hospice Journal, 9*(1), 21–32.

Smith, E. D., Stefanek, M. E., Joseph, M. V., & Verdieck, M. J. (1993). Spiritual awareness, personal perspective on death, and psychosocial distress among cancer patients. *Journal of Psychosocial Oncology. 11*(3), 89–103.

Smith, H. (1982). *Beyond the post-modern mind.* Wheaton, IL: Theosophical Publishing.

Snygg, D., & Combs, A. W. (1959). *Individual behavior.* New York: Harper.

Stoddard, S. (1992). *The hospice movement.* New York: Vintage Books.

Sutich, A. J. (1968). Transpersonal psychology: An emerging force. *Journal of Humanistic Psychology, 8,* 77–78.

Sutich, A. J. (1969). Some considerations regarding transpersonal psychology. *Journal of Transpersonal Psychology, 1,* 11–20.

Suzuki, S. (1970). *Zen mind, beginner's mind.* New York: Weatherhill.

Tillich, P. (1948). *The shaking of the foundations.* New York: Scribners.

Truax, C. B. (1967). A scale for the rating of accurate empathy. In C. Rogers (Ed.), *The therapeutic relationship and its impact* (pp. 555–568). Westport, CT: Greenwood Press.

Walsh, R. N., & Vaughn, F. (Eds.). (1980). *Beyond ego.* Los Angeles, CA: Tarcher.

Watts, A. (1968). *Myth and ritual in Christianity.* Boston: Beacon.

Weisman, A. D. (1972). *On dying and denying.* New York: Behavioral Publications.

Weisman, A. D. (1974). *The realization of death.* New York: Jason Aronson.

Wilber, K. (1977). *The spectrum of consciousness.* Wheaton, IL: Quest.

Wilber, K. (1979). *No boundary.* Boston: Shambhala.

Wilber, K. (1980). *The Atman Project.* Wheaton, IL: Theosophical Publishing.

Wilber, K. (1982). Odyssey: A personal inquiry into humanistic and transpersonal psychology. *Journal of Humanistic Psychology, 22,* 57–90.

Wilber, K. (1983). *Eye to eye.* Garden City, NY: Anchor Books.

Wilber, K. (1986). The spectrum of development. In K. Wilber, J. Engler, & D. P. Brown, *Transformations of consciousness* (pp. 65–105). Boston: Shambhala.

Wilber, K. (1988). On being a support person. *Journal of Transpersonal Psychology, 20*(2), 141–159.

Wilber, K. (1991). *Grace and grit.* Boston: Shambhala.

Wilber, K. (1993). The great chain of being. *Journal of Humanistic Psychology, 33,* 52–65.

Wittine, B. (1993). Assumptions of transpersonal psychotherapy. In R. Walsh & F. Vaughn (Eds.), *Paths beyond ego* (pp. 165–171). Los Angeles, CA: Tarcher.

Wolberg, L. R. (1967). *The technique of psychotherapy, Vol. 1.* New York: Grune & Stratton.

Wood, R. E. (1969). *Martin Buber's ontology.* Evanston, IL: Northwestern University Press.

Index